WILD in the HIMALAYAS

Loves and tragedies from Paris to Kathmandu

FRANCISCO PO EGEA

Copyright © 2017 Francisco Po Egea.

ISBN: 9781980778837

Original title: De Ejecutivo a trotamundos

Translated from the Spanish by Cristina P. Wenger

Cover design: © Pablo Serrano

TO BARBARA AND CRISTINA... MY WINGS

Wild in the Himalayas

At the beginning of time, the mountains had wings. They flew in the distance, crossed rivers and seas, oceans and continents and landed where they wished. But one day Indra, the Vedic god of lightning and storms, jealous of so much freedom, cut off their wings and held them to the ground. The wings, free but without self-will, became helpless and turned into clouds. This is why they always float around the mountains.

Rig Veda (1400 B. C.)

Do not believe in anything simply because you have heard it. Do not believe in traditions because they have been handed down for many generations. Do not believe anything because it is spoken and rumored by many. Do not believe in anything because it is written in your religious books. Do not believe in anything merely on the authority of your teachers and elders. But after observation and analysis, when you find that anything agrees with reason and is conducive to the good and the benefit of one and all, then accept it and live up to it.

Buddha (600 B. C.)

I think that men are also born with wings or, at least, with a seed waiting between the shoulder blades. A conservative education, social and religious conventions, policies of the leaders and conformism join forces to prevent its development. You must release it. In addition to one's teachers, one must also read and listen to the heterodox and the aesthetes, the rebels and the iconoclasts. They are the ones that create change. You have to travel, see the world with the body and the spirit, with no company, and no ties. This way, little by little, we will spread our wings.

The author (Paris – 1982)

Francisco Po Egea

A journey is always made three times: First in one's dreams, in the imagination, on maps. A second time along roads, in old buses, in stations waiting for hypothetical trains, in dusty shelters and radiant forests. And, finally, a third endless time in one's memory, in the presence of instants which will last indefinitely and which nothing and nobody can ever erase.

Elisabeth Foch
L'Echappée Indienne

Four large birds were circling above us, they looked like vultures, under an intense blue sky where grey clouds were forming. "There must be a dead animal nearby," I thought. "*Merde!* it's going to snow again." It must have been around three in the afternoon. We had been walking all morning and had stopped a few hours ago due to a soft and wet snow in which we were sinking more and more with each step. We made the most of the time by eating what food we had left from the previous night, some rice, chapattis and a tin of tuna fish. We wanted to get as close as possible to the pass before the sunset, to be able to cross it the next day before it became impossible due to the increasing level of the snow. If we didn't manage it, our hopes of getting out of there would vanish.

I was in the heart of the Indian Himalayan range, in the gorges of Rishi Ganga –a tributary of the Ganges which drains part of the glaciers of the area– at the foot of the practically impenetrable walls that protect the Nanda Devi Sanctuary, presided by its peak with the same name. The date: mid-October 1978.

I had read a fair amount about the mountains of the Garhwal. First, in a few libraries in Paris, and afterwards, in the library of the illustrated Nepali aristocrat, Kaiser Bahadur Rana. His splendid collection of books on the Himalayan range was stored in his old palace in Kathmandu, and accessible to all those who showed any interest. I had learned that these mountains were especially rich in legends, myths and traditions, as they were the birthplace of Hindu religion and the traditional abode of its gods, as well as the terrene setting for their great deeds described in the Vedas, the sacred books of Hinduism.

Over these mountains reigns the Nanda Devi, which at 25,643 feet (7,818 m) is the highest peak in India, one of the most gorgeous, the most isolated and the subject of many legends. A glorious mountain, its ragged peak like a spear leaning on its shoulder, ready to tear the sky or the sail of a vessel made to fly through space. All the routes to reach the summit, either by climbing one of its faces or ridges, are long, steep and abrupt: rock, snow and ice. From its base, one needs weeks to reach it, and very few have managed to do so.

Its name means Goddess of Happiness, one of the denominations of Parvati, the wife of Shiva. Until 1934 nobody had found the key to penetrate this sanctuary –in the sense of a place of shelter and protection– and the peak remained unclimbed until two years later. It became the highest peak ever climbed by man until the ascent of Annapurna in 1950. Since then, fewer than a dozen climbers have reached its summit and almost as many have died in the attempt. The sanctuary itself is enclosed within another great circle of mountains and sharp peaks more than 21,000 feet high (7.000 m.) –the so-called outer sanctuary– and

2

can only be reached via two passes 13,500 feet high (4.500 m.), passable according to whether or not they are snow-covered and how much of it they have accumulated.

I had been trekking for several months now, sometimes alone and sometimes accompanied by a porter when I needed to take a tent and food and there were no villages or shepherd huts where to sleep. I had walked through the valleys and mountains of the great range, trying to get as near to its central peaks as my limited experience and little equipment would allow me, to Everest, Cho Oyu, Annapurna, Kangchenjunga, etc., as well as some of its more remote regions. Had I not been such an optimist –no doubt due to how well my adventures had gone so far– I would have never dared to embark on this current one: reach the upper border of the cited shrine, take a look at its interior and photograph the beautiful mountain and its environment at my leisure.

There were no guarantees that I would achieve my purpose. The trek would cross uninhabited land, outside the usual trekking routes and where mountain expeditions were extremely rare. Without a doubt, Nanda Devi was gorgeous, and to me, its environment resembled paradise, but it was also true that its ascent required a long and complicated trek for the porters to be able to approach its base. Moreover, it was not an "eight-thousander" - even though it is harder to climb than several of them - so of what interest would its "conquest" be? In these times of marks and records, it seemed that only the peaks of more than eight thousand metres, with Everest in the lead, mattered.

"Conquest": Too much of a word to describe stepping on a summit for a few minutes. A summit which will immediately become as inhospitable and hostile as it was before, and which will demand of its next "conqueror" the same or even more effort, perhaps even his life, to allow for this fleeting, precarious "conquest".

I had read the stories of the first explorers/mountaineers who had travelled to these places in the first half of the 20th century: Tom Longstaff, Frank Smythe, Eric Shipton, and Bill Tilman. Characters devoted to the discovery of these remote lands without thinking about triumphs and glories, but only for the pure pleasure of feeling the freedom of the explorer. I had become infatuated with the bohemian and romantic spirit emanating from their narrations.

"Francisco, the snow is getting hard again; we can go on now," Pemba said standing next to me.

He was my guide and porter. I had found him in Joshimath, the village that supplied the whole area and also the start of the pilgrimage to the four temples that mark the sacred sources of the Ganges. Pemba was a Bhotiya, a Tibetan ethnic group which, like the better-known Sherpas, came from Tibet hundreds of years ago and settled in the southern slopes of the Himalayas. While the Sherpas occupy the Everest region, the Bhotiya villages extend throughout the West of Nepal, and much of the Indian Himalayas and are also more numerous than the Sherpa settlements. The owner of the hostel where I was staying introduced us, and from the first moment I met him, I felt I could trust him completely. He was of medium height and solid body, but with the agility of a mountain goat and the sharp vigilance of a feline. His mountain gear, anorak, trousers and boots, were of high quality but very used. He had probably received them from a member of a previous expedition when it had ended. There was a constant smile on his lips when he talked, and his slightly slanted eyes were sincere and cordial – after a couple of weeks, we had forged a brotherly relationship.

His words brought me back to reality. The vultures in the sky continued circling above us but there were around twenty of them now, and they had come down a little lower. Without further ado, I got off the rock where I had been sitting for the past hours, grabbed my backpack and resumed the trek. We had only advanced a few dozen steps when a red patch, a hundred meters higher up on the same slope in the direction of the sharp summit of the Dunagiri, caught our attention. It was my partner, with the experience of a dozen expeditions, who first saw it.

"There is a man there."

"Can't be. It must be a tent or some canvas."

He didn't answer but started walking towards it. When we got there, I saw he was right. I couldn't believe it. It was a man, lying against a rock in a foetal position, face covered in snow and looking lifeless. I could see that he was big, blonde and well equipped with a red down anorak, trousers and climbing boots. We knelt beside him and brushed the snow off his gaunt face.

"Look, Francisco, he is barely breathing."

"He probably hasn't eaten for days," I said, looking at his haggard face. He wasn't wearing any sunglasses. "He might be blind by now as well."

"He's also probably been sleeping out in the open."

We sat him up and started rubbing his body, trying to bring some life and warmth back into it. We had warm tea and tried to get him to drink some. Impossible, his jaw was locked together, as if frozen shut and even though we kept massaging his face and chest he didn't seem to be able to open it. He hadn't opened his eyes yet.

"I think he is one of the Americans of the Dunagiri expedition."

"You must be right, who else?" answered Pemba.

After ten minutes of insisting we managed to get him to separate his lips and ever so slowly we were able to get him to drink. It took him a while to react, but when he finally opened his eyes, they were opaque and empty.

"He is dying," said Pemba. "We can't carry him back with us."

His face was bluish, his lips purple, and his beard and eyebrows had completely frozen, but I could still see a young, brave face. He would have parents, maybe a wife and children, friends. This image, just a few inches away from my eyes, became that of José Ignacio, my inseparable friend from school, dead in our arms after drowning in a dam when we were sixteen years old. It had happened during a school trip, and even though we hadn't been allowed to, we had jumped into the water right after lunch, with fatal consequences. In my memories, I could still feel his bonhomie and fraternity. And now I had another dying person in front of me. A new tragedy in the mountains like all the others I had heard and read about, stark and impassive. It wasn't the stage for a tragic emotional event, but a natural, simple one. But here I was, with a feeling of dread and uncertainty rising in my chest. I was going to cry.

Pemba seemed unmoved and had walked a few metres away. One knows the risks when one aims to conquer a Himalayan peak. Sometimes you win, and sometimes you lose.

"We have to try, we can't just leave him here," I looked at him pleadingly. "We can set up camp and see how he progresses till tomorrow."

He didn't answer but started creating a platform on the snow. I continued rubbing Jack. I had just baptised him. When the tent was set up, we pulled him inside and while Pemba prepared some soup and more tea I started to undress him, which wasn't easy. He had lost a glove, and his fingers showed clear signs of frostbite; his toes, however, seemed fine. I rubbed them until some warmth returned and continued with his hands, arms and back. So much exercise and in such a small space, I was roasting. He seemed to feel it too and started mumbling. We couldn't understand a word he was saying, so we wrapped him up in my sleeping bag and fed him a few vitamins, aspirin, soup and more tea. After this he fell asleep or passed out, I am not really sure which.

"What about the other American, do you think he is around here somewhere?" I asked Pemba.

"I was wondering the same thing, but I don't think so. This one seems to have been lost a few days now. But I am going to climb up to that rise anyway and see if I can see something."

He left me there, reflecting on our dire situation: "As if it wasn't tricky enough…What the hell are we going to do now." After an hour had passed, I heard Pemba return.

"I didn't see anything. They must have become separated. Or the other one has fallen off the precipice."

He said it with such ease; it was alien to me how easily he accepted death. But I assume they were used to it, the quiet, reflective porters, who accompanied the western mountaineers to fulfil their dreams, and knowing that there was a significant possibility that those dreams would lead the expeditionary to his death. I, on the other hand, had a constant feeling of dread in the pit of my stomach and could feel the bile coming up my throat. But there was no point focusing on feelings and reflections of our uncertain future, in these situations you live in the present and follow the necessary steps to survive.

With this thought, we started getting dinner ready and organising the tent to spend the night. The three of us had to fit inside the small tent, so we left some of our possessions outside, but under the protection of the double roofing. While Pemba cooked Dhal Bhat (rice and lentils) on our tiny gas stove, I stood facing the towering mountains that I had travelled so far to discover. The last sun rays of the day were caressing the highest of the peaks, colouring the pure white snow with a pinkish golden hue giving them a feminine and more beautiful touch, while the shadows from the gorge started creeping up, like deadly fingers predicting what could very well happen that night. I couldn't help thinking how unpredictable life was and how my good fortune that had been accompanying me during all my travels had changed so much since the morning before.

That day, the morning had started as usual, with Pemba's soft words waking me up:

"Morning tea, *sahib[1]*."

His words reached me through a sea of puffy clouds where I was resting, surrounded by sensual and semi-naked Apsaras[2] who danced in front of a proud and satisfied Shiva, while down his long locks flowed the waters of the Ganges, deluging from the skies upon his head, offered by the God himself to protect the Earth. We were only a few kilometres away from the source of the sacred river and a few days before, I had been ambling between temples boasting ancient frescos, depicting idyllic scenes of Gods entwined with their partner's prominent breasts and sensuous lips.

---

[1] Sir, master: Used especially among the native inhabitants of colonial India when addressing or speaking of a European of some social or official status.

[2] In Hindu mythology, a celestial nymph, typically the wife of a heavenly musician.

"Francisco, good morning, your tea." I wasn't ready to give up my pleasant dream, but I could hear Pemba insisting, loyal to the firm tradition of morning tea introduced by colonial Britain and still very much a daily routine in this area of the Himalayas.

Reluctantly, I bid farewell to the beautiful priestesses and slowly opened my eyes. The white clouds turned into the greyish ceiling of the cave where we had spent the night, covered in soot due to various fires of previous guests. In his altar at the entrance of the cave, Shiva had his back turned on me. Someone had written on the walls: *Best five stars in the whole trip*, and someone else: *Putain de merde de cave*. Typical, the relaxed humour of an English gentleman and the usual complaining habit of a French.

"It is snowing very much; we should leave as soon as possible," warned Pemba.

I could see the snow falling heavily through the irregular entrance of the cave.

"And can't we wait to see if it stops?" I grumbled.

"Look, if it continues snowing like this and we don't get to the Duranshi pass soon we might not be able to get out of here at all."

I sat up, shocked by his statement.

"What? Do you mean we have to hurry back to the pass we crossed the other day? But the monsoon ended a long time ago!"

"Yes, exactly, this is not the end of the monsoon but the first snows of winter that seem to have arrived a bit too soon and caught up with us. And you never know whether they will only last a day or the whole week," he answered, with an excusing tone rather than an urgent one.

Taking into account our current situation, we hurried through a breakfast of cereal and powdered milk diluted in water, packed our

9

bags and at around 7 am started walking. Not in the direction of the gorges of the Ganges and the walls that would take us up to the sanctuary of the Nanda Devi, my initial plans, but back to the Duranshi pass and the deadly gorges of the Satkula, which we had crossed a few days earlier on our way to our current position. It was too risky; we were heading back.

While we trudged along surrounded by snow, I recalled the idyllic, pastoral scene from previous days.

From the last pass, we had descended more than a thousand metres to meadows encircled by Alpine forests of birch and rhododendron, sprinkled with poppies, primroses, anemones, calendulas, and the daisy, a great colour palette painting the landscape. Corollas and petals, pistils and bulbs vibrating with insects sang the great chlorophyll fornication while dragonflies pursued each other in their game of lovemaking and bumble bees buzzed around undecided. We had seen golden eagles dominating the skies, bharals or blue rams of the Himalaya with their large twisted horns, their silhouette camouflaged against the rocks, and Imperial pheasants scampering in front of us, slightly startled by our presence. Under that stratospheric sky, where a few white clusters floated dreamingly about, each step was a taste of all those visions and essences while the nostrils trembled with pleasure as they absorbed all the fragrances that turned the walk into a voluptuous symphony.

I had been enraptured by the scene, delighted taking pictures of the flowers and the eagles soaring through the skies. I had patiently waited for the rams to lift their lustrous heads to portray them proud and dominant and had been frustrated by only being able to photograph the pheasants' backs as they ran away from us.

But today, the atmosphere was completely different, a menacing grey. The thundering of the river accompanied our steps, eroding the rocks and lifting up whirlpools of foam with its impetuous current, covered by a threatening dark sky that hid the peaks and turned the trees into ghostly silhouettes. Inevitably, I thought about how, at the top of the pass, the dangerous path had seemed to "fly" at various points, hundreds of metres of eternal precipices above the gorges of the Satkula or Seven Gorges. I looked back at the moment when we had had to stop at the start of one of these "flying" stretches to give way to a group of twenty porters that had already begun the careful journey of crossing it.

We could see them edging closer, one after another, in a single file, stuck to the wall. On their backs, their heavy baskets and massive rucksacks. Careful steps, their torso leaning forward due to the weight and their eyes fixed on the ground, searching for a safe place to place their next footstep. The *sirdar* reached us first, and Pemba started talking to him while I took some pictures of the porters crossing and the Nanda Devi which could be seen on the horizon, towering above the other mountains, a powerful mistress dominating them all.

Suddenly, something unexpected. Tumbling stones. One of the last figures leans dangerously away from the wall. It looks like a big rock. No, wait, two. But it's a porter and his basket; separated from each other. He screams, twice. Both shapes fall and crash into the ground at a gradient of eighty degrees. The basket explodes and pans and pots fly everywhere. The man hits the ground with a thud and continues rolling down amidst screams of desperation, trying to grab something that will save him from a tragic end while his companions stare without comprehension. He keeps falling and disappears. Abrupt and eternal silence.

The screams of the porters echo in the gorge. They call out his name again and again but no-one answers. They argue among themselves and Pemba translates. One of them, his brother, wants to go down to look for the poor man. Desperately he calls for a rope to what the *sirdar* replies with more shouts. There is no rope, they don't have any. We don't either, we can't help them. The unanswered cries continue. One after another they arrive at the ridge where we were standing. They unload their packages. Some are still arguing; others remain silent. They have decided that two of them will run up to Lata, the village from where we started, to get some ropes and try to rescue their comrade. They do not believe, however, that he is alive.

The *sirdar* talks and Pemba transmits. They were coming from a failed expedition to climb the Dunagiri (23,182 feet; 7,066 m) – which stood there, on our left, its base camp a few days walk– and the *sahibs* had taken the ropes with them for climbing. But the two Americans had not returned. They had waited for them for several days and then decided to go and look for them but had only found one of their rucksacks abandoned at the foot of the wall. They then had decided to return home, convinced that the mountain had claimed two new victims.

The memories, Pemba hurrying me up constantly, and the thought of his concerned face that morning, made me start to realise the situation I was in, for which I was surely not experienced enough nor prepared for. But we had to continue, climbing without pause. It had taken us six days from Lata, the last inhabited village in the area, to get to the cave at the throat of the gorge, halfway between the last mountain pass and the edge of the inner sanctuary. We had crossed the gorge and the pass the evening of the third day but had set up camp closely after. So we would need at least four days to reach the pass again, if not five, taking into account that the greater part of the journey was now uphill and walking on snow. If it continued snowing with this intensity, there was no doubt we were going to get lost and if we did manage to get to the pass, after all, it would be uncrossable.

If I hadn't stayed that extra week in Leh with Hildegard, waiting to see if she would or not be evacuated by plane to Delhi, I could have started the trek one or two weeks earlier and I would not have been in this mess right now. I thought of her permanent good mood and her snub nose between those clear and serene eyes. No, I wasn't fair. I had stayed because I liked her, and I had enjoyed spending time with her. I remembered her aversion to speaking well about herself and ill of others; a generous and gracious dove. She had been an exceptional travel companion, with her good judgement and a good heart. I wondered what had happened to her in the end. For a moment, I eluded all thought of danger and uncertainty and began to hum a Jacques Brel song in her honor: *"Y en a qui ont le cœur si large qu'on y entre sans frapper... "[3]*

Ah, Paris! I remembered fondly the years I lived there. I had a story to tell from every corner, every street in the Latin Quarter, Saint Germain, Montparnasse, on the banks of the Seine, the Opera and even from the Champs-Elysees I kept an ethereal souvenir. A café, a bistro, or a cinema were the stages of dreams, thoughts, visions, a hug, a longing, a kiss... I had spent two significant periods of my life there, and how different they were from each other! The first, young, naïve, with little money but fervent to conquer the world. The second, a mature adult, with a good salary, relationship issues and disillusioned professionally. I certainly preferred the first one, with its life lessons, its revelations and its surprises.

They say cloudy days are better for contemplation than sunny ones. It was without a doubt very true in my case. About to turn

[3] *"There are some who have a heart so wide that one can enter without knocking ..."*

forty, I started reflecting on my past years and on everything I still wanted to live and experience. I thought of my mother and her despair if I did not return; of my father who had never understood why I had suddenly quit my career, after so many years of studying and working until I had achieved my goal of being a high executive at a prestigious multinational company, to then throw it all overboard. And Ursula: Would she now realise that she really did love me more than anything else in this world and wanted to live with me even though that meant leaving Munich? And did I still want that? A six-year relationship with no visible future. Agreements and disagreements. Intensity and evasion. Passion and confrontation. A love as sharp and rugged as a saw, with sharp peaks and deep grooves. But at the end of the day, we always ended up together again. But when I returned home she would probably say: "Francisco, you are the one that left." And she was right. A pure and straightforward truth for her; a more debatable one for me.

And Monique? My last minute new love, sweet and fragile. So idealistic and in need of affection. It had hurt immensely to leave her in Kathmandu a little more than a month ago. But I had had to do it. And I had left her only for a few days and in good hands, safe from the temptations of the drug addicts that swarmed around the backstreets of Freak Street and Thamel, waiting for her flight back to Paris where we would soon be reunited.

The trek required all my attention, so I stopped dwelling on the past. The path climbed steeply from the gorge through the meadows which were now covered in snow and rocks which we carefully navigated, flanked by giant fir trees and rhododendron bushes. We had had to cross the sacred Rishi Ganga river over a slippery log lodged between the two shores. The current roared beneath us. I thought that maybe a swim in those turbulent waters would have rid me of all my troubles. In the present situation, the fear of the immediate future, and the Gods, good and evil that lurked around every corner, no wonder I was questioning my own extremely rational convictions. Pemba crossed the river with ease but stepping delicately on the precarious bridge. I, on the other hand, crossed it on all fours, at some point hugging the log, and without feeling any shame whatsoever. Pemba had obviously carried my rucksack to the other side after leaving the bag with all the supplies first.

Around five hours later we stopped to have some lunch: leftover rice from the previous night, a tin of sardines and some chocolate. Shortly after we resumed our walk it stopped snowing, the sun came out and illuminated the forest and mountains, warmed us up and fed our hopes of getting out of there, energising our steps. Just before sunset, we set up camp, cooked the usual rice and lentils, tea and biscuits for dessert and got into our sleeping bags, waiting for morning to arrive.

When we woke up, it was snowing again. At our altitude, around 12,200 feet (3.700 m.), the layer of snow was already about thirty centimetres thick, but it was still hard due to the cold of the morning, so we were able to continue steadily and without much effort. However, the temperature started rising quickly, and the thickness of the snow increasing and we were soon struggling to maintain our pace as our boots sank more and more with each step. The sun appeared at around twelve, and the snow became too soft to continue, so we decided to stop and have some lunch. We estimated that we were almost halfway to the pass so, if we walked all day until night time, the situation didn't get any worse, and it didn't snow the next day, then we would be able to make it to the pass mid-afternoon the next day. It was then that we found Jack.

Since I was a child, I had always loved walking in the mountains. When you walk, you see the world and yourself more clearly. You have the feeling of purifying the mind and soul. Perhaps it is due to the better irrigation of the brain. I had never looked to defeat or conquer the mountains, but to immerse myself in their unfathomable vastness, to learn to combine the desire to do something different with overcoming the difficulties it entailed; to feel the humility before their supremacy and pride of their proximity and beauty, and savour the feeling of evasion and freedom they provided. And above all, to relish the purity of the air that surrounds them, the wonders of their landscape, their forests and the animals that inhabit them, the rivers and the love dialogues between light and water, and the encounters with the people from the valleys and elevations. As I had read often, "the mountains touch your soul, they are addictive and shower you with rewards, but they also make us conscious of our temporality and the fragility of our existence."

And there, next to me, I had the proof; again in my arms, a man about to die. He was a complete stranger but I felt close to him; it could have happened to me or could still happen in the near future while I tried to escape the terrifying situation in which I was in. Throughout the afternoon and evening, we fed him, every two to three hours, taking turns to rest. A couple of hours before dawn, the most critical for his state, the man was still breathing although somewhat agitated. If he woke up of his own accord, he would live, I told myself. Maybe I was fooling myself. I didn't really have any experience in situations like these. Pemba, on his other side, slept in a foetal position. He really did resemble a big child or a bear.

With first light, Jack seemed to have recovered slightly; he opened his eyes and asked us a question, which we did not understand. He muttered for a few minutes and fell asleep again. If he had not died during the night, then he should be able to survive. But he was in no condition to walk and we could not leave him. I went outside to give Pemba more space to prepare breakfast and when he came out to offer me some I suggested:

"Why don't you go to the nearest village, light and with no weight except some food? It will only take you two or three days and you can come back with help to get us out of here."

"Yes, we could do that. Alright." He answered.

But he was looking at me with certain reservations, he wanted to say something. He started getting his things ready. When he emerged out of the tent, I gave him a big farewell hug. It was then that he spoke.

"Are you sure of what you are doing? Do you realise the danger you are exposing yourself to?" he said. "If we can't cross the pass we will turn back and go home. You, on the other hand, will stay here," he added gravely.

I felt a blow in the pit of my stomach. I nodded, while doubts, fear and anxiety swelled up inside me. I looked upwards at the mountains and the sky. Dawn had broken bright and clear, there were hardly any clouds and the vultures had disappeared. "He was right," I thought, "but my conscience or sense of good doing wouldn't have allowed me to leave a man in this state, at least for the moment." I felt ashamed of this last selfish thought but I knew there was a possibility I would have to.

"I trust you Pemba. I know you will do whatever it takes to get us out of here. You will be rewarded, you and whoever comes back with you. Anything you ask for."

I hugged him again even though he, like all Asians, was not prone to effusive displays of affection, but he was now used to mine and he tolerated them. He presented me with his usual open

17

and sincere smile, grabbed his bag, turned around and started uphill. I followed him with my eyes. "I will wait for you, my friend. I know you are a brave man and you would not abandon us". He arrived at the summit of the slope and turned around. He raised his arm to the sky, joined the palms of his hands and turned his gaze upwards. I understood. He entrusted us to the gods. I imitated him. I also raised my arms, joining my palms together. "Which God was I entrusting myself to?"

II

¿From what immortal desire, what sudden sight of the unknown, surges that desire? What flint of fact, what kindling light of art or far horizon, ignites that spark? What cry, what music, what strange beauty, strokes that resonance? On these hangs the future of the world.

Nancy Newhall

Who would have thought a year ago, during my first trip to Kathmandu, with the sparkles of adventure dancing before my eyes and a whole new world before me ready to be discovered, that I would find myself in such a dire situation? There I was, alone and abandoned in the middle of the Himalayas with a dying stranger agonising beside me. I had the whole day ahead of me. This one and the following ones with nothing to do, except take care of this man and wait for our rescue party. Would Pemba come back for us? Would this be the end of my new self? Was my new life of experiences, travels, unexplored roads and fascinating encounters going to end so quickly? What would my destiny be, had the Gods sealed my fate?

I had to calm down. If I allowed such dismal thoughts to dominate me, I was going to have a tough time. I had made it my mission to save Jack. I looked at him. "Poor boy, who was he? What was he thinking? What would he say when he woke up?" I started melting snow in our small gas stove. I envisioned the living comforts I had left behind but didn't feel any nostalgia. I didn't regret it, quite the opposite, I was proud.

I saw myself on that plane again. I remember that as soon as I had settled in my seat, I had chuckled at the thought of no more business class for a while and that I didn't care one bit. As well as in my radical change of appearance, goodbye to the suit, tie and shiny shoes; hello to the short sleeved shirts, mountain boots and anorak in the baggage compartment above my head. There was now no doubt about it; in the past, I had been a repressed bohemian.

I wasn't the only one dressed like that. There were three or four couples dressed in a similar outfit and with rucksacks of varying dimensions. Just like me, they had felt "the call of the East", very much in fashion in France since "May '68". But were any of them leaving like me, having broken ties with their past? Leaving work, career and love? Had I taken a reasonable decision? Yes, I had changed a foreseeable life for a new one of uncertainty and adventure. Or maybe I hadn't made the right decision, but it was too late now, and the boots I was wearing were made for walking.

There were also a few people who looked like businessmen, and also some tourists on an organised tour. Some Hindu *dhotis*[4], Sikh turbans and colourful saris indicated where we were going: New Delhi. There, after a couple of days visiting the city, I would board another plane towards my final destination. Instead of opening my

[4] A garment worn by male Hindus, consisting of a piece of material tied around the waist and extending to cover most of the legs.

20

grey briefcase, typical companion of all executives of the time, to look over some offer for electrical equipment which I would later present to some client in Frankfurt or Milan, I drew open the zipper of my small rucksack – the big one was stored in the hold – and got out the *Guide du Routard of Nepal*, a country which till very recently I had never heard of. Behind me, I was giving up, at least for the moment, fifteen years of professional life. My enthusiasm for what was to come erased for a moment the doubts about the wisdom of my decision. And funnily enough, I perceived it as both the premiere of a great adventure as well as the triumphant final chords to my previous life.

The process of deciding to change my life had started a few weeks earlier with a simple phone call. It was a sunny afternoon at the end of June 1977, and I sat in my office on the 24th floor of the tower of France contemplating the great arch of La Défense, and feeling heavy after yet another business lunch. Then the phone had rung.

"Herr Schneider on the phone," I heard my secretary through the receiver.

"Hello, Klaus. How are things in Frankfurt?"

"How are you, Francisco?" and without waiting for my answer, our man in Germany added, "I have just had lunch with Hans Brücken, the head of purchases of Mannesmann and we have him under our thumb. The order is a sure thing, all the electrical cabinets for their ring-rolling mills."

"Fantastic. Well done."

"Yes, but let me get to the point," Klaus continued while I paid close attention. "He wants us to go to Paris next Wednesday to see the France – Germany football match, and afterwards to go and celebrate the outcome dining on oysters and Château Margaux.

"No problem."

"He wants to meet you, and probably try and get a discount," I could hear the enthusiasm in his voice.

"We'll see about that. Anne will take care of the tickets and of finding a restaurant with good oysters and a Château Margaux at a discrete price. If not I will have the auditors at my throat."

"Forget the auditors. It's a three-million-dollar contract!"

"All right, all right. And congratulations Klaus, good job. I shall see you Wednesday."

I was then, a highly paid executive with credit cards, American Express or Diners Club, always ready and with a Samsonite briefcase strapped to my wrist. I had two secretaries: A Swiss lady, mature like me and as discreet and efficient as a Swiss bank and another girl, French, young and slightly punk. I also had a boss of whom I thought very little and a salary which out of modesty or embarrassment I had not told either family or friends. I drove a BMW, latest model, which the company had put at my disposal, and I lived in a luminous apartment facing the Bois de Boulogne, the largest park in Paris. I dined in the best restaurants, dressed in Yves Saint Laurent and Ted Lapidus suits, and played squash twice a week with my former colleagues from the INSEAD Business School of Fontainebleau, where I had obtained my MBA a couple of years earlier.

I travelled frequently. Once a week I would fly to Milan, Frankfurt, Brussels, Copenhagen… tedious day trips. I would get up at six in the morning to catch an early flight and wouldn't return home until nine or ten in the evening if there were no delays, of course. From the car to the plane, taxis, offices, meetings with future clients, back to the airport, parking lot, car, motorway at night time, exhaustion. Fortunately, I could sometimes combine these business trips with a weekend of skiing in Innsbruck or Crans sur Sierre, or some tourism in Venice or Amsterdam. I used to go to London a few times a month and to our headquarters in Chicago twice a year, where I enjoyed the open and honest American hospitality. In all of these cities, I would stay in the best hotels. My life was that of the perfect executive and well paid. However, I was not happy.

In the company, where I held the position of Marketing and Sales Director for Europe, things were not going very well. The French company, the headquarters for all the European subsidiaries of the American company Cutler Hammer – manufacturer of electrical equipment for large-scale industries – had failed to make any profits since its opening ten years earlier. They had hired me again, after my fantastic results as general manager at the Spanish subsidiary, with the mission of increasing sales and in consequence the turnover and profits. And yes, sales had grown considerably, but we then faced the problems of the inability of the factory, situated in the North of France, to meet deadlines and the technical specifications of our clients.

Thus, the losses continued, to the subsequent frustration of all of us. Especially mine, tired of the endless meetings with the international vice-president or other envoys of the headquarters in the USA to discuss marketing plans for the next five years, forecast sales and the reasons as to why we were not managing even to break even. Moreover, I despised my boss, a Dutchman, who in his previous profession had been an accountant but who now, the only thing he knew how to do was lock himself in his office to count our losses and hold long telephone conversations with our correspondent in Chicago. The general manager at the factory was a former French Navy Officer and the perfect example of order and discipline, but also of ineptitude. The facility was impeccably organised and spotless, but had barely produced any proper amount of work since its opening and was incapable of establishing a decent rhythm of manufacturing. Its engineers and workers were like a football team which only trained for pleasure but never to compete.

After nearly two years, my disappointment had reached its limit. I asked myself, what would become of me: CEO in Paris? Vice-President of the international division in Chicago? More people to be in charge of and more money until I reached retirement age? I felt I had nothing important to fight for, and no one to do it for. My body was tired of these express trips; my stomach, tired of all those business lunches; and my brain was exploding with talks of riches and power: Mercedes or BMW, Rolex or Breguet, Saint Tropez or Portofino. I was aware that material things alone did not satisfy me. I had already felt it three years ago when I had left my job in Madrid to study for an MBA. But of course, one can't give up on something without having had it first.

I was also convinced that life was not pre-determined by the circumstances in which we were born. Quite the opposite, the circumstances are the dilemma on which we have to make up our minds and the ones who shape our character and attitude towards life. On the other hand, during my travels, I had perceived the width and complexity of the world and wanted to get to know it thoroughly, without any ties or deadlines. I felt the need to renovate myself, maybe even rejuvenate myself, to live new experiences completely different to all that I had lived until then.

My professional life wasn't going well, and my sentimental one not much better. For the past five years, I had had a girlfriend: Ursula, aquamarine eyes and the body of a Valkyrie, a degree in Art History from the University of Heidelberg and a degree in Philosophy from the University of Munich, where she currently resided. But for the past couple of years, our relationship had remained stagnant. There was nothing in the world, not even her, that would make me want to move to Germany. And there was nothing that would make her leave her job as assistant professor in the university and her doctorate on the Venetian *Settecento*. I admired her for her determined ideas on politics, society and ecology, although there were many times when due to our age difference – I was twelve years older than she was – and the educational differences between Spain and Germany, I thought they were somewhat too advanced for me.

She would write some very intelligent and affectionate letters. But when we were together she was too introvert, and it was hard for her to open up to me. When she did, she was wonderful. We would see each other once a month, and we would spend three or four weeks together during the summer. It was mainly I who insisted on us seeing each other. In my last letter, I wrote: *I am tired of letters, the communication of absence. A practical and idealistic replacement of a relationship, the thoughts of what we want or would like to be. Not real enough. I want, I am, spontaneity, feeling and pleasure. I reject spirituality at a distance. I admire Plato, but it is Epicurus who moves me.*

Wednesday arrived, the one I had planned with Klaus by telephone. At the Parc des Princes, France and Germany tied at two goals, which left the Germans satisfied enough. We celebrated with a shot of whisky on leaving the stadium; we had already had one during half-time at the insistence of Hans Brücken. We then went to Elysée-Lenôtre, located in the middle of the Champs Elysees' gardens, - a restaurant with a magnificent reputation due to the freshness of its seafood as well as the sumptuous decoration below its *Belle Époque* style dome – to dine on oysters and drink Château Margaux. But our guest had not warned us of his intention of having both at the same time. So after enjoying a glass of *kir de champagne* as an aperitif, we ordered two dozen *fines claires* to

25

start with, and when the *sommelier* brought us an Alsatian Riesling, the stubborn *Teuton* insisted on his Bordeaux. "What an idiot! Wanting to have a red reserve instead of a dry white with the oysters, like everybody else," I thought, "but he is the client, although he is going to cost us a substantial amount."

It's not that one can't make exceptions once in a while. But what I could not have imagined was the devastating effect the combination would have on my very gastronomically educated stomach. During dessert, I started feeling sick. The old wood and the tannins of the vintage 70's wine had brought the oyster back to life and they were fighting to get out of my stomach, preferably through the upward escape route. I broke into a cold sweat. I felt so ill I didn't even bother hiding my agony. I went to the bathroom a couple of times but could not rid myself of the torment. My German colleague looked at me, worried about the possibility of losing the deal while the head of purchases smirked in my direction, with the contemptuous superiority of the Aryan vigour in comparison with the weakness of the Latinos.

After finishing dinner, I took them to the Crazy Horse on Avenue George V, which boasted of having the most beautiful women in Paris, dressed only in shimmering light. I left them there and sped back home, literally dying. After massive heaving and effort, I finally liberated myself from the oysters, the sirloin steak with *chanterelles*, and the *tarte Tatin* dessert. A defeated man looked back at me from my bathroom mirror. I promised myself that this would not happen again; I had to be more careful.

At six a.m., I left home in the direction of Charles de Gaulle airport. It was raining lightly, but I sped down the motorway, at a hundred and forty kilometres per hour. I didn't care. I got there just in time to catch my plane to Helsinki where Lukas, the general manager of our Stockholm office, was waiting for me. From there we travelled to Tampere in the North of Finland where we had a visit planned to a paper paste factory, a possible client. In the afternoon, a prelude to one of those Nordic white nights at the end of June, where darkness never comes. Our customers, with the typical hospitality of small towns, led us to a sauna in a cabin located at the edge of a forest on the shore of a lake and afterwards took us out for dinner at a nearby restaurant.

The next day, at four in the morning, Lukas and I took the first flight to Helsinki. We arrived half an hour late and had to rush through the terminal to catch our next flight direction Stockholm. From there, we flew to Oslo, where we rented a car to go and visit another client near Bergen. The road meandered close to the coast for the most part of the way. It was a sunny day; the North Sea shone, calm and tempting, untouched beaches appearing between the cliffs and ancient rocks. We stopped for a while, and I jumped into the freezing waters to prove to myself that another life still existed. A minute to breathe between flights, running through airports, ticket desks and polite conversations on this speedy trip. As Scandinavian tradition dictates, our client was waiting for us with a delicious *smorgasbord*; a varied selection of delicious canapés on black bread. Butter, smoked salmon, herrings, also smoked, marinated or pickled accompanied by various sauces. I can't remember now whether we managed to seal the deal or not, but I do remember that we ate an enormous amount and very well.

After the meeting, back to Oslo, and from there to Copenhagen, delayed again. The Hilton was full, and so was the Crowne Plaza. "You won't find a free room in the whole city. There is an international machinery fair, and the annual Cardiology Congress" informed the receptionist. So we took a taxi towards Helsingor but no luck. We did, however, manage to catch the last ferry to cross the strait between the Baltic and the North Sea to Helsingborg, in Sweden, and finally, at twelve o'clock at night and after twenty-two hours non-stop rushing through four different countries, I collapsed on a bed.

Back in Paris, I spent much of that weekend reflecting on the type of life I was leading and the absurdity of it all. *"Success is not the key to happiness; happiness is the key to success,"* I reminded myself. I was so tired of these speedy trips, airports, highways, offices and restaurants, a compressed succession of haste and meetings. So, how many more years was I going to stand this? There is no greater torture than to work on something useless and meaningless. And that is how I often felt, empty. And that emptiness had become my own reflection, which stared back at me every evening after a tiresome day at the office or on my return from one of those express trips. Or on those lonely weekends when I missed Ursula's presence the most.

All through Saturday, I tried to call her, but to no avail. She wasn't at home. Afterwards, I would know that she had been working in a "Biergarten" to earn the necessary money to pay her expenses. It rained all weekend. It was a wet and depressing Paris, emphasising my feeling of loneliness. Sunday awoke equally depressing, and I spent the morning contemplating the rain falling on the trees in the park. After lunch, I downed a Remy Martin, got into my BMW and drove to the Guimet Museum of Asian Art. I had read in Le Monde that they were that afternoon showing a documentary on Nepal.

I barely knew of the existence of this country. But the images of the exotic Kathmandu, with the hustle and bustle of its picturesque markets, the curved roofs of the unique pagodas and the temples flanked by sculptures of strange gods, together with the scenes of the cheerful people in those beautiful valleys sheltered under the snow-capped mountains, enraptured me immediately. Especially, the image of a nomad family walking across a hillside carved into rice terraces and sown with prayer flags and Buddhist stupas. "Freedom, freedom!" My thirst for adventure had awoken.

"But would freedom bring me closer to happiness? Yes, it would. It would allow me to choose my own destiny," I thought as I walked down Iena Avenue in the direction of the Palais Chaillot gardens, where the car was parked. "But was happiness the only thing I was seeking? Wouldn't that alone be rather dull? No, what I was looking for was the novelty of the unexpected, for adventure, for discovery. To be able to choose what paths to follow; to fall in love, to be passionate about something again, even if I knew it might cause suffering or lead me down dangerous roads. I wanted to live; I needed to live, to be somebody else somewhere else."

I felt very optimistic when I got home. Disregarding the elevator, I ran up the stairs two steps at a time, the three floors that separated the garage from my apartment, my heart pounding with excitement. I heated up the vegetable stew from the previous night, got the Camembert, the Roquefort and the Pate de Canard from the fridge and opened a bottle of Châteauneuf du Pape. After the second glass, the trees of the Bois de Boulogne on the other side of the balcony had turned into the snow-covered mountains of the Himalaya.

> *"Hier encore j'avais vingt ans.*
>
> *Je caressais le temps*
>
> *Et jouais de la vie*
>
> *Comme on joue de l'amour*
>
> *Et je vivais la nuit*
>
> *Sans compter sur mes jours*
>
> *Qui fuyaient dans le temps*
>
> ....

Et j'ai gâché ma vie "[5]

sang Charles Aznavour on the radio while I got ready to go to bed. No, not I. That would not happen to me. I still had time. The decision was made. For the time being, I would take a year off; after that, well, who knows.

As soon as I got to the office on Monday, I dictated my letter of resignation to a profoundly stunned Anne. With it in my hand, I presented myself in my boss's office. He hadn't arrived yet but Solange, his gorgeous secretary, with her curly hair, tight black skirt and revealing blouse, was standing next to his desk. She greeted me with her usual slightly provocative smile and her big blue questioning eyes. I handed her the letter.

"What is this?" she asked.

"My resignation."

Her mouth dropped open in surprise and I, overexcited by the bold decision I had just taken, grabbed her by the waist and sealed her lips with the kiss I had wanted to give her for a long time.

"*Ah, mais non!* You can't leave now that you've finally dared…"

Oh, but I could! I ran away from it all as if my life depended on it, and a few weeks later I was smoking a *chillum*[6] with the hippies and *sadhus*[7] at the old Royal Square of Kathmandu. A few days

---

[5] *"Yesterday I was twenty.*
I was caressing time
And played of living
As we play of loving
And I lived at night
Without counting my days
Which were fleeing in time
....
And I wasted my life "

[6] A small pipe used for smoking cannabis.

later, rucksack strapped to my back, I had joined a group of Frenchmen on what would be my first trek down the adventurous paths of the Himalaya, in search of the flying mountains.

---

[7] A religious ascetic, mendicant (monk) or any holy person in Hinduism and Jainism who has renounced the worldly life.

III

A man goes on a trip and it is another one who comes back.

Peter Matthiessen.
The Snow Leopard.

It was snowing again; our second day in the tent. Dawn had broken covered in clouds but calm. They had disappeared for a while mid-morning, a few hours after Pemba had left, but it had started snowing again in the afternoon with no sign of stopping. I assumed that Pemba would be close to the pass by then, but wondered whether he would be able to cross it before night time caught up with him or if he would wait until the next day. I imagined that in a few days he would have reached the village. So in another four days, five at the most, he would be back, only if the snow allowed them to cross the damned pass. We had around one kilo of rice left, a quarter of lentils and half of muesli; tea, coffee and milk powder, four instant soup packets, a head of garlic, a couple of onions, a can of tuna, another one of sardines and some cheese. "That should be enough for five days. We won't do much exercise, so we don't really need to eat that much," I told myself.

Jack looked uncomfortable. He kept complaining about his left shoulder; it was swollen and blue. I was giving him Paracetamol every eight hours, but I feared it was broken. When he had woken up, he had looked at me in amazement. "You, you, who...? Peter,

Peter…" he had repeated in a faint voice. I tried to talk to him, but he had kept asking for his friend and then fell back asleep. I assumed that Peter was his friend and expedition partner, lost in the snow. Later in the afternoon, after explaining to him how we had found him, that he was safe and cared for, he seemed to recover, but not enough to get out of the sleeping bag.

"Are you in pain?"

"No, yes…, my shoulder," his answer was barely a whisper. "I can't see very well."

I looked at his face. His lips were still blue, and his eyes lifeless. I didn't have much experience in these cases, but I thought that the worst was over and that, right now, what he had was temporary blindness due to the days he had spent lost in the snow without sunglasses. Maybe I should have put a bandage over his eyes, but I didn't want to scare him.

"You should probably put my glasses on," I said as I handed them over and helped him put them on. "It will give your eyes some rest. You'll be fine soon enough, you just need to sleep, eat and get hydrated again. You'll see, you will feel better tomorrow."

He didn't answer but didn't complain either. I examined his hands. The fingers on his right hand had not improved much, but his toes seemed fine. However, he didn't look too distressed taking into account the condition he was in. He dwelled on his friend's unfortunate destiny and on his return home:

"What am I going to tell his parents?" he whispered, clearly heartbroken.

I didn't know how to answer. What could I say? But Jack – surprisingly, he was actually called that – didn't expect me to answer. After a few minutes he continued:

"He was dying…right there, next to me…and I didn't do

anything."

"I am sure you did everything in your power. But one can't fight against mountain and ice. It's impossible."

But he wasn't listening. He muttered something else and resumed his state of contemplation. His words made me think of my childhood and my parents. My mother had always taken care of me, supportive and encouraging in my studies. And I got on well with my father. As a child, he had taken me along to football matches and on a few trips, first in a lorry and afterwards, in one of his buses which he had for tours and excursions. He had followed my studies without showing much interest but had been proud of my professional successes. But now he was wary of my latest decisions. He just could not understand why I had quit my job after achieving such a good position and with such a good salary. We were very similar: independent, restless, curious, I had learned a great deal from him; especially to take advantage of my knowledge and skills and to deal with problems and find solutions with ease. This reminded me of one of my first trips with him, at the end of the 1940's, when I had just turned eight.

Many years had passed, but I could still see them. Two silhouettes emerging from the fog at the edge of the road, right in the middle of the stream of light projected by the lorry's headlamps. One of them stepped forward and lifted his arm, the palm of his hand extended as a signal for us to stop. As he got closer, I could see that he was a civil guard. The other didn't move, but remained alert and at close range, with his gun pointing downwards. During that time, the years after the civil war, the Civil Guard had a terrible reputation. Only their presence, or the knowledge that they were close by, resurfaced an ancestral fear and torturous memories in the minds and hearts of many; the result of collective executions, tortures, illegal confiscations and other heartless activities which were attributed to them.

I looked at my father and noted that he had sat up straight and his face looked tense and severe, his jaw locked. I shuddered.

"Are they going to hurt us?" I whispered.

He didn't have time to answer me. The lorry had just stopped, but the first guard was already at our window. He lifted his right hand up to his "Tricorne" and asked us authoritatively:

"Where are you headed?"

"To Lerida," answered my father, as he switched on the cabin lights.

"What's the load?"

"Sugar. Five thousand kilos."

"Please, don't take me for a fool. A lorry full of sugar in these times? Let's see, documentation."

The guard examined the documents of both the goods, the property of the National Supply and Provisions Service – if it hadn't been so, it would have been contraband and confiscated, including the lorry which was my father's. I shrunk fearfully in the furthest away corner of my seat, as far away from that man as possible. During that time, anyone wearing a uniform scared us, especially civil guards and the "grey ones".

"I wouldn't mind a coffee right now," said my father, trying to sweeten the atmosphere and release some of the tension created. "We've got enough sugar," he added, forcing a smile.

"Drive carefully," answered the driver, ignoring my father's joke but visibly more relaxed. "We have noted the presence of *Maquis*[8] close to Candasnos, and if they find out what your load is..."

"Perfect, just what we needed." You could hear the frustration in my father's voice.

The guard had already taken a few steps back to let us pass but immediately stopped and stared at my father suspiciously.

"Why so?" he asked with interest,

"One of the piston rods is burnt out, and I don't dare go faster than forty per hour."

"Good grief! Well, keep on going, and hopefully, you won't meet any trouble. Good luck." With this, he bid us farewell. He even sounded friendly.

The fog, typical of the Ebro valley at this late time of the year – it was the end of December, next day would be Christmas Eve - had started creeping upon us right after crossing the river, on the outskirts of Zaragoza. If you looked out of the window, you could only see darkness, but if you looked forward, through the windshield, you could see the creeping finger of fog, in yellowish waves, outlined by the light of the headlamps. In some stretches, the trees on either side of us looked like skeletons which had escaped from a nearby graveyard and were trying to grab me and drag me into the depths of the forest, while the silhouettes of the hills, a wall of earth to our left, resembled a fortification that was about to collapse on us at any second. I could not expect, at such an age, where one's head is full of fantasies and stories, a creepier and more mysterious setting than this. It reminded me of some of the stories and books I had read. While my father focused all his attention on the road and the real dangers outside, I crouched on

---

[8] Spanish guerrillas exiled in France after the Spanish Civil War who continued to fight against the Franco regime until the early 1960s.

the worn-out leather seat, huddled in a blanket, chin on my knees, trying very hard not to look as weak and scared as I felt.

The tarmac melted into the darkness of the night. It was a straight road, relatively even and flat. Our old Hispano-Suiza, with its nose crowned by a slender stork spreading its wings, the emblem of the brand, and its wooden box carrying fifteen thousand pounds of load, once encouraged, flew swiftly and steadily down it. To make myself feel better and safer, I started thinking about school and the small adventures my classmates and I had had during the year. At that age, I went to the French Institute.

My mother was quite a Francophile herself, she had attended the same school as a child and had travelled to Biarritz many times to learn about the latest fashion in hats. She had a workshop where she designed and made them for the high society ladies of Zaragoza. I started singing the first song I had learnt in school: "*La Chanson des Voyelles*".[9]

> *Où sont passées les voyelles?*
>
> *Elles se baladent dans les mots*
>
> *C'est le grand jeu des voyelles*
>
> *Elles rendent les sons si beaux!*
>
> *.........*
>
> *Entends—tu le A dans « chat"*
>
> *Entends-tu le U dans «lune»?*
>
> *Oui il joue même avec*

[9] *The Song of the Vowels*

Des «bulles» et des «plumes»[10]

My father accompanied the song by honking the horn, and I jumped up and down on my seat following the beat. Years later, I learned that for Pythagoras, as well as for other philosophers, the sound of the vowels corresponded to the position of the planets. The sun is the centre. The planets evolve harmoniously, and their movements and oscillations produce a sound called "the music of the spheres". In Greek, there are seven vowels, and each vowel represents the sound of a planet. Therefore, this melody of the planets and of the vowels possesses a celestial essence. As a result, the believers of this theory during ancient times would invoke the gods by singing the sound of the vowels. At the end of the 19th century, in France, the esoteric and theosophical musician and writer, Edmond Bailly, had collected information on this tradition through numerous ancient sources and had captured it in his book: *Le Chant des Voyelles*.

We passed a few villages. It was around nine o'clock in the evening, and there wasn't a soul to be seen, not on the road either. We crossed paths with a vehicle once every three or four kilometres. A few metres after crossing the Pina intersection, the road started to gradually get steeper. At this point, my Dad leant forward with a worried look on his face. He swore.

"What's wrong Dad?"

[10]*Where are the vowels?*
They wander in the words
It is the great game of vowels
They make sounds so beautiful!
Do you hear the A in "cat"
Do you hear the O in "moon"?
Yes it even plays with
"Bubbles" and "feathers"

"Can't you hear it, son? A clack, clack, clack. It' a piston rod, it's burning out."

We stopped and he jumped down, lifted the bonnet and put more oil in the sump. We then continued but at a much slower pace.

"I have no idea at what time we will get there, but we will, so don't worry."

I trusted him blindly. He was very smart and knew how to solve any problem that would arise. However, I had started worrying after the civil guard had told us that the *Maquis* were roaming around the area. At such a slow speed, we were an easy target. If at least my father had brought his shotgun with him, we would have something to defend ourselves with. I had no idea who the *Maquis* were really, I only knew what people said about them, that they were some sort of brigands or bandits who roamed around the villages, stealing and killing people.

Every twenty kilometres we had to stop so that my father could fill up the sump again to keep the oil level as high as possible. By doing this, he would ensure that the piston rods and the crankshaft were properly lubricated all the time.

"Dad, tell me something. What do you enjoy more, driving a bus or a lorry?"

"Well, that's easy. The buses load themselves and you don't travel alone. They also have a better suspension and go faster." He answered. "Although to be honest, the passengers fall asleep immediately most of the time and if you are tired you can't stop, you have to drive all through the night."

"And during the war, the fascists took them away from you."

"Don't use that word, it's not allowed. Even if you mother and grandfather use it."

"And why did they take your buses, father?"

"They needed them to take the soldiers to the front. Who knows where those buses are now."

"But what upset you the most was that they took the new one, right?"

"Yes, I see that your Mum told you the story. The Dodge. It was getting the finishing touches in Arbucias, in Gerona, before being sent to me in Zaragoza. The Catalan Republicans seized that one.

"Grandfather is a Republican and he is a very good person," I answered defensively.

He stopped looking at the road for a second and focused his eyes on me.

"Look, you can't walk around saying those things. Your mother should not talk to you about such matters. It is family stuff; you will understand when you are older."

My mother had told me how my grandfather had been in prison, but only a few days, as his son, my uncle Jose Maria, had managed to get him released quite quickly.

My uncle was short but strong, like everybody else in the Egea family. He knew everybody in Zaragoza and when I went for walks with him, he would stop or would be stopped every five minutes to greet someone. He was also very brave. On two occasions, he saved a boy and a man from drowning in the Ebro river, and the city council awarded him a diploma. But he was also quite stubborn. Right after the end of the civil war, he would walk around Zaragoza wearing a red shirt. It cost him a few arrests until his friends from the Falange told him to stop being provocative or next time they would not go to the police station to get him out.

He had no children of his own, and I was his favourite nephew.

Every Sunday, my auntie Mari, my uncle and I would go on a day trip. First by bike, cruising down the road on the banks of the Ebro, or exploring the hills of Torrero. Later on, when he got a car, we went to the Pyrenees. This is where my love for the mountains began. He also encouraged my love of reading. He would buy adventure books for me, "Tarzan King of the Apes" by Zane Grey or Jules Verne novels which he purchased in Allué, a magnificent second-hand bookstore in Estébanez Street, right in front of the olive and pickle warehouse that my grandfather had founded. He had another store, where he sold goods to many shops and bars in Zaragoza, situated in the bustling street of San Jorge, in front of the offices of the bank "Caja de Ahorros".

I remember the place vividly. The walls were packed with cabinets and shelves, rammed all the way up to the ceiling, filled with cans of all sorts: sardines, tuna, squid, mussels to name a few. In the back store, gloomy and cold, could be found gigantic barrels, filled to the brim with green and black olives in brine. On one side, the office, and on the other, a small room where three young women stuffed olives with pieces of anchovies, sitting around a solid wooden table which was most certainly older than my uncle. I would spend some afternoons with them, observing their work and chatting. They liked hearing my stories about school, they found them funny. A few years later, when my curiosity had surpassed my manners, I asked them to show me their breasts. The youngest one would boast about them and would let me touch them sometimes. They would tease me, they had fun provoking my naïve naughtiness.

My memories returned to the truck on our way to Lérida. Just before arriving at Candasnos, the fog disappeared. We had actually risen above it and a full moon was now visible, as yellow and as round as a peach. We certainly were an easy target now, I remember thinking. Huddled in my blanket, I was pondering about possible escape routes or plans but I couldn't think of any and felt increasingly afraid. Suddenly, from a distance, we saw another lorry stopped at the side of the road. My father slowed down and stuck his head out of the window.

"Could it be the *Maquis*?" I asked as I withdrew into my seat.

"I can't see anybody."

He stepped on the brakes, had second thoughts and stepped on the accelerator.

"Lie down on the floor", he ordered.

There was no need to repeat it twice. I could already hear the gunshots in my head, trying to take us out as my father, leaning over the steering wheel, accelerated to get us out of harm's way. But just as we were about to pass the stranded lorry, a man jumped out of the cabin and waving both arms, empty-handed, signalled us to stop. And we did. The poor man had run out of petrol. During those days, everything was rationed and people would try draining the fuel tank to the limit. With the help of a rubber tube, we poured a few litres from our tank into a tin and the man emptied it in his.

"What about the *Maquis*? The civil guard said they are roaming around this area", asked my father cautiously.

"Bah! Don't worry about it. I go up and down this road every day and I still haven't seen one. If there are any they will probably be further up in the Pyrenees, past Barbastro", answered the man.

He gave my father three pesetas for the petrol and a pat on the back.

"What about you, boy? Already learning the ways of the road? Not a job that I would recommend, you´d better concentrate on studying as much as you can."

"I already do", I answered proudly, "I got a nine in Arithmetic."

We bid our farewells and continued. He went first and slowly started picking up speed, increasing the distance between us. We continued at our leisurely pace, wondering when we would finally arrive at our destination.

We passed a stretch with a few gentle curves and then a long black river of tarmac. In the distance, we could see the road slowly rising again. Down the road, there were two short walls made of stone, one on each side. There was probably a creek and next to the wall on the right, a couple of trees with bare branches. As we got nearer, five men stepped forward from between the trees.

They ordered us to stop by lifting their guns in the air and approached the lorry. I suddenly noticed that I needed to go to the toilet, but with difficulty managed to control myself. The men looked a sorry sight, unshaven, emaciated, wearing pitiful rags, and crude blankets thrown over their shoulders.

"Where are you heading? What are you carrying?" one of the men asked with bitterness. His beard was speckled with grey and he looked like being in charge. He was also the only one wearing boots. The rest were wearing cloth shoes, one of them without any socks. He positioned himself next to my door while the rest remained a few metres in front of the lorry.

"Good evening", answered my father. "Are you hungry? Pass me the sandwiches son."

With shaky hands and failing courage, I gave up the cloth bag with our cured ham sandwiches and the two oranges.

"Alright, they won't come amiss", he said as he grabbed the bag. "Juan, Antonio, share it out. Where did you say you were heading?" he added, now in a much friendlier tone.

"We are on our way to Lerida, if we ever get there, the engine is failing. The Civil Guard stopped us a moment ago and scrutinised our documents for quite a while" lied my father with composure.

"Where?"

"Just nearby, at the entrance to Candasnos. The traffic police were there too."

"Hey! This man says that those civil guard bastards are in Candasnos, and on top of that, the police are with them," shouted the boss to his colleagues. "And what are you carrying?"

"Sugar."

"Lift up the canvas."

Quickly, my father jumped out of the cab and walked towards the back of the lorry. I got even more worried when I saw the man following him with his gun still in his hand. In the meantime, the *Maqui* standing next to my door put his head through the window, examining the cabin. His foul breath reeked of decay.

"Don't be scared, boy. We are not going to harm you. You are nearly as miserable as we are."

I could hear the boss addressing the others:

"Grab a couple of sacks. We don't have time to take any more," and then to my father, "If you need to justify them, say that `El Botazos´ took them." He chuckled bitterly.

The mention of the civil guards had clearly alarmed them. So they grabbed the sacks and without further ado, disappeared up the mountain. My father sighed and looked at me gravely. He started the engine, put it into gear and we slowly continued on our way. It was at that moment that I decided that he should sell both his lorries and start another business. This one was too hard and too risky, too many villains roaming around. I was certainly not accompanying him again. And not only that…

"Why did you give them the sandwiches? I'm hungry," I grumbled, "If only we had eaten them earlier..."

"Because I didn't want them to steal the thirty pesetas I have in my pocket, son."

The explanation was convincing enough and after a while, due to the monotony of a straight road, the sound of the engine and the exhaustion from all the excitement, I dozed off. When I woke up, we were descending down the Fraga pass and my father seemed in higher spirits.

"If we manage to get up that hill on the other side of the village, we will be in Lerida in no time," he announced, optimistically.

It was four in the morning when we finally arrived in Lerida; our initial plan was to get there before twelve. We left the lorry in the courtyard of the provisions office and headed to a hostel nearby to get some sleep. The sheets were humid.

"Father, I'm cold."

He hugged me and rubbed my back with his calloused hands. He smelled of sweat and gasoline.

"Try and sleep a bit. Tomorrow we'll catch a train and will be home by mid-afternoon, with your mother, your brother and your sister, just in time for Christmas Eve dinner. Your mum will have prepared your favourite vegetables and the large chicken we got from Borja.

"And for dessert, Christmas sweets," I added, right before falling deeply asleep.

IV

To tell the story of my life...
I don't know where to begin.
A life you remember in jumps, in blows.
Suddenly a passage comes to memory.
And the scene of memory is illuminated.
Josefina Aldecoa

On the third day, I woke up feeling like I was suspended in an ethereal space, timeless and still. Jack slept quietly next to me; he slept better now, his mind seemed to rest. I unzipped the flap of the tent and put my head outside. Dawn was breaking, and I smiled. One always welcomes a new day with hope, and at this point, I really needed it. A halo of pink light coloured the sky behind us, where darkness was slowly fading away. The bottom of the gorge remained engulfed by shadows and darkness, but the glaciers up above us shimmered in the morning light, tongues of ice slithering down walls of sheer rock, coarse and unforgiving. The silence was absolute, so much that it seemed to become something tangible, perceivable. It was fascinating, the continuous sound of a single, musical note, like the vibration of a Tibetan bowl, with an infinite sound, vibrating in the sacred metals long after you have ceased to hear it. I tried to listen to the silence, immobile. But it wasn't the silence I was hearing, it was the pounding of my heart, resounding the echoes of my past.

Memories and more memories, like a defence mechanism protecting me from reality and solitude. The ones about one's childhood always seem happy, we tend to forget the painful, unhappy moments. Although I don't think I really had any. I was a happy child and a happy teenager as well. But it is now that I understand that the reason why we were happy was that we were really quite ignorant and naïve. I had actually lived through a very dark period in the history of Spain. I had grown up in a country recovering from a cruel civil war. But for us, children, we had never known better times. How different my life would have been had I not moved to Paris when I was only twenty-two.

From the small and homely French Institute where I had studied until I was nine, I transferred to a Jesuit school to start my secondary education. The teaching method of the French Institute had proven to be so effective that the priests awarded me an honorary distinction when I did my entry examinations. But after that, I don't recall any other moments where I felt the slightest gratitude towards them or that school. Every day, we had to endure a long and suffocating mass, a poisoning of the brain – I won't use the term brainwashing due to the positive connotations of the term "to wash" – as well as a discipline based on punishment and terror. Half a century later, I still conserve a slight hearing defect, the consequence of a slap I received from Father Lahuerta in the second year. Father Melitón Laquidain was, however, subtler, despite his name which translated from Spanish would mean something along the lines of "the one who hits". He would place a big iron key in his hand, with only the sharp end of it visible between his fingers. Then he would walk between the desks and approach you from behind. If he saw you whispering with your neighbour, or merely distracted, Wham! He would hit you in the back of the head. A couple of examples of "*La letra con sangre entra*" which could be translated to "The lesson will be better learnt if blood is spilt." They interpreted it meant to mean the blood of the student, although I am sure the man who invented this saying was referring to the effort of the teacher. That, however, would not have agreed with the Jesuit's teaching philosophy.

Father Félix Gómez on the other hand, "loved us". He was what was then called a "spiritual father" and so, would very often summon us to his office where he would proceed to show us his affection. Seated in his chair, he would signal us to stand next to him. He then would place his right arm around our waist and gently sit us on his lap and cradle us. A kiss on the cheek, a caress on the back of our thighs. Being ten or eleven years old, I saw nothing wrong with it; I saw him as a loving grandfather. Father Fonoll, a sensible Catalan priest, was my maths teacher during the first three years of secondary school. He was so good that he could make algebra and equations seem as simple as playing marbles. His character was the same as the subject he taught, fair and accurate. After the third year, I learned that he was leaving for the Americas, to become a missionary. I went to say goodbye, and to express my gratitude to him. When I wanted to kiss his hands, he took them away and placed them on my shoulders saying: "Study as much as you can, be restless and remain curious!"

Jack shifted uneasily next to me. I had been stuck in that miserable tent all morning. This was probably the reason why so many childhood memories were suddenly coming back to me. Could it be because there was finally enough silence to be able to listen to my soul? Was I assessing my life because I could feel the closeness of death? Waiting for "the cold hand of snow", as the witty and nutty poet José Bergamín used to say. What does a man feel when he is dying? What was going through Jack's mind? How

48

helpless one must feel if, at the time of one's death, there is no-one to look at, no-one to talk to or no-one that will listen. A complete and authentic loneliness.

"No way, this will not happen to me, and it is stupid to think about it. I am in perfect health and very fit. Surely Pemba will return to get us, and if he doesn't, as soon as Jack recovers, we will get on with it and find our own way home. And if he dies, I'll go alone, the village can't be that far, and I remember the way but...what if there is fog or too much snow...?" I felt guilty thinking that way, but there was still a chance Jack might not make it, and I had to be realistic.

My companion was now awake, rubbing his shoulder with his right hand. I offered him a plate of rice which I had cooked a few hours before. Helping him to incorporate himself and holding him up with my left arm, I fed him with the right. For dessert, black tea, vitamins and anti-inflammatory medicine. He thanked me with a faint voice a couple of times and lay down again.

I, on the other hand, needed to move and breathe. I left the tent and stretched my legs. The skies were clearing, and the sun shyly peeked through the clouds, but not enough to warm up the afternoon. I fetched the survival blanket from my bag, stretched it out in front of the tent and sat down. There I was, alone, with no other company than that of the mountains, the blue and grey sky, my memories and my worries. "I should think less and keep my mind blank, like the yogi's teachings to be able to relax."

I spotted a group of bharals, those Himalayan blue sheeps, of thick grey skin and bluish backs which, from a distance and when they are immobile, look like rocks. Males have large horns in the shape of an arch, while those of the females are straight and short. There were about a dozen of them, two hundred metres down the mountainside, right at the edge of the woods. They were grazing on the tall, hard grass protruding from the snow and nibbled on the branches of small bushes. Slowly, they ambled upwards, towards our tent. They had become used to our presence now and were not alarmed by either me nor the strange shape that was the tent.

Suddenly, the silence was broken by the pounding of hoofs, as they started running in every direction. I was startled but immediately understood, as the memory of what Peter Matthiessen had written in his book *The Snow Leopard* came to mind. I had read it a few months ago, in Kathmandu. It describes the experiences of the author as he accompanied the famous zoologist George Schaller on his expedition to the Dolpo Valley in Nepal, in search for the famous and evasive feline. They only found footprints and excrement. What they did see were a lot of bharals, as the author pointed out, the snow leopard's favourite meal.

My eyes wandered around the scene, taking it all in, the snow, the rams, the tension, and then stopped, incredulous, unbelieving. It couldn't be, impossible! But it was, right there, right before my eyes. The most elusive and mysterious of all cats, the majestic snow leopard. He must have appeared from the same spot as the rams a few minutes earlier. My senses were alert, but I did not dare to move an inch. I was about to witness something only very few have been lucky to see and worthy of the most impressive nature documentary. Slowly I raised my camera, which I luckily had brought with me to take pictures of the sunset. Thank god that the zoom was on and with it at 200 mm so I could get closer to the scene.

The leopard had chosen his prey: a baby lamb that ran, glued to his mother's flank, in complete panic. He went for it, the distance separating them growing smaller and smaller. A few more metres and he would have his prey under his claws. Spellbound I followed them. The law of the jungle, inevitable and eternal. It was now only a matter of seconds. But then, instinct took charge. The mother stopped and turned around, facing him who dared threaten her child. She lowered her head, horns pointing towards the leopard while her small baby sought refuge and protection between her hindquarters. The feline was startled and slowed down, hesitated, moved to the right and then to the left, searching for a gap, a weakness to attack the stubborn protector. But she stood her ground. The leopard kept on searching for the right angle to pounce, but could not find it. He simulated an attack and was met with horns and a mother's determination. The lamb did not leave his mother's side. I could hear his inconsolable bleats.

Meanwhile, the other bharals observed the scene from a cautious distance, without showing any intention of intervening. Two black crows landed on the white snow, around twenty metres from the battleground, waiting for a favourable outcome. After trying a few more times in vain, the leopard stopped. He lowered his head, almost grazing the floor as if to say: "I surrender" and opted to withdraw. Every few steps he would turn around and assess the situation again but the mother did not take her eyes off him, attentive and firm. Finally, the leopard disappeared into the trees, no doubt, with his tail between his legs, I thought. The bharals regrouped and started ascending the slope, after a while, they were out of sight. The crows spread their wings and also left the scene, and so, the landscape returned to its quiet indifference and me to the memories of my youth.

What I remember from my student days resembles what many other students who attended university remember. During the first two years, I tried to combine both a degree in Law and a degree in Industrial Engineering, but it turned out to be an impossible task as the timetables clashed and so, happily really, I quit law. Moreover,

I didn't really like subjects which involved a lot of studying and memorising, I liked those based on logic and reasoning.

All the reading and experiences through which I lived during my adolescence and youth piled up in my mind, overlapping and forming the wings that allowed me to grow, learn and fly. Despite the fact that it was during this time that I discovered that my deepest philosophical thoughts had already been enunciated by the ancient Greeks and Romans. Also by Goethe: "in man, the more intelligent, the more unhappy".

Yes, my wings grew and grew, but without any apparent consequence. There I was, stuck in Zaragoza, my hometown, restless but not knowing where to go or where to focus my efforts. Until the day that Thermodynamics appeared in my life. They allowed me to spread my wings, leap, and fly. I am not referring to the physical phenomenon of the effects of changes in temperature, pressure and volume of a body, and how the power thus generated infuses movement. But that, thanks to an unexpected good grade in this subject, the bane of my last years, I found myself that month of June with my degree complete and freer than the then famous singer Nino Bravo's song *Libre*, free in Spanish.

I had the whole summer ahead of me and no plans. The example of my friend Daniel's latest adventures kept hovering in my mind. Last summer, he had spent a month in Paris, unloading trains in the "Gare du Nord" and the year before, another month washing dishes in a restaurant in Stockholm. But he had returned without having slept with a Swedish girl – a myth at that time – and of Paris, he only talked of hardship and misery, he had earned very little money and his French had not improved.

But then a providential encounter. One morning at the end of June, while I was walking down the Gran Vía near the School of Medicine, I met Bautista, the friendly and ever helpful teacher of technical design at the School of Engineering.

"How are you?"

"I passed everything."

"Congratulations! What are your plans now?"

"I would like to go to Paris two or three months to work and improve my French."

"Why don't you do an internship with the Télémécanique? We went to visit their manufacturing plant last year as an end of year trip, and they told us that if anybody wanted to go and work with them, they should just write them a letter."

I rang the French embassy, and they gave me the address. My sister helped me write the application letter, she had spent the previous summer in Toulouse at a friend's house and had been able to improve her French. A few days later I received an answer. I had been accepted but with one condition: I had to bring with me a certificate from the IASTE, the International Student Association for Technical Exchanges. They gave me an address and a telephone number in Madrid, and without losing a minute, I rang.

"How did you manage to get the internship? We only give the certificate to those who apply through us, and the deadline for this summer ended in April," they answered.

What a disappointment! What to do? But my father, used to fighting for what he wanted since he became an orphan of both parents at sixteen and with three smaller brothers to take care of, urged me to keep on trying:

"Just go without the certificate and if they say no, then you look for something else. Here, take these three thousand pesetas to live in Paris for a week and to buy a return ticket if after that week you haven't found anything. "

Two days later, at two in the morning, I boarded the night express to Irún/Bilbao, accompanied by my friend Daniel who was travelling to Tolosa to visit the paper factory he represented. My friend had stopped studying after finishing higher secondary school and since then, had been working with his father as a sales agent representing paper manufacturers and steel plants until, a couple of years earlier, he had become independent of his father and found his own clients. He was the only one of all of us who had a real income and this, together with his generosity, was something that suited us perfectly. He would frequently invite us to have Vermouth with Gin in The Avenida, under the porches of Independencia Avenue, where he would relax at midday after having made his work rounds visiting present and future customers.

Daniel was also a poet and an avid reader. His poems were very postmodern and lacking in rhyme, and he only showed them to his best friends and that after many hesitations and only if he considered them perfect enough. At that time, he already knew about and read Alberti, Bergamín and Guillén; and taught us about Solzhenitsyn and his *Gulag*, Sholokhov and his *And Quiet Flows the Don* and Pasternak and his famous *Doctor Zhivago*.

We arrived in Hendaya, and I changed trains, but not before the customs officers and gendarmes inspected my passport thoroughly. It was nine o'clock in the morning. My train compartment companions, from Mondoñedo in Galicia, opened up their cardboard suitcase which contained only a shirt, a change of underwear and a big loaf of bread stuffed with meatballs and green peppers. I was cordially invited to have lunch with them. The meatballs tasted a bit earthy and were not as juicy as my mother's, maybe because they had been made a couple of days ago. Then, I fell asleep. When I woke up, the gothic towers of the Cathedral of Chartres protruded over the landscape. I admired the symmetry of the wheat fields and the abundance of forests and their large trees.

It was almost night time when we arrived in Paris. We arrived at Austerlitz Station, next to the Seine, the entrance through which so many Spanish citizens had passed, during that time and previous years, after and in consequence of the civil war, with their hearts overwhelmed by feelings of defeat and exile. Those of us who arrived now, however, had our hearts full of excitement and enthusiasm, but I must admit also in awe of the superiority of a more developed country. At least, that is what I thought back then. I knew that my priority was to find a hotel to spend the night, but I found myself dragging my suitcase across a wide bridge over the Seine, enchanted by the amplitude of the views, the light of the lanterns extending left and right through the streets and along the tranquil riverside walkways between massive walls. In the distance, the illuminated towers of Notre Dame. I leant forward on the parapet with my suitcase between my legs contemplating the scene, completely enraptured.

What a difference to the one I was witnessing now. The clouds had descended, seeking shelter in the gorge below us. Until a few minutes before they had been reddish pink, but were now of a threatening grey as the Sun had already set behind the mountains which blocked my views to the West. But its essence remained. As the day drew to a close, the snow of the highest peaks turned purple. The light on the Nanda Devi was the last one to extinguish itself. The sky grew dark but remained clear. There was hope for tomorrow.

My thoughts returned to Paris, to the evening of my arrival. When my practical sense took over, I finished crossing the bridge and took the underground on the other side. I stayed at a cheap hotel near Pont de Neuilly, as the next morning I would catch the bus nearby, to Nanterre, a village in the suburbs where the factory was located. The next morning, I introduced myself to the Training Manager and explained why I had not been able to bring the certificate with me:

"No problem, we can get it at the Paris office," he answered.

And so, as easy as that, my three-year stay in Paris began. A universal city where a walk down a boulevard, a bridge or a square evoked a great past, in every corner of the city an important piece of History had occurred. I discovered Charles Aznavour, who had arrived in Paris only a short while before me at the age of eighteen – *a dixhuit ans, j'ais quitté ma provence*[11], he sang –, the filmmakers of the Nouvelle Vague, and the famous Ingmar Bergman and his film *Wild Strawberries*. I was impressed by the scene where a funeral carriage passes next to the main character. The horse rears and the coffin falls to the ground and opens, showing his own corpse. I was no less impressed by the films made by Luis Buñuel: *Las Hurdes*, a symbol of the backwardness and lack of justice in many areas of rural Spain, and the surreal *An Andalusian Dog*, with the shocking scene of an eye cut open with a shaving blade.

In the cafes, the Deux Margots in Saint Germain and La Coupole in Montparnasse, I discovered the existence of the last existentialists and bohemians. I also learned about the editorial *Ruedo Ibérico*, and its collection of books, forbidden in Spain, such as *The Spanish Labyrinth* by Gerald Brenan, *The Secret History of the Opus Dei* by Jesús Ynfante and *History of the Civil War* by Hugh Tomas. These three books changed my perception of the recent history of Spain; I learnt many truths, very different to the history I had been taught in school, or what press and radio had

[11] *"At eighteen, I left my province…"*

reported and what I listened to during my youth had told us. I met Republicans and Anarchists and attended their gatherings in the Latin Quarter. And I discovered the real significance of words such as politics, socialism, democracy, strike…

And my first real love. And sex. I also felt real freedom for the first time, but also true loneliness. They tend to go together. I learnt that in reality, we are angels with a single wing. We must attach ourselves to another angel if we want to fly. And it did not take me long to find her. Rather than an angel, she was more of a devil, and her name was Marianne.

"Voulez vous danser avec moi?"[12]

It had taken me a while to summon up the courage to stand up and go and ask her to dance with me. I was scared she would reject me, as she had a few others who had also dared approach her. But as I walked towards her, my insecurities vanished as I forced myself to think: "If she rejects me, who cares, she won't be the first nor the last". She looked at me, with those clear eyes that held a touch of indifference and, to my surprise, stood up, raised her arms, entwined her right hand with mine and placed her left on my shoulder. I brought her close, hugged her waist, and we launched into a sensual dance to the torn chords of a tango.

Three weeks had passed since I had first set foot in Paris. It was Saturday evening, and we were at Le Jardin de Montmartre, a dancing venue at the Place du Tertre; a Spanish friend from the factory had taken me with him. Through a glass door and to the left, the bar, with a dozen men leaning on it, Pernod or beer in hand. Some, like us, wore simple summer suits, or a summer shirt with a sweater casually thrown over the shoulders. Others, the vast majority, in fact, wore tight open shirts, showing off their hairy

---

[12] "Would you like to dance with me?"

chests, flares snug at the hips, thin moustaches and elongated sideburns. They clearly had Johnny Hallyday or Elvis Presley as role-models. Not to forget the handkerchief tied around their necks and a cigarette, Gitanes or Gauloises, hanging from their lips.

Beyond this scene, the access to patio and garden. It was a moderately illuminated dance floor, surrounded by small tables and iron chairs under the shadows of a glorious but old vine. Quite a few couples, a tourist group or two, and single girls, in duos and trios. We found a table next to the dance floor and ordered two glasses of the cheapest wine on the menu. The ambience, without being roguish, was slightly mischievous and it seemed like everybody more or less knew each other. After an hour, I had only managed to dance once. With a small brunette with a bob, with whom I had had no connection whatsoever, neither verbal nor carnal. My friend had not even managed that. We were already accepting our defeat and planning our retreat when she arrived together with a friend. Marianne was blonde, but a pale blonde, not the striking type; light blue-grey eyes with a serene gaze. Medium height, petite waist and a well-defined bust as it was the fashion then: Brigitte Bardot was all the rage.

They sat down. Their presence encouraged the impatient ones, but they all received a negative answer to their proposals. I suppose I had to summon up quite a bit of courage, but my experience helped as well – I was an avid dancer and had frequented many such places in Zaragoza – and cautioned me to wait until the girl had made evident that she did not just go with anybody, especially not with the first one that asked her.

In any case, the fact is that there I was, with this beautiful girl in my arms, her splendid breasts pressing against my chest and our thighs brushing against each other to highlight, as it should be, the positions, the surges and stops that the plaintive violin and the imitator of Carlos Gardel indicated. They say that one dances The Tango "listening to the other's body". Starting with the embrace of one's partner, one tries to express sensuality to a maximum. Everything within the Tango is about connection: eyes, arms, hands, every movement of the body accompanying the rhythm and the experience. The Tango achieves a three-minute romance between two people who might have just met, like us, but it unites and excites like no other dance. Afterwards, we danced sambas, boleros and even a *pasodoble*.

I remember nothing of my friend or hers. Only sitting at a table alone with Marianne. She was Danish but had been living in Paris for a couple of years as a teacher. Alone, she and I. My arm wrapped around her shoulders, our heads locked together, rehearsing our first kisses. I didn't really have much more experience with women than that, a bit of breast touching and rubbing against each other, but that was it. Spain at that time was a country of much prayer and little flesh. We had been brought up in ignorance of such things and society had imposed on us a repression of all impure desires, as our alleged educators, the priests, would call the natural inclinations of the living being.

More tangos and this time Marianne surrendered herself with pleasure to my embraces and would press against me openly. At around three in the morning, we had to leave as it was closing time. The square was already empty, neither artists nor tourists. We walked towards Sacré Coeur, entwined in one another. A few verses of Federico Garcia Lorca came to my mind, the ultimate example of erotic literature that we had been able to access in our youth, and obviously not in literature class:

> *En las últimas esquinas*
>
> *toqué sus pechos dormidos,*
>
> *y se me abrieron de pronto*

como ramos de jacintos.

We arrived opposite the Grand Basilica and sat at the top of the legendary stairway that precedes it. The moon was waiting for us, always exquisite, melancholic, sullen, romantic, the queen of beauty that night. And Paris with all its roofs, domes, towers, arrows and lights was at our feet. As expected, I allowed myself to get carried away by the poet and be swept away by the joyful passion that immediately appeared in Marianne. My hands fumbled with her breasts, her tongue in my mouth. The desire and urgency grew, with an uncontrollable hunger. The "Nordic infidel" (as they were then considered in Spain) took the initiative, and we penetrated the foliage of the adjacent garden. I followed García Lorca's orders:

> *Bajo su mata de pelo*
> *hice un hoyo sobre el limo.*
> *Ni nardos, ni caracolas*
> *tienen el cutis tan fino,*
> *ni los cristales con luna*
> *relumbran con tanto brillo.*

My hands explored and she expertly guided them down her body, while I offered my manhood with all the anxiety of the submissive innocent.

> *Sus muslos se me escapaban,*
> *Como peces sorprendidos,*
> *La mitad llenos de lumbre,*
> *La mitad llenos de frio.*

And it was there, in the shadow of the famous expiatory neo-Byzantine church, that, oh, sacrilege! in two shakes of a lamb's tail, I had lost my virginity.

Aquella noche corrí

el mejor de los caminos,

montado en potra de nácar

sin bridas y sin estribos.

The night went by, and we lay there in our embrace until the morning dew forced us to react. Recomposed, we went back to the staircase. Dawn was breaking, and from down below, from the square of La Bastille, the first fireworks exploded against the pink sky. For a moment, I thought it was in my honour. But no, it was 14th of July, the anniversary of the French Revolution. And finally, I had become a man.

In the farthest street corners

I touched her sleeping breasts

and they opened to me suddenly

like spikes of hyacinth.

Underneath her cluster of hair

I made a hollow in the earth.

Nor nard nor mother-o'- pearl

have skin so fine,

nor does glass with silver

shine with such brilliance.

Her thighs slipped away from me

Like startled fish,

half full of fire,

half full of cold.

That night I ran

on the best of roads
mounted on a nacre mare
without bridal stirrups.

V

I'm going into an unknown country where I will not have name or past, and where I will be reborn with a new face and a virgin heart.

Colette

It was my third day in Jack's company. Loneliness and uncertainty were already starting to weigh me down. I took out a painting I had bought a few weeks ago in Kathmandu, and which I kept rolled up in my bag: it was the portrait of a Nepali woman, a hundred, or maybe even two hundred years old. I had been immediately captivated by her serene beauty. It must have lain abandoned for a long time, forgotten in an attic or a closet, waiting for someone to discover it. Even though someone had carefully restored it, there were still a few tiny holes in her hat and dress. Except for a few marks on her forehead, her face remained intact. Maybe the painting was an idealisation; she looked more European than Eastern. Her skin was white and smooth, her mouth small with well defined red lips, her eyes were of clear amber, her nose broad and straight, and her long hair was jet black and smooth. Three layers of pearls encircled her neck and another one, made of turquoise stones, adorned her cleavage. Various other delicate pendants hung above her chest, and a large golden hoop dangled from her right earlobe. The left was invisible to the eye, as her head was slightly tilted to that side in a demure pose, looking downwards.

She made me think of Ursula but also reminded me of Monique. I was amazed at the way I was always complicating things further. Hadn't I wanted to break up with everything and start a new life? Instead of worrying about the complicated situation I had got myself into, there I was, daydreaming about my two impossible loves. But what was evident was that if I didn't get out of this mess, there would be no use worrying about my love life as I would never see either of them ever again. But thoughts and affections are untameable. And anyway, I liked thinking about them.

So that is what I did, in the precarious refuge between peaks and snow, the fear and the silence, loneliness and the wait, and accompanied by Jack's restless sleep, I thought of the time I had spent in Kolkata with Monique. It had only been a few months ago, on this my second trip to the Himalayan region. First, the surprise of meeting such a charming woman and then, the intensity of our relationship, more platonic than carnal. Buried feelings, maybe inappropriate for my age and experience. Remembering that scene moved and transported me; it brought a smile to my lips, a smile of longing. I remembered her with such affection. And more than that, with sadness. I closed my eyes and allowed myself to see her again that morning, at the break of dawn.

The white linen sheet barely covers the lower part of her body. She is lying on her left side, with her back turned to me. I admire her smooth skin, naturally tanned and probably incredibly soft to the touch. The light of the early dawn enters the room through a worn-out curtain that covers the entrance from the balcony. Old English furniture, the photographs of British officials and Maharajas posing vainly alongside the lifeless bodies of wild tigers become sad remains, plaster mouldings blackened over the years, a hobbling ceiling fan and naked light bulbs hanging from where bohemian crystal chandeliers had probably hung in the past.

Once an ancestral colonial mansion it was now a decayed hotel in Sudder Street, the street where we, the majority of the backpackers, stay when they arrive in Kolkata. It was called Fairlawn and was run by an elderly couple, an Englishman and his Armenian wife, as pleasant and charming as they were bizarre and for whom the days of the Raj had not seemed to end. They guarded the past grandeur of the British Empire in India when Kolkata was its pompous capital city. Manuel, Monique and I shared a triple room; strictly speaking, a double room with an alcove where the subject of my attention and desire was now sleeping.

She turns. Her young face, innocent in her sleep, her beautiful teenage breasts and her left hip exposed. I feel a great tenderness towards her. Maybe even more than that. That is why I observe her from a distance, leaning against the wall. She fascinates me, but there is no lustful desire in my eyes, I don't feel like a voyeur. I approach her and lean over her, slightly. I am attracted by her mouth and fight a desire to put my hand over one of her golden breasts, fruits of paradise crowned by a discreet areola slightly darker. She opens her eyes. Her smile is spontaneous, interrogating. I move closer, and she looks at me, a spark of amusement in her eyes. She places her right hand behind my neck and brings me closer. We kiss. A sweet, light kiss, almost childlike. She then covers herself, turns around and falls back to sleep.

I had met Monique and Manuel two days earlier, on the flight from Paris to Kolkata via Kuwait. It was April 1978, and I was returning to the Himalayas after my adventures from the previous year, with the intention of exploring it for five or six months and create a photographic book about its landscapes and people.

Monique was French and had been sitting to my right, next to the window. Manuel, seated to my left, came from Argentina and was around thirty, tall, lanky and blonde, which denoted his German ancestry. Monique was around twenty years old. She was from Orleáns, and she told me she was a Buddhist. A failed love relationship had driven her to go in search of the meaning of existence. After three weeks in a community in the Alps and eight days locked up in a tiny room meditating, she was on her way to Nepal for the big test: three months of isolation and fasting sitting in the Lotus position in the cell of a Lamaist Monastery, facing the snowy peaks of the great mountain range. She was a brunette, brown eyes and had a pretty oval face, with a boyish haircut. I saw her as an idealist, naïve and full of enthusiasm. Another "Joan of Arc."

The three of us had spent the nine hours between flights together, exploring Kuwait, until a friendly and apparently unoccupied native had taken us to visit the desert. An excuse to show us and show off his assortment of whiskies and other spirits that he kept hidden in the trunk of his grand American car, and to which Manuel and I had no other option but to please him by tasting a few of them. The consequence of this, we had slept like a log the whole flight, abandoning Monique to her thoughts. When I woke up, my head was resting on her shoulder but she, following the doctrine dictated by Buddhist compassion, had suffered this patiently and without complaint.

It was midnight by the time we exited the airport in Kolkata, after the typical immigration procedures and waiting for the bus to start. The three of us had read about the emotional shock that the misery, chaos and diversity would inflict upon us and we were mentally prepared. I had even been to Indian cities before, like Delhi, Varanasi and others. But as we drove down the streets of the Bengali capital, the spectacle was as surprising as it was tragic.

The whole city was covered in darkness. You could not tell if it was because the already scarce public lighting went out regularly at a particular time or if there was a power shortage at that moment.

The night was completely black, and as I looked out of the window, I could barely see anything. But if you looked in front of you, through the windscreen of the old bus, the beam of the headlights depicted a shocking scene that of dozens of bodies lined up on the pavement one next to another, wrapped from head to toe in a sheet. They looked like corpses covered by their respective shroud. My emotions evolved quickly from shock to excitement. Monique had dozed off next to me, unaware of the scene in front of us but Manuel was as surprised as I was. A few seconds later, we understood the scene that we were witnessing. If one looked at it rationally, they were just ordinary citizens sleeping, either because they didn't have any other roof over their heads than the starry sky, or because in their own presumably over-crowded homes it was way too warm to sleep. I wouldn't describe it as heartbreaking, but it did impress us tremendously. A gloomy and unexpected introduction to the city, the old "Jewel of the British Crown", and now called alternatively "The City of Joy" or "The City of Death."

We arrived in Sudder Street with the hope of finding a couple of rooms in one of its cheap hotels, but it was late, and they were all closed for the night. Only the Fairlawn, a decrepit three-star hotel, had a remaining light over its Victorian porch. A lanky Bengali, with red teeth due to the *betel* – pouches of leaves filled with areca nuts that the Indians chew as a digestive-, was lying on a cot next to the reception, but he jumped up when he heard us and with a complacent smile offered us his services. He gave us a triple room, as palatial as it was ramshackle, but for a reasonable price, so we stayed there for the couple of nights we were planning on remaining in the city.

The next morning, we immersed ourselves in the hustle and bustle of the city. After the dry atmosphere of Kuwait, the air in Kolkata hung over the city, enveloping you like the retches of a hippopotamus drowning in a clogged sewer. Apart from that, the city looked as if it had suffered a dozen floods in the past years, alternating with another dozen fires. Such was the appearance of the streets and buildings, with huge damp stains in the basements and black soot and dirt on its facades and roofs. Ironically, only the monument to Queen Victoria, Empress of India, was pristine in its majestic magnanimity of white marble, between two ponds on the side of the wide esplanade of the Maiden.

The streets were heaving with people. *Rickshaws*[13] pulled by men clothed only from the waist downwards in their *dhotis* leaving their squalid torsos and legs exposed, wagons pulled by skeletal horses and beat up buses, their bodies hanging dangerously to the left due to the number of passengers hanging from both their open doors on that same side. On the wide pavements, whole families had their permanent camp set up, dirty and covered in rags, and protected from the sun by old awnings hanging from tree branches and fences, and surrounded by a thousand flies. The crows cawed from the power line cables, a few cows ambled along, searching for something green to ruminate on while the dogs rummaged through the rubbish piles next to the road.

In Park Street, a long line of mothers with their babies waited for their turn next to a clinic of benevolent doctors, many of them Western, lodged in tents. A beautiful example of charity. Manuel had come to Kolkata to do something similar and I, for the first

---

[13] A light two-wheeled passenger vehicle drawn by one or more people, chiefly used in Asian countries.

time, was aware of the intense need to help developing countries. We stood there for a while, contemplating the comings and goings of the mothers, their patient attitudes and their faces of hope or concern while the doctors listened attentively, examining the children with a stethoscope and explained the treatment or gave advice.

There were queues everywhere, men and women lining up around the central building of the post office and in front of every other public building. Sellers of *betel* and *beedies* (cigarettes made from a single sheet of tobacco), peanuts, postcards, knives and garlands of flowers to offer to the gods occupied each corner under large posters announcing movies of powerful, singing heroes and dancers covered with silks and jewels. A couple of tailors sitting under a fig tree seemed to compete to see who pedalled faster on their old Singer sewing machines, their wrinkly hands guiding pieces of orange fabric under the needle. A group of barefoot children observed them. Here, a *sadhu* sitting next to a statue of Ganesh, the elephant God, helped passersby with their offerings and accepted their alms. A toothless old woman sold a handful of green chillies and another, young and robust, dressed in a bright red Sari and with her hair in a bun, so oiled it looked like being varnished, split a huge rambutan into pieces with an old machete and offered its juicy pulp to the pedestrians.

Despite the number of visual stimuli, the new impressions, noises and smells, I could not stop thinking about the image of Monique half-naked in her bed at dawn. If I walked behind her, I became absorbed by her figure now covered by a simple cotton dress floating over her body to the rhythm of her walk. If I walked next to her, I took advantage of any opportunity to touch her bare arms with the pretext of guiding her, help her cross the crazy traffic or avoid the most minimal obstacle. At times, it was she who would, I wouldn't say press, but yes bring her body closer to mine. I felt the desire to hug her and kiss her right there, a demonstration that would have raised cries of surprise and indignation among the prudish Bengali.

In a large square, presided over by a huge banyan tree, we noticed four men, a distance of around five meters separating each other, and squatting over a large basin in front of each of them. In front of one of the men, a queue of about 20 people with a plate in their hand had formed. When it was their turn, they received a ration of rice and lentil soup. The benefactor, who was pointed out to us, was leaving the scene wrapped in a white sari with blue and black stripes, a traditional widow's outfit.

We each gave twenty rupees, five dollars in total, and gave it to one of the men so that they could serve another thirty people. Immediately a queue formed of around forty, while others emerged from every corner. We gave him sixty rupees more and slipped away before we attracted half of Kolkata, discussing amongst us whether it was charity or exoticism what had driven our action.

We ate at a local restaurant. For eight rupees per person, we were served the typical *thali*: a mountain of white rice served on a banana leaf plate, and various small bowls with different thick soups made of lentils and vegetables, chutney with coconut and chilly, pickles and a few *poori* which are wheat flour fritters. All of this we ate the oriental way, without using cutlery, just making a ball of food with our right hand and trying to stuff it into our mouths without losing half the meal. We had a great time and laughed a lot at our inexperience, especially Manuel who would have never imagined that he would one day eat soup and rice with his fingers, and this relaxed the tension which the street scenes had produced.

After lunch, I proposed we take a *rickshaw* to visit the Kalighat Temple.

"No way, I am not sitting in one of those things like a duchess expecting a poor man to drag me around!"

Monique's exclamation sounded as spontaneous as appalled.

"You shouldn't look at it that way" I answered. "There is nothing dishonourable about it. For them, it's a job like any other. You are doing the one you choose to "drag" you around a great favour. He would charge an Indian four or five rupees but will charge you twenty or thirty. With that, he can pay the daily rental of the rickshaw, because they are usually not theirs, and he can feed his family for two or three days.

"If you look at it that way, I don't think it's a bad idea," said Manuel.

"I still think it's a degrading job" replied Monique, "but anyway…"

"Of course, compared to the Buddhist monks who do absolutely nothing throughout the day…" I said, without stopping to think about the effect of my words. She stared at me in amazement.

"What do you mean?"

"Well, that with so much prayer and meditation they don't have much time to do anything else," I tried to save the situation.

"Every man has the right to choose his path" stressed Monique.

"Come on, let's take a *rickshaw* each and go and worship the famous Kali" concluded the Argentinean, trying to avoid a squabble.

What I most wanted to do at that moment was to hug her, she was so attractive with that point of outrage in her eyes.

Following Manuel's suggestions, we chose a young and strong driver for Monique from the half a dozen which had already surrounded us a while ago and who offered their services by tapping with their open palm the withered seats of their respective vehicles. I got the oldest and weakest looking. I lit a cigarette and offered him one before settling into my seat:

"For later," I told him, handing him one.

But he rejected it:

"I don't smoke."

Instead, he spread a thin layer of white cream on his bottom lip.

"To me, this has the same effect as tobacco," he explained. "But what I like is opium. I take it twice a day: at eight in the morning and four in the afternoon. Without it, I can't work. If you don't have cigarettes you don't smoke; but if I don't have opium, I can't work, my arms and back will hurt too much," he concluded.

With those last words, he adjusted the strap around his chest, grabbed the bars of the carriage and began to jog in pursuit of his colleagues. Despite my previous argument to persuade Monique, I could not help feeling a bit uneasy as I contemplated the man's fragility.

We discovered that the temple was of little artistic interest, but at that time of the evening, it was heaving with devotees. The entrance and surrounding streets were crowded, turned into a bazaar where one could buy all sorts of offerings for the goddess, as well as pictures representing the black effigy covered in blood with snakes and skulls around her neck and a variety of weapons in her five pairs of arms.

"All this fanaticism is absurd, it repulses me," said Monique.

"Yes, I completely agree, this is the worst form of Hinduism," I replied.

"Well, this is the more popular form of Hinduism, one should

72

not mistake it with Brahmanism, which is the real Hinduism," Manuel pointed out. "This can happen in all faiths. One must distinguish between doctrine and ritual, the philosophy of the religion and the need of the people to believe in things which frighten them and don't understand, the mysteries and superstitions.

"And in how dirty it all is. So much plastic, and wrappers and cow dung," Monique added, wrinkling her nose.

"Do you know what an Indian once told me when I first visited India?" I asked, smiling ironically. "That it was us, the Western tourists, the ones who taught them how to be dirty; before us, they didn't have anything to throw away.

"Hmm, interesting," said Manuel, who then took out his guide and proceeded to read to us a summary of what we were seeing.

Kali, "the black goddess" and the patron saint of Kolkata, is one of the forms of Shakti as a consort of Shiva. According to Hinduism tradition, in the mists of time when the gods still walked on the Earth, King Daksha, father of Shakti, decided to perform the great Vedic ritual called *Yajna*. But he did not invite Shiva. Distraught by the affront made to her husband, Shakti died during the ceremony. Shiva, furious and blinded by rage and pain, appeared as lighting and destroyed everything in his wake. Before the awed spectators, he took the corpse of his bride on his shoulders and began his dance of destruction of all created.

The rest of the gods, alarmed, sent Vishnu, the protector, who with his *sudarshan chakra* or wheel of energy, cut the body of Shakti in fifty-one pieces, which fell scattered all over India, to hide them from the desperate husband. They became places of pilgrimage. The toe of the Goddess fell in Kolkata, right in the place where the present temple stands. For the devotees of Kali, the devourer of human skulls, Kalighat is the most sacred temple in the world.

Meanwhile, we had arrived at the main door. A young Brahmin approached us and offered us a *puja*[14]. I encouraged my friends to share this experience with me. We took our shoes off and followed him. He stopped in front of one of the stalls that sold offerings.

"One doesn't approach the deity empty handed," he told us and chose a coconut, flowers and a few sticks of incense.

"Hundred rupees," said the vendor.

We had seen the previous client paying ten, so we offered him twenty. It is normal in the East that foreigners pay something more than the locals. After haggling for a while, we came to a deal and gave him thirty. Pushing and shoving our guide led us through the crowd, and we arrived right at the side of the steps which led to the main altar, closed by heavy ancient silver doors, behind which we assumed the deity was hiding. The Brahman confirmed this and asked for our names to repeat them to the goddess together with some invocations in Sanskrit which we did not understand. We placed the flowers on a platter overflowing with similar offerings, lit the incense, and the Brahman halved the coconut by hitting it against an iron fence. He then poured the milk over our heads.

"You have to offer Kali some money," he pointed out.

Monique murmured something along the lines of "when are we going to stop behaving like fools" and Manuel deposited a ten rupee note.

"Two hundred rupees minimum," the Brahmin insisted.

"We are not rich, let's see what Kali can do with ten," answered Manuel. The Brahman re-directed his contemptuous look at me,

14 The act of worship in Hinduism and Buddhism.

but I remained impassive.

Suddenly, the tone of the invocations and chants rose, and the heavy plated silver doors were thrown open by two Brahmins. And there she was. Her red eyes stood out from her charcoal black face like two flares while her tongue sprang from her mouth, a golden waterfall half a meter long between her golden fangs. Her body was covered by red brocade and from her neck hung a myriad of flower garlands. We barely had few seconds to submerge ourselves in the spectacle then the doors were shut again.

"They don't want the people to get used to seeing the devil, it's essential to maintain the mystery," you could hear the irony in Monique's voice, but she was speaking in French so only I could understand her.

"What is she saying?" asked the Brahman wearily.

"Oh! That we are very impressed, it was fantastic!" I assured him.

This time he seemed pleased. We were then led to a large platform on one side of the temple, overlooking a large patio where an excited crowd was gathered, uttering chants and screaming. In the centre stood a man holding what looked like a scimitar, an ancestral executioners tool used in the Middle East and Western Asia, a sword with a large curved blade. He was visually measuring the distance between his blade and a live goat's neck who stood there bleating and held still by two other Brahmins. He raised his steel, and with a precise hit, split the goat's head from her body. Other Brahmins collected the body of the goat and with the blood that spurted from her neck, sprayed the dozens of effigies carved in the walls of the courtyard. The people directed their victory cries to Kali, while they smeared the blood over their arms and faces, in complete ecstasy. We felt like throwing up.

"What sort of place have you brought us to, this is disgusting," Monique remonstrated.

"I know, you are right. I wasn't expecting this," I replied apologetically. "But I think it has been a fascinating experience. This is how this land is, not only spiritualism and yoga."

"I think that in this country there is little mysticism and too much ritualism," Manuel added.

We returned to the hotel, this time by bus and for a while on foot, as the centre of the city was a chaos of cars, pedestrians, cows, bicycles and a few elephants transporting heavy loads. After dinner, Monique and I went for a walk around Maiden Park, which was next to our hotel. We sat on a bench, and she told me a little more about her life. Her parents had divorced when she was only seven years old, and her father had barely shown an interest in her afterwards. She lived with her mother and her new husband, who annoyed her. She had had a steady relationship till a few months ago when her boyfriend had broken up with her without any explanation. But now, she had found her way.

"But I am scared," she admitted.

"It's normal. I think that what you are going to do, lock yourself up in a cell, alone with your thoughts and with an unhappy past stalking you, is not a good idea."

"Meditation is not about thinking about one's past. It is about leaving your mind blank," she lifted her chin and closed her eyes. "One must reject all that is negative, not allow oneself to be wrapped in emotions, one must think in positive."

"Yes, ok, but how does one achieve this in solitude? I can assure you that it is by interacting with other people and being active in new scenarios and environments. Nature is perfect for it, being in direct contact with her makes you feel much better. Come with me to travel the paths of the Himalaya," I continued, as I held her hands, "to discover, to learn about other people other cultures, to experience the joys and sufferings of the trekker. Afterwards, you can always go to your monastery."

"But I don't have the adequate equipment, no boots, no anorak…"

"You can buy that easily. With the money you were planning on donating to the monastery, and you will still have some left over," I told her.

She looked at me and smiled.

"Look, I like how you are, and I trust you; although I am not so sure, now that I think about it, those eyes, half brown half green… I am not sure whether they are trustworthy." Her smile broadened. "Look, let me be," she continued, "I appreciate your interest but…"

"Those who are not able to change their minds are not able to change anything", I argued.

"And when someone has a new idea, they are considered crazy, until his idea succeeds."

"Well, you are not lacking in bravery, and you are a bit crazy."

She leant on my shoulder. I felt a heavy heart, seeing this little girl on her way to an empty and illusory experience. "What to do, I am forty years old, and I am already a sceptic about everything," I thought. However, her future did matter to me. I couldn't help suffering for that beautiful youth, hopelessly doomed to another disappointment, another let-down. I wanted to tell her: "Let me teach you something about the realities of life. Let me love you, show you. Let me take you with me. But I'll have to settle for accompanying you in the distance and wish you luck. But from now on, I will dig my nails into the Earth, or hide my face into the pillow, or I'll raise my arms up to the sky and desire, more than anything else in this world, to see you again." But I thought it would be useless, so I kept quiet.

We returned to the hotel in silence. She to her alcove, and I to my adjoining room, where Manuel was already asleep. A few hours later, I woke up to her preparations to leave. As I listened to her packing her things I lost the little hope I had left. "I was going to lose her. In only a few days, her idealism, her ingenuity and her beauty had penetrated into my innermost self, and in a few minutes I would never see her again," I thought, as I started getting dressed to accompany her to the airport. But she didn't let me.

"It will be harder for both of us," she said.

We hugged. I couldn't let go of her.

"It has been wonderful meeting you. I wish you happiness."

"I will think of you," she answered; we'll see each other in Paris in a few months."

She had given me her address, but I knew it was improbable. She was saying it to comfort me.

"I have to leave now, please."

I opened my arms. She touched my lips with hers and let go. After saying goodbye to Manuel, who had pretended to be asleep, she took her rucksack, opened the door and crossed it without turning back.

I let myself fall onto the bed. My eyes, staring up at the ceiling. I closed them. "It seems I enjoy suffering", I told myself. But, after a few minutes, I recovered: I also had plans. After a warm hug, Manuel and I went our separate ways: he, to spend a few months with Mother Teresa, as planned, and I took the small train to Darjeeling, and from there, to continue my journey in search of the flying mountains. But I knew, that when I got to Kathmandu in a few weeks, I would look for Monique until I found her.

VI

And now here is my secret, a very simple secret:
It is only with the heart that one can see rightly;
what is essential is invisible to the eye.
Antoine de Saint-Exupéry
The Little Prince

Jack, huddled next to me, started stirring, bringing me back to reality, back from my thought of Kolkata, back from my short stay with Monique which I was longingly reminiscing. The Paracetamol and the tranquillisers had knocked him out, so it took him a while to wake up every morning. How long had we been here? How many days and nights? I should have started a calendar, marking the tarpaulin every morning or even easier, making a note in my notebook. I was writing down my thoughts but not the dates, where had my rationality gone? I stood up, opened the flap of the tent and looked outside at the scenery before me, still covered in shadows. The sun was rising from behind the Nanda Devi massif, and it would still take a few hours for it to shine upon us. But only if the sky remained clear.

I decided to go for a walk and stretch my legs for a while. Climbing up the hill, I noticed that it had snowed again during the night. One hundred meters, two hundred meters…I lost sight of the tent and silence surrounded me giving way to my thoughts and memories. The landscape slowly brightened and transformed, and new shapes and colours began to appear. I was aware of the beauty and calmness that surrounded me, and the loneliness it transmitted; it was like an invitation. For a few moments, I felt free to continue walking, even if that meant leaving Jack behind and continuing each on our separate ways, following our own uncertain destiny.

A bird's cry shattered the prevailing calm, and reality imposed itself. My freedom depended on when, how and who would come to rescue us. I was not alone, and I didn't think I would be able to find my way back to the other side on my own either. A bird, dark blue, rose behind me and glided over my head with motionless wings, its head facing downwards, scanning the area where I stood. I stopped for a while to admire it. It twisted its tail and leaned to one side, gliding gently parallel to the mountainside until it got close to the gorge. It became a dark silhouette contrasting against the clarity of the snow. It then turned again and disappeared in the direction of the Nanda Devi. It must have felt attracted to her, just like me. It was by far, the most beautiful mountain in sight, as well as the highest, its fresh snow glistening in the sun, its silhouette elegant and daring, dominant over the other crests and peaks.

The sky had been crisp and clear until a second ago, but now, without me noticing, it was slowly being invaded by masses of cirrus clouds, of wonderful tones and strange shapes. They resembled exotic flowers, large birds, winged horses…They were coming from the East, and we were on the south-west side of the massif. As suddenly as they appeared they began to dissipate, as if by magic, mysteriously and stealthily; until one of them did not. Without warning, the sky turned dark, as if a gigantic dragon was soaring above us. I could feel the cold seeping through my body: another storm was coming. I returned to the tent, as fast as I could, but careful not to slip on the icy snow. Jack greeted me with a smile and a wave of his hand. If he had missed me, he did not say. I answered his greeting, wrapped myself in my sleeping bag, lay on the camping mattress and returned to my memories of past adventures.

I had arrived in Kathmandu three weeks after saying goodbye to Monique in Kolkata, but with her memory still glued to my skin. It would soon be a year since I had first visited the Nepali capital. I had arrived then, after abandoning my job in Paris, with an urgent desire to get away from everything that had until then been my life. I had spent the least amount of time possible in renouncing my executive post, with dignity of course, and separating myself from other earthly ties. In no time I found myself in the plane in the direction of this old hidden kingdom at the foot of the Himalayan range.

Kathmandu, with its profusion of colours, its razzle-dazzle, its anarchy, its poverty, its joy, had surprised me in such a way that I had the feeling not that I was on another continent, but that I was on a different planet entirely. I had spent three months exploring the Kathmandu Valley and had gone on a couple of treks in the Himalayas. The first one had been easy, with a French group, a guide and porters, and no higher than four thousand metres. The second one, more ambitious now after the previous experience, I did alone, in the company of only one porter and destination Everest Base Camp.

During these months, I had discovered one of the richest, most exotic and well-preserved cultures in Asia, a fraction of the Hindu and Buddhist religions and had been able to get close to some of the highest peaks in the world. I had met the simple and good hearted people of the valleys and mountains; the uprooted dreamers come from Europe and America; and the travellers who, like me, were in search of new horizons and experiences. As a result of it all, I had fallen in love with Nepal and the Himalayas, and had resolved to return the following year to travel across the whole mountain chain with the intention of writing a photographic book on the region. I would go from East to West, from Sikkim to Cashmere and Ladakh for five or six months, walking, by bus or by whatever means of transport was available.

And so it was that I found myself in Kathmandu again, excited and motivated by a project which was already underway. After leaving Kolkata, I had followed the southern trails of the Kanchenjunga massif −the third highest mountain on earth− and visited the Tibetan Buddhist monasteries of Sikkim. I had even slept in some of them. I had been quite fond of the lamas and Buddhist monks, but now, despite their hospitality, I saw them as those who had taken Monique away from me and saw them, quite irrationally, as primitive, uncouth and lazy − they spent their days either praying or playing football.

The god Shiva and his consort Parvati welcomed me one more time, facing out of one of the carved windows of their home temple, looking like just another couple of neighbours, as they benevolently contemplated the curious and animated scene of Durbar Square, the Royal Square of Kathmandu. A variegated spectacle of temples and palaces, merchants, tourists, occasional guides, peasants, beggars, holy men and children engrossed in their games.

Like on my first visit, I did not know where to rest my eyes first. In this square, with a medieval atmosphere and imprecise perimeter, one finds many of the countless architectural marvels and treasures of the valley. Facades of old but solid red brick, windows and enclosed balconies made of the most laboriously carved wood, a dark wood moulded and crafted to the limit, and statues of stone or bronze, representing gods, demons and mythological animals. Pagodas with overlapping roofs, topped with golden pinnacles, banners and bells, and eaves supported by goddesses of swollen breasts, three heads and seven pairs of arms, or by couples or threesomes in daring lovemaking positions, the fruit of the carefree as well as arousing interpretation of the manners of procreation.

Hanuman, the monkey god, painted in red, protected the entrance to the ancient Royal Palace, next to a soldier armed with a rifle from the 19th century, and in the middle of the square, the terrifying, black and gigantic image of Bairav, one of the demonic interpretations of Shiva. Men and women came to offer him handfuls of rice and flower garlands to appease his ferocious character. They then received his beneficial vibes by taking their hand to their forehead in a respectful gesture.

In the porches of the houses and temples, traders and shopkeepers displayed their goods. Papier Mâché masks resembling the faces of demons and animals, multi-coloured fabrics, polished bronze figures and *thangkas*, some antique, others brand new, depicting religious scenes, images of Buddha and monks in peaceful and meditative positions as well as terrifying pictures of terrible demons. On the wide stairs of one of the temples, a couple of farmers sold a handful of tomatoes and another a few bunches of freshly picked onions, with earth still attached to their roots. A woman massaged her baby son's body with oil, while another stretched out a bucket of rice to dry.

At the top of the stairs leading to the temple, a westerner with his blonde hair tied up in a ponytail was playing his flute surrounded by curious Nepali girls. And a bit further along, in the open temple of Kasthamandap - the gigantic structure built with the wood of a single tree and from which the name Kathmandu originates - a group of aesthetic *sadhus* were sharing a *chillum*. I again remembered my first visit to this square and how these wandering monks had invited me to share a pipe with them. And just like last time, the sweet smell of hashish spread around us and mixed with the pungent scent of the incense and the fresh vegetables.

Two western girls were sitting on a window sill almost at floor level. One of them looked like Monique, but she had her back turned to me. The same short brown hair and the same graceful figure. I felt like hugging her tightly. However, when I got closer, I realised it wasn't her. But I didn't feel disappointed; it would have been too good to be true, and too easy.

A couple of small children dragged me into the interior of a courtyard surrounded by laboriously carved windows.

"Come and see the Kumari."

After a few shouts to get the caretaker's attention and after a short wait, a very made-up, adorned and striking little princess appeared briefly at the enclosed balcony. She looked at me for a few seconds, without acknowledgement and hid again. She was the living child divinity of Kathmandu. The other two ancient towns of the valley, Patan and Bakthapur, had their own child god as well. Worshipped like the incarnation of the Hindu goddess Durga, the Kumari is selected at the tender age of five among the Newari families (a Buddhist ethnic group) of the capital, for her beauty and courage: a sample of the religious syncretism of the Nepali, who mixed Hindu and Buddhist traditions and beliefs. The children told me how the little goddess, always on her throne and carried everywhere, only left her home to preside over various religious festivals where even the king prostrated himself before her.

I continued my walk, and in front of the façade of the old palace of the ancient Malla Kings, I discovered a very peculiar character. Tibetan leather boots, a *chuba* knotted at the waist, a dagger with an ivory hilt, necklaces made out of coral, a large turquoise earring and a cream-coloured felt hat. Clean and spotless. He looked like one of those Tibetan noblemen from the old photographs from the times in which the famous adventurer Alexandra David-Neel attempted to reach Lhasa, back then in the 1920's. Or maybe he was a Mongol; his physical features puzzled me.

I greeted him in the traditional Tibetan way joining the palms of my hands at chest level:

"*Tashi delè*," I ventured.

"*Tashi delè*," he answered.

"You look magnificent!"

"Thank you."

"Where do you come from? Tibet? Mongolia maybe?"

He smiled and took off his sunglasses, uncovering his clear blue eyes.

"What do you think? I come from Paris."

"*Merde alors*!" I couldn't help but swear.

We shook hands and laughed.

"What did you think of the Kumari?", he asked.

"I saw her last year. But she looked younger this time."

"Yes, that is because she is, this one is new. Her reign has just begun. The poor thing doesn't know that she will be miserable for the rest of her life."

"Oh!"

"Yes, exactly. As soon as she gets her first period it is all over; she will no longer be a goddess. You see, she will bleed, and so confirm that she is only human," my new friend began to explain.

"From then on, her life won't be easy; it is tough to stop being a deity suddenly," he lifted his arms in sign of helplessness and continued to observe me with interest. "Later, if you want, we can go and visit the girl who was the Kumari until last year. But first, why don't you come over to my place? I live nearby," as he pointed his head in his home's direction. "You can meet Cesar, my flatmate. He comes from Colombia and is dying to speak Spanish. He claims he will forget how to speak it soon."

Jean-Pierre and César lived in a beautiful old house. On the ground floor, you had a sort of workshop, a kitchen and the living quarters for the Nepali boy who worked for them as both a servant and a cook. On the first floor, a large spacious living room, furnished quite anarchically, with an old couch, large cushions, low tables, and antique Hindu and Tibetan objects of those used in religious rituals. Thick curtains separated this room from the bedrooms and the bathroom. César, sturdily built, dark eyes, black and long locks fastened in a ponytail, was very fraternal, talkative and likeable. Maybe even a bit too much, I thought afterwards. While the boy served the tea, they started telling me their story.

"We arrived here from Paris nine years ago. What a journey; long but full of dazzling adventures down the Asian roads," Jean-Pierre started. He immediately got interrupted by César; it was clear that he was dying to speak and he continued the story with that elegant and baroque Castilian typical of the Colombians.

"During that time, for us, travellers of the infinite, which is how they used to call us, Kathmandu was our only goal in our pilgrimage of the East. A journey of initiation and discovery, the break for all those rebels from the May 68 student revolution, for the hippies of Berkeley and the followers of the famous *On the road* of Jack Kerouac."

"Yes, I have read something on the subject..."

"That trip is now unrepeatable. The good old times…" César interrupted me this time, as he lifted his hands up to the heavens. "There, in the Pudding Shop of Istanbul, where backpackers from all over the world met at a kebab and a Turkish cafe, is where I met this crazy Frenchman. And look, we are still together!"

"That fraternal seedy little café," continued Jean-Pierre, "was not only the meeting point to share experiences, but also the bulletin board to find a shared vehicle, share petrol, adventures and dangers in the deserts of Iran and Afghanistan."

But César interrupted again.

"An Iran where the Ayatollahs were pondering a revolution in their mosques, and an Afghanistan still happily anchored to biblical times. What a trip!" he leant back and raised his arms again to the heavens as if he was holding tribute to a spirit. He continued, "Unlike the *Machadian* trip, here the goal was as important as the journey to reach it: Kathmandu! Nepal! The veil of mystery and spirituality, heightened by the distance, surrounded this hidden corner of the world.

"There he goes again, hyperbolising," said Jean-Pierre, laughing loudly.

But César ignored him; he was in full swing. He continued with passion, exacerbating his speech with grand hand gestures.

"Far away horizons, hidden between the mountains, Shangri-la was waiting, the Kingdom of wisdom and eternal youth. We didn't really know what we were looking for nor what awaited us, but none of us felt disenchanted when arriving in this valley, you see?" he continued. "We were all hooked on this simple life, this relaxed anarchy and denial of the western materialism. Moreover, hashish and marijuana were grown and sold freely. It was paradise."

"After four years of this, I returned to Paris," It was Jean

Pierre's time to interrupt, "but I wasn't able to fit in anymore, so I returned. But it is no longer the same. The time has come to go back home."

"Yes, that is why we want to sell some of our stuff. We need the money for the trip," added César.

And the two of them proceeded to show me the numerous treasures that they had accumulated from their adventures around the country. Their collection was made up of authentic religious ritual instruments, beautiful antique *thangkas*[15], oil or carbon portraits of 19th-century Nepali nobles and bronze statues depicting different gods or Buddha.

"You have gorgeous things. I love them, really, but I can't buy anything at the moment," I excused myself. "I won't be going home for at least a few months, I will be travelling around, going from one place to another. I'm taking pictures and collecting information to write a book on the Himalayas. If when I return from my journey, you are still here, I'll definitely buy a *thangka* or statue from you," I promised, intending to keep it.

They didn't insist but, thinking that they might be able to help me find Monique –they seemed to know many people– I changed my mind and bought from them, for twenty dollars, a portrait of a beautiful Nepali lady. Properly rolled up, it must have measured around forty centimetres. I could carry it around in my backpack, and it would keep me company during my lonely nights in the tent.

"By the way, I would like to find a French girl I met on the plane. She was on her way to Nepal, to stay in a Buddhist monastery to follow a meditation course and afterwards retire to a

[15] Tibetan Buddhist painting on cotton, or silk appliqué, usually depicting a Buddhist deity, scene, or mandala.

cave. Any idea where she could be?"

"She is probably somewhere in Bodnath," they both agreed. "It's full of monasteries, and it's nearby, just half a dozen kilometres away."

"But come, let's go and visit the ex-kumari first. It will be interesting for your book, and you can take a few pictures of her," Jean-Pierre suggested and sent the servant boy to the girl's house to warn them that we were coming to visit.

We were received by her mother, affable and modest, with a child a couple of years old clinging to her left hip, a red dot in the middle of her forehead and large gold hoops hanging from her earlobes. I slid twenty rupees into her hand (one dollar) as Jean-Pierre had suggested and we followed her up a very narrow and steep staircase to the room on the first floor. The door was open, and we had to bow down to be able to cross it. The room was tiny, with a low ceiling held by blue painted beams and a packed earth floor covered by thick orange fabric. A naked light bulb hung from its cable. There were two cushions on the floor prepared for us to sit on.

Sunina had just turned thirteen but seemed older due to the makeup, quite excessive, which accentuated her dark eyes and coloured her lips and cheeks. She wore a burgundy skirt and a jacket of the same colour, trimmed with navy blue lace, and had her black hair held back in a bun. She adorned herself with a long necklace made of old silver coins. Even though she was sitting in an old armchair made of wood and leather, one could see that she had a small, underdeveloped body. I assumed it was due to the lack of exercise. We gave her the sweets and the golden pen we had brought as gifts. She made a gesture with her head, a mixture of shyness and lack of interest, and lay them down next to her, barely looking at them. Her mother thanked us again, and between her and Jean-Pierre, who translated, they began to tell me her story.

At the age of five, and after passing a few tests related to the perfection of her body, her horoscope and her serenity facing difficult situations, she had been chosen as the new Kumari and she been installed in the palace temple. Her life was governed by a very strict code. Every morning, she was bathed, dressed and made up. Her wishes, if they didn't violate any of the established rules, were immediately fulfilled. She would only go out in the street seven times a year, and it would be on a palanquin or on the top of a lavishly decorated carriage. The crowd would prostrate themselves as she passed by. One inevitable day, puberty arrived and proved that she was only human, and so Sunina finished her career as a goddess.

Now, after seven years of being adored even by the King himself, Sunina was trying to be a normal girl. She had to learn how to walk again: as a goddess, she had been carried everywhere because her feet were not allowed to touch the earthly ground. Now, however, she had to mingle with the other children in school and help with the household chores.

"I need to forget my previous life in the temple and not talk about it," she explained. "I was happy there, but I am happier now as I can take care of my siblings."

"And how is school?" I asked.

"Not bad. I learn English, but I don't like it," she grimaced, "it reminds me of the tourists shouting underneath my window so I would look out."

"Can I take your picture?"

She answered with a forced smile and straightened her figure. I quickly set up the tripod, aimed the flash towards the ceiling and fired half a dozen pictures at different angles. To my surprise, she then lifted her hand and with a gesture indicated the interview was over.

"That girl is going to have it tough," I told Jean-Pierre.

"Of course she is. It is going to be practically impossible for her to find a husband. Who wants a wife who is used to being served? Moreover, they say that those who marry ex-kumaris die at a young age."

The next morning, I rented a bicycle to go to Bodnath, the main Buddhist sanctuary that César and Jean Pierre had told me about. Before arriving, I left the road and took a small path following the river. I passed small temples inhabited by ascetics in orange tunics, *sadhus* dressed only in ash and air, and yogis in deep ecstasy sitting on rocks or under trees. Two logs cast over the waters served as a crossing, and after this, the path zigzagged between the rice paddies and up to the great stupa. On its white dome, the prayer flags fluttered in the wind and on the base of its golden tower, the eyes of Buddha watched over the world in all four cardinal points. The Tibetan refugees, who had fled their country after the Chinese invasion, had rebuilt their world here. In the doorways and porches of the houses, they sold their arts and crafts and copies of their religious relics. I entered several temples. In the gloomy and dimly lit interior, the monks and novices sat on cushions on the floor or on top of platforms, depending on their rank, and recited their monotonous and repetitive prayers, like chants, accompanied by the sounds of gongs and the wavering light of the oil lamps. Would I find Monique among them?

Thus, and as Jean Pierre had recommended, I went to pay my respects to the Chini Lama, the head of an influential Lamaist sect, and one of the foremost authorities in Bodnath, also well known for his commercial interests. I knelt before him and deposited at his feet the usual white neck scarf as an offering, bought especially for the occasion, with a twenty-rupee note hidden between its folds. He pocketed the money expertly, blessed my soul and tied the scarf around my neck. Then, he proudly showed me the photographs that were hanging from the wall with their corresponding frame, memories from his trip to London by ship almost thirty years ago, to attend the coronation of Queen Elisabeth II.

I answered with the expected admiring comments and followed by showing my interest in his *thangka* collection. An assistant extended the paintings on the floor, paintings drawn on canvas and depicting many figures of Buddha, demons or monks, sometimes accompanied by tigers or monkeys, situated around the central figure of a god and drawn in great detail between cottony clouds and monasteries at the top of mountains. After a while of contemplating them, I chose one which represented Vajradhara, the central Buddha in his form of a tantric *bodhisattva*[16].

"Three hundred dollars," he announced without further explanation, lounging between the cushions of his couch."

"I am not a wealthy American, but a poor Spaniard," I said apologetically. "I don't want it as a decorative souvenir, but as a source of inspiration to meditate. I would only be able to pay fifty or sixty dollars."

"Two hundred," he said without moving.

I insisted. Finally, I handed him five twenty dollar bills while I made a deep reverence and claimed that I would remember his great generosity for the rest of my life. He took the money and looked at me as if to say: "You are not as dumb as the others." I decided it was the right moment to ask him about what I was really after.

[16] In Mahayana Buddhism, a person who is able to reach nirvana but delays doing so through compassion for suffering beings.

"Sorry to disturb you, but I am looking for my niece. I would like to know how she is. She is enrolled in a course around here and meditating in a cave. Would you happen to know where I could find her?"

"What is her name?"

"Monique. She is French. She is my sister's daughter, she married a Frenchman. I would also like to make a donation to the monastery where she is," I added, as I had learnt that here, money and religion were also strongly related.

"Ok, I will find out. Come back in an hour," as he lifted his right arm in what could have well been either a blessing or a farewell.

I killed some time by wandering around the area and checking out the shops. I saw the Lama's assistant go into and out of some of the nearby monasteries. My hopes grew and with them well rooted I returned to the Lama's house. His assistant met me at the door and told me that at the moment there was only one monastery in Bodnath giving a course to foreigners, and there was no French girl enrolled in it. Hugely disappointed, I wandered off and went to eat some *momos* (Tibetan dumplings stuffed with meat and steamed vegetables) as a consolation, in a small local restaurant at the edge of the stupa.

A while later, as I was unchaining my bike, a young lama, who wanted to practise his English, approached me. We introduced ourselves, his name was Tashi. I asked him where I could find the westerners who came to learn about Buddhism. He seemed happy to help and led me down the narrow streets until we left the buildings behind and were out among the fields again. Several groups of young monks were strolling up and down the road, avidly chatting. A hundred metres from us there was an imposing square monastery, three stories high with a white façade and

94

crowned by a yellow and red tinned roof with several golden tigers in each corner. We went in. There were various monks in the courtyard practising archery, while a few others observed us. Tashi asked one of them. "No, there is currently no course and not either in the monastery across the road," was the answer.

"But wait. If you say she came to meditate, she must be in Kopan. They have meditation cells near the monastery," he said as he pointed in the direction of the hills situated around 30 kilometres further north.

At the top of one of them, one could distinguish the shape of the monastery. Further away, in the background, the white, distant and appealing summits of the Himalaya.

"Ok, shall we go there then?" I suggested.

"I am sorry; I apologise but I can't come with you. I need to return to my *gompa*[17], prayer time is about to begin."

I thanked him for his help and went on my way. Several Tibetan women worked in the fields, and I crossed paths with a few old men carrying heavy bundles of wood over their heads. "The young men become monks and do nothing but pray and play, while the women and the old men need to work to feed them," I thought to myself. "But of course, religions don't keep anybody; they are the ones that need to be kept. They don't work the land and don't produce crops. They have always lived from the others' work, and then the priests have the arrogance to dictate our ways of living."

With this in my mind, I arrived at the base of the hill. I left my bike between the trees and a little more than half an hour later, and after a steep last climb, I found myself before the entrance door to the monastery. The figures of two antelopes lying face to face

[17] Buddhist monastery.

framing the wheel of *dharma* or cycle of life crowned it. From the main temple, I could hear the isochronous chanting of prayers, punctuated every now and then by cymbals, drums, sea shells and trumpets. Two hundred lamas, monks and novices in the lotus position occupied the room, sitting on top of long rows of cushions on the floor and under the attentive gaze of three gigantic Buddha statues. To the left, and positioned on a dais, sat the principal Lama with a yellow pointed hat. Facing him sat the musicians. The scene in the gloom had a daunting and mysterious touch to it. I settled on one side of the door and waited while I admired the paintings, some of them of terrific demons, that covered the walls, as well as the magnificent *thangkas* hanging from the columns.

After a long hour, the ceremony ended. The monks stood up and returned the books of prayer, long oblong leaves enclosed between two wooden panes and covered by red and yellow fabrics, to the shelves where they were stored. Some disappeared through a side door and others, a smaller group, came towards me in the direction of the central courtyard. I followed them, but none showed the least interest in talking with me. I heard someone speak in English with an American accent. It was a small group of Westerners.

"Hello, how are you?" I greeted as I approached them.

"Fantastic," they answered in unison.

"Is your life here interesting?".

"Oh, very much so, this is fabulous," the tallest one answered.

Two of them walked away.

"They don't want to get contaminated with useless conversation," the same one said jokingly.

The other three laughed and lifted their hands up quickly to cover their mouths.

"So, what do you do all day?" I continued.

"We train on the Buddhist canon, we pray…"

"And we eat very little," a second one added.

They laughed again.

"And don't you lock yourselves away to meditate?" I continued, showing my interest.

"We are learning. We have only been here for a few days."

"Do you happen to know Monique? A French girl who has been here for a month or so. She basically came to meditate isolated in a cell. I would like to know how she is," I added.

"She must be in the caves then," the most talkative of them answered. "They are on the north slope of the hill; the opposite side to the one you climbed up from. But if you are going to go over there, be careful; it's going get dark soon, and there might be leopards," he added, as he mimicked pouncing on me with his hands in the shape of claws. "You also need a permit from the Chief Lama," he finished.

"Ok, thank you so much; I'll come back tomorrow," and I bid them farewell.

I left the monastery and went around it. Indeed, there was a path which sloped downwards between the bushes and trees and I followed it, penetrating the vegetation with a slight fear, but which I was slowly overcoming with the determination of finding my subject of desire.

After around twenty minutes, I saw the silhouette of a small house. As I got nearer, a lama emerged and came up to meet me. I greeted him. He answered kindly but lifted up his hand with his palm extended towards me, as a sign for me to stop. I tried to start a conversation, but he shook his hand to show me that he did not understand.

"I am looking for a friend, Monique."

"Monique? Monique! No, no!" he answered, suddenly becoming aggressive, as he indicated with strong gestures of his hand that I should leave.

"But…" I tried to insist and put my hand in my pocket with the intention of offering him a few rupees.

"Out, out!" he shouted as he moved towards me shaking his fist in the air.

I had to turn back and return the way I had come from. After a few minutes, I found a small path to the right. Quite apprehensive, as it was already getting quite dark I walked down it for a few metres. I came to a clearing and distinguished a figure and the ember of a cigarette. He was a young man, practically naked despite the cold air of dusk, with blonde hair tied up in a ponytail and smoking a joint. The smell was unmistakable. He greeted me by raising his right arm. I approached him, and he smiled and patted the ground next to him, suggesting I join him.

"I'm Ted," he said. "Are you lost? Where are you from?"

"I'm Spanish. My name is Francisco. I thought Buddhists didn't smoke," answering his friendly attitude with a smile.

"I don't know what I am doing anymore. I have come to the conclusion that this is not for me."

He passed me the weed, and I accepted, waiting for him to continue.

"Yes, I am quitting; it is too hard, and I don't see the point," He spat towards the grass.

"Have you been here long?"

"Yes, three weeks trapped in that shit cave."

"I see; it must be quite hard. By the way," I dared ask, "do you know Monique, a French girl?"

"Yes, of course, a gorgeous girl," he answered as he shook his head in sign of admiration. "We got here at the same time. But we didn't see each other much while being here, we sometimes ran into each other when we went for walks outside of the cells. But I haven't seen her for a few days now."

We heard a sort of howl. We were silent, but apparently, nothing had happened.

"Monique, you think she left?" I started again.

"I'm not sure. She seemed happy. Although…she told me that the monk that brought us the food was being a bit annoying. He was always trying to touch her, and it seemed like he insinuated himself."

I felt the rage boiling in my stomach. I threw a stone into the thicket.

"What a pig! I just met him. When I asked him about her he went crazy and got very defensive and kicked me out."

"Oh, it's an ugly affair then. I'll see if I can find out something. Come back in two or three days, at around ten in the morning when that guy isn't here, and I'll tell you."

"It would be great if you could find out what happened. I would be very grateful," I said as I placed my hand on his arm as a sign of gratitude and trust. "I'm worried now."

I said goodbye to Ted and went back to the main path, trying not to think about the leopards that were surely lurking in the shadows. Suddenly, about twenty metres in front of me, I saw the tall grass move. Holding my breath, I stood still. I thought I heard something moving, stealthily. Nothing happened. I hesitated, to continue or to turn back. The grass at the edge of the road parted, and a silhouette emerged: Was it a fox? A jackal? It turned his head towards me and was still. I lifted my right hand as a sign of peace. Like a flash the creature crossed the path and disappeared. I admired its lightness and grace and it soothed me.

I continued uphill. I walked around the *gompa* and started descending again. At the base of the hill, I recovered my bike and pedalled quickly towards Kathmandu surrounded by darkness, well disappointed at not having found Monique and without any idea of where she could be. As long as the monk had not harmed her or kidnapped her...!

I slept poorly; partly due to the large meal I had rewarded myself with after such an intense day. I was worried and had nightmares. I remember one. I was running across the mountains, dressed as a *sadhu*, nearly naked, barefoot and with my hair braided with wild herbs and tied back in a long ponytail. The lama from the caves was running after me, armed with a baseball bat and shouting: I am going to shove it up your arse! Suddenly, an immobile leopard in the middle of the road. I protect myself behind him. He goes into attack position and roars in the direction of the lama. This one turns around and runs away at full speed from where he came from. I am about to thank the leopard when it turns into Duna, the gentle Pyrenean mastiff from the house in the Pyrenees where I spent my summer holidays as a child.

What a rough night. And to all the above one had to add the symphony of barking which enlivened my nights tirelessly in Kathmandu. A symphony without adages or pianos, only errant and rabid allegros. Every three or four months, the army would clean the city and get rid of the dogs. The government wanted to protect the tourists' sleep and stop epidemics. It was a long time since there had been a canine raid and I, at four in the morning, could not stand it any longer.

So, as soon as dawn broke, I grabbed my bike again and went to Pashupatinath, the Nepali Varanasi at the banks of Bagmati river, a miniature Ganges. The temple was three storeys high covered with golden and curved roofs. It was dedicated to Shiva, but they didn't let me go inside. "Hindus only" read a placard. I had to settle to witnessing the unusual scenes from the door. The faithful poured butter, honey and flower petals on the *lingam*, the phallus made of black stone that represents the fertile power of the God. They then groped another giant statue, also made of stone, which represented the Nandi Bull, the God's vehicle.

The remains of a corpse were being consumed on a crematorium pyre in the *ghats*, stairs that descend to the River, while a group of faithful performed their ritual ablutions and submerged themselves three times in the sacred waters. Men bathed naked; the women, wrapped in their saris.

An ambulance appeared. The occupants descended with a stretcher carrying a young man, covered by a white sheet and with plastic tubes coming out of his nose and mouth. His family surrounded him, one of them holding the dropper. They brought him down the dirt road to a shed next to the *ghats* and removed the tubes and serum needle. Then, they sprayed him with water. I was interested in his condition and asked one of the men that was supervising the whole operation: cancer, it was hopeless, he would die in a few hours, they told me. However, everyone was calm, and he seemed happy. What greater bliss than die by the sacred river and so, secure oneself an optimal reincarnation?

When I got back to the hotel there was a note from Jean Pierre: "Come over when you can". But it was hot, and I was tired, so I waited until the following morning.

101

"Here you are, I was expecting you yesterday afternoon," he said as we shook hands. He had not lost the French habit. I apologised for not having come the previous day.

"I have been thinking, maybe my friend Jang can help us find Monique. One of his uncles is the home affairs minister.

"Fantastic!" I answered enthusiastically.

Son of one of the richest families in the country, and at only twenty-five, Jang Rana lived in a palace wing, mostly uninhabited, between screens and Chinese silks, Turner landscapes, methacrylate tables, the latest in electronics and signed pictures of the then young singers Mick Jagger and Carole King. He had studied in Eton and Harvard and even though he had not been a brilliant student, he had learned fencing, polo and skiing.

He welcomed us in the living room, or was it maybe his bedroom? He lay in green satin underwear on cushions between food scraps, empty alcohol bottles and a few syringes strewn on the floor. On the cushions, enveloped in clouds of smoke, one could distinguish two female bodies judging by the hair and a couple of arms and a naked leg protruding from them. After a few minutes, Cindy appeared: from California, golden skin and locks, ecstatic smile, and following her, Monique. I felt my heart miss a beat.

"Monique! Weren't you meditating? I looked for you."

She looked at me, weary. She stood up, opened and closed her eyes a couple of times. She leaned on her right arm and got up with difficulty. She was only wearing a short white skirt, made of translucent light material.

"Oh! The Spanish adventurer!"

She didn't remember my name. She walked towards me unsteadily, gaunt, with a deep pastiness, not only from her

102

colourless skin but from her face, hair and lips, while her lovely honey coloured eyes had lost the entire spark from before. She lifted her arms and let them fall on my shoulders and kissed me on the mouth like an automaton. Her lips were cold, lifeless; this is how death's kiss must be. I felt a huge disappointment, disenchantment, bitterness. My world fell apart. I remembered her warm and delicate kiss a few weeks before, in the alcove of the old colonial hotel of Kolkata. I did not know what to say, the thrill of having found her was now disillusionment, more painful because it was unexpected, and it transformed into pity.

The woman that I had met with so much emotion, and who I had hardly embraced or kissed. The girl with whose image I had walked for days and days, searching and searching again, remembering those great eyes which had looked at me full of eagerness, excitement and honesty, captured by her natural and open smile, her clear and soft words, her plenitude, her calmness, the self-confidence that her whole being emanated. And here she was, transformed, weak, indifferent and apathetic. I kept her thin hand between mine while I tried to recover.

Meanwhile, Cindy, much more awake, took a guitar that was leaning on the wall and after a few strums started singing. She had a faint voice, but her intonation was good. I tried to focus my attention on her and her melody to detach myself from the situation with Monique. I did not understand the lyrics very well, and when she finished I asked her.

"Very nice, is it yours?

She laughed, with amusement.

"Don't you know it? It's *Blowing in the wind* by Bob Dylan."

"Oh yes! Of course, I am a bit detached from the world right now," I answered a little embarrassed while I remembered the lyrics of the song: *"How many roads must a man walk down, before you call him a man?"* And there I was, walking down so many roads, but...I was already a man. I turned to Monique.

"What happened? Were you not happy in the monastery?"

She looked at me anxiously and took a while to answer.

"Well, yes," she hesitated, "I don't want to talk about it."

"Come on, let's go, you can't stay like this," I said as I took her arm.

"No, leave me; I'm fine here.

"Hey, you," it was Jang, "it's not your business, she's telling you."

I didn't answer him and insisted again that she should come with me. She looked dispirited and downcast and stared at me with indifference. She gestured so I would let go and I did, already discouraged. I went up to Jang, trying to get him to understand and help me. His rejections made Jean Pierre intervene. He asked him how he had met Monique. Someone had brought her to one of his parties, and the girl had liked it. He had invited her to stay and...there she was. According to what she had told him, she had to run away from the monastery because the monk that brought her water and food every day was annoying her and trying to take advantage of her.

A superficial conversation followed while we finished the drinks we had been offered. I was silent. The situation had become uncomfortable so Jean Pierre made up an excuse and we said goodbye. Monique did so with an uninterested gesture from the cushions from where she was lying again. I didn't even notice Cindy.

As we left I felt confused. On one hand, I was disappointed, hurt. So much interest in her, so eager to find her, so many thoughts, so many desires to have her next to me and, when I finally had found her, not only did she not feel anything for me, but she was well on the way of becoming a vulgar drug addict. On the other hand, I couldn't believe it. The scene I had just witnessed could not be true. It wasn't possible that Monique had already abandoned her ideals. It was a phase, something temporary, the consequence of something terrible which had happened. I had to find out, understand, forgive her. Was she entitled to my forgiveness? Of course she was. What is more, it was my duty to help her. Already on the street, I told my friend,

"I am coming again in the morning, first thing. I'll talk with that guy to make him understand that she is sick. She needs help."

"You won't achieve anything. These men are very proud. They consider themselves above everybody else, and, even though they imitate us in a lot of things, they despise Westerners. You are in his country, and he will tell you not to get involved in his business. He is in charge."

Nevertheless, I returned the next morning. Two lackeys met me at the door. Their master was not there, nor were the ladies. I insisted. One of them placed his hand on the handle of his machete. I had to retreat. Later on, I told Jean Pierre.

"See? What did I tell you? Be careful. You might find yourself lying in a dark alley with a dagger in your back. Forget her." He warned.

I returned to the hotel, overwhelmed by reality and with the prospect of new days of despair and melancholy. The world could not be that cruel. All the plans that I had unconsciously made for when I found Monique had been shattered. I had to forget a future with her. But when, after a few hours, the sun shone through my window announcing a new day, I pushed aside my grief. I decided that I had to continue with my project, I had to finish it. It was May, in a month the monsoon would arrive and I would have to interrupt my trekking in the mountains. Without more ramblings and misgivings, I went to the Immigration Office to request the trekking permit to Everest.

VII

This ground is not prepared for you. Is it not enough that I smile in the valleys? I have never made this soil for thy feet, this air for thy breathing, these rocks for thy neighbours. I cannot pity nor fondle thee here, but forever relentlessly drive thee hence to where I am kind.

Henry David Thoreau

"It was my fault…it was my fault that he died. Had I been in front, nothing would have happened to him."

Jack began to sob weakly, huddled up, hugging himself, his face between his arms. I was silent, waiting for him to calm down and continue with his newly begun story. But he didn't speak again for a long while.

It was the night of our fourth day stuck in that tent. During the previous days, despite the problems of having a man likely to die next to me and not knowing whether we would get out of this trap in which we found ourselves, the romantic side of the situation had made me feel optimistic at times.

But in reality, our situation was worrying. As agreed, Pemba had left the morning of the first day to find help. I had barely left the tent since then, only a couple of times to fetch water from a nearby torrent or to go for short walks taking advantage of the moments when it didn't snow. The rest of the time I had spent feeding and taking care of Jack. That afternoon, I found him quite recovered. There was no doubt that he was a strong man and very well trained. After a dinner of rice and lentils and our last tin of sardines, we sat at the entrance of the tent and contemplated the sun slowly descending and turning fiery red as it neared the distant mountain group presided over by the sharp Nilkanta in the west. That was when Jack, despite his weak condition, began to tell me his odyssey.

He was indeed one of the North Americans from the Dunagiri. With his words, he remembered his dead friend. During the previous day, we had spoken a little, had exchanged names, nationalities and a few other details, as well as how we had found him and that Pemba had gone to look for help. I made some coffee and offered him a cup. He took it with both hands and thanked me with a gesture of his head. Then looked into my eyes for a moment, looked down at his cup, took a sip and lifted his eyes up to me again, this time more determined:

"I need to write a letter to his parents and tell them how their son died."

"I feel for you, it's a distressing situation, but maybe it would be a better idea if you waited and told them in person."

"What if we don't get out of here?"

"I'm sure we will. Look, the weather is improving. There are many deaths in the mountains. It's inevitable; it forms part of the risk and the adventure."

"Yes, but Peter's was terrifying. What is normal is when someone falls off a precipice. A slip, a hook that fails and "Wham!", a fall, a blow against some rocks and it's over. Or you have reached the summit later than expected, at midday or two or three hours later. You come down very tired, you stop for a while, you think, you doze off, night comes, and you freeze to death. You don't even realise it. But Peter…From all the stories I have heard, I have never known one so terrible and harrowing.

"Would you like to tell me? I'd like to hear it."

I could see the hesitation in his eyes, but after a few seconds, I could also see that he was dying to tell me so that in some way, he could free himself from those dark distressing memories.

"It will help me put my thoughts in order," he answered.

He thought for a few seconds and even with a few interruptions to recover and some hesitation in remembering how the events had happened, I remember a very coherent story.

"After six days of the approach march, on a route more or less familiar to us, we reached the place where we set up base camp. It was a good spot, a grassy plain encased between steep hills dotted with loose rocks at the edge of a stream. The following day, the porters left, and we continued upwards, following the torrent and close to one of the slopes. Our excitement at finding ourselves at the beginning of the adventure grew as we gained height and sky rocketed as the sharp tip of the Changabang appeared to our right. Just when we reached a position where we could see the whole peak, a symmetric cone of curved walls like a space projectile, another bristly icy peak, the Daunagiri, our goal, emerged at the head of the valley. Our first aspiration had been to climb the Changbang, but as we gathered information and learned about the generalised opinion of the enormous difficulties of climbing it, we gave up this idea and focused on the Daunagiri.

While the Changbang had only been summited once, a few years ago, and by a team of experienced British mountaineers, the

Daunagiri had, been conquered at least three times. Indeed, from the position in which we were standing it didn't look so terrible, it resembled even one of those mountains that we had climbed in the Alps. It was a magnificent day, equalling our mood:

"In three days we'll be at the top my friend," Peter had said.

"And I'll be the first to reach it," I had replied showing off.

"I'll let you pass; it is your right by age and experience."

"Well, if you behave I'll let you summit at the same time as me," I had answered as I patted him on the back, "but let's not count our eggs before they've hatched. Let's think about from which way we are going to attack the summit."

The west face of the mountain began with an ice fall between two rock foothills which led to a ridge, long and not too steep, which in turn led to the summit. It had been the ascent route of previous expeditions, and we had planned on using it as a descent route if indeed we reached the top."

I interrupted him for a moment. "Yes, I remember it, it's clearly visible from the top of the pass, I took pictures of it and studied it through the camera's zoom."

He listened to me without making any comments, took a break, and continued. His face had begun to light up as the story unfolded.

"In front of us, on the other side of a field of moraines of old ice and stone, the Southeast foothill of the mountain had a very steep climb with a nearly vertical wall of about two hundred meters high, located approximately in the centre of the ridge. From there, the ice ridge continued, continuously very steep, straight to the summit. We weren't able to see the whole of the East face, but from what we perceived, a wall above another one of rock and ice, it looked utterly impracticable. So we evaluated and finally

110

dismissed ascending from that side. We had come in search of a challenge, difficulties and uncertainties, and didn't want to follow the footsteps of our predecessors, but we were not going to attempt impossible tasks either. The decision was obvious; we would try the Southeast foothill and ridge.

We seemed to have agreed on it but, a few hours later, when we had already crossed the moraine and set up camp at the base of the wall, and while we prepared dinner, Peter brought up the subject again:

"And if we finally decided to climb up the East face?" he said. "I think no-one has ever attempted it before."

"But didn't you see what it was like? Do you think we have that much experience in the Himalayas to get ourselves into such a mess?" I tried to get him to reason.

"You do, and I don't see it much more challenging than the Eiger," he insisted.

"Except that here, we will be at an altitude of five to seven thousand metres, and there we were only at three thousand," I answered.

"Yes, of course, altitude sickness," he grumbled.

"And, on top of that, have you not seen the reddish tones in the rock? It's fragile, and the pitons will not hold, they will tear at the rock every time we try to hammer one in.

"Yes, you are right, it's obvious," he finally agreed.

"Sometimes Peter upset me with his fantastic suggestions and made me feel uncomfortable thinking that maybe I was too cautious. I asked myself whether I was realistic and more balanced than Peter in my judgements or whether I was just lazier and more of a coward than he allowed himself to be. It was evident that he was a brave and generous man."

"It hurts me to think that we sometimes argued about stupid things. He was a bit childish sometimes, but of course, he was so young!" he said with bitterness.

"I am sure that you were a perfect pair," I said. It came out spontaneously, from the heart. He thanked me for it with a gesture and continued:

"At the crack of dawn, with our heavy backpacks on our back, the crampons tied to them and a roll of rope on our shoulder, we started up one of the hollows of snow and ice that led to the ridge. There were several of these hollows of about three hundred metres in length, but we chose the steepest one because it was a more direct route and we felt strong. We had not yet learned to conserve our energy for when we were higher up. Even though the weather continued crisp and clear and I felt fit, I couldn't help having the usual doubts one has when immersing oneself in a new climbing adventure, and they twisted my stomach. Peter, on the other hand, like usual, seemed indifferent to such thoughts and was completely sure of himself and his condition. This, of course, encouraged me."

"Ok Frank," Jack called me like that, "I am not going to bore you with the details."

"You are not boring me; quite the opposite, I am very interested, but you must be tired. If you want we can leave the rest for tomorrow," I offered. But, after another short break, he continued:

"I don't know how many metres of rope we must have gone up the first two days, more than three hundred metres in altitude. The third day, night caught up with us when we were still halfway up the great rock wall, it was a climb between a sixth and seventh degree, and we had to descend to sleep at the foot of the wall, but we had left a large part of the ropes fixed. So, by the next day we were above the wall, and two days later, in the early afternoon of the sixth day, we reached the top of the mountain.

We hugged each other and jumped for joy as much as we could taking into account where we were standing. Peter was exhausted and somewhat worried about it. To the East the Great Goddess magnificent and majestic; nearer by, the Changabang and the Kalanka; further away, the Trisul and other peaks, other names. They all emerged from a sea of clouds that covered the valleys. We planted a flag from Peter's University; another one from my town, Flagstaff in Arizona, near the Grand Canyon, and took some pictures."

He interrupted himself.

"Damn! The camera!" he exclaimed. "What a shame! Damn, damn! It's in Peter's bag!". Desperate, he hid his head again between his knees and mumbled, "his parents won't be able to even see him at the summit of the mountain. At the summit of his dream." There were a few minutes of silence. I placed my right hand on his shoulder. Then, with the sorrow still visible on his face he continued:

"As soon as we started our descent we thought that we might have problems. We barely had any food left and the ridge down which we had decided to descend was more complicated than it had looked from afar. However, we calculated that in two, maximum three days, we would be able to reach base camp. But we were too tired to continue. "Danger of an accident," we thought. So a hundred metres below the summit, at the spot where we had left our bags while climbing, we dug a hole in the ice and spent a relatively comfortable night.

More rested and with our lungs receiving more oxygen the lower we got, we started to feel better, and the satisfaction of

113

having achieved our goal made us ecstatic again. We had nearly reached the foot of the mountain, and we were descending down the glacier, at times almost skating on the ice. Peter went in front, tracing a secure way between the cracks, some very wide but others very narrow and hidden by the snow from the previous night. We were roped together but had left a large span of rope between us to advance more comfortably. We are both from Arizona, and even though he is ten years younger than me, we get on very well in all aspects."

I noticed that Jack still referred to his partner in the present. And also that, despite his low physical state, remembering his partner seemed to give him strength. "We had climbed a few times together, in the Rockies and the Andes. We had summited the Huascarán with its nearly six thousand eight hundred meters, and other peaks. In the Alps, we had climbed the Matterhorn and had attempted, without succeeding, the north face of the Eiger. For me, it was the third expedition to the Himalaya. I had formed part of the American expedition to Everest in 1976, although I hadn't gone further than Camp 3 at nearly seven thousand metres. And with that other expedition where we attempted Makalu the following year; but we had to desist after an avalanche destroyed the camp we had set up and from which we were going to attempt the summit and left us without any equipment and a dead team member…poor Michael, buried in the snow.

For Peter, it was the first time he came to Asia and therefore to these mountains. I think the success made him feel very happy and confident at that point. Maybe that is why he was descending so quickly. We stopped for a moment to take a rest, and I suggested I go in front for a while. He refused, he felt very well. And I didn't insist, but we shortened the length of the rope that tied us together. A measure we thought prudent at the time but which turned out to be fatal."

Jack interrupted his story again: "In essence, I am guilty of his death. If I had gone first…," he searched into my eyes, seeking my comfort.

"I don't think you should feel guilty", I said, "You did what you thought was right at the time."

"We arrived at an area which was less steep, crossed from time to time by strips of ice like a wide staircase. We walked fast. An hour later, suddenly, when Peter jumped one of those drops, the crust of snow gave in. He disappeared, suddenly, having sunk into a crevasse and dragging me with him.

"Jaaaaaack!" his cry shattered the landscape, a loud, terrible, desperate scream. "Hold me!"

And I did try, but his fall caught me off guard as we had been walking on a land which had not seemed risky. I quickly turned the ice axe and with all my strength tried to thrust it into the hard ice of the slope, but I couldn't. "But the rope, the rope…, I need to keep a hold of it," I kept telling myself. But Peter was plunging down the slope at an incredible speed, and he dragged me behind him. I held the ice axe with both hands and repeatedly tried to sink it into the ice, but it would not hold, and I continued to be towed by the weight of my partner, increasingly faster.

An overwhelming fear paralysed me, and I flew down the mountain, powerless, propelled down the snow as if were a skier in the Olympics.

Soon I found myself at the edge of the crevice. Peter's fall had stopped all of a sudden. Afterwards, I saw why. The walls of the crack met at 15 metres deep and narrowed the gap between them. His backpack had gotten stuck there, and him, underneath it, trapped. A prisoner, face down and with his legs hanging in the void. His left arm had become imprisoned between the backpack and the ice wall and it seemed like one of his legs had broken with the impact because his foot was dangling at a strange angle. And on top of that, as we had been closely attached by the rope, I couldn't stop as I reached the crevice and fell on top of him, with all my weight, digging him deeper into the crack. At the same time, I felt a severe blow on my left shoulder as I hit the wall. I couldn't understand what had happened. Still stunned, I heard Peter cry: "Jack, get me out of here".

For three hours, I did nothing else but try and try, every way possible. My shoulder was killing me, and I could barely move that arm. All my efforts as well as his to turn him around or unhook him from his bag were useless. The cold was getting more intense by the minute, and I feared that my hands and legs would freeze before I had been able to achieve anything. I also thought that, if I cut the straps from his backpack, he would sink even deeper into the void. "Stop and think, don't let yourself be carried away by panic," I said to myself. I remembered my father's advice to me when I was young: "If you do things fast and without thinking, you don't live very long."

I wanted to cut into his bag to try to empty it, but it was compressed against the walls of the glacier and with the cold had become a big block of ice. Centimetre by centimetre, thrusting the front ends of the crampons and ice axe on the wall, I managed to climb up to the edge of the crevice. From there, I tried to move him by pulling the rope. Impossible. I wasn't able to move him. My friend, in a state of panic, wouldn't stop urging me and begging me to get him out. He fought against the intense cold and the fear. He said, "You have to do it, you have to find a way".

But I was completely exhausted, I couldn't do it any longer. We had barely eaten in the past days. After a while, I don't know if it was hours or minutes, I had to yield myself to the inevitable. I would not manage to get him out of there. I collapsed on the snow in a state of total confusion. What could I do that I had not yet tried? Through my mind, the scenes of other mountain accidents I had lived, heard or read about. None resembled this one. That trap made of ice, with the rucksack lodged between the walls, transformed by now into a complete block of ice, was something entirely new to me. It was not a matter of going to find help. It was evident that he would freeze to death long before I could find some."

I looked at him while I listened to his terrifying tale, and saw him gesture in pain. He raised his hand to his shoulder. The memory of Jose Ignacio's agony came to me again, my school friend, when he was dying, and we couldn't do anything, while we waited for the doctor that someone from the house next to the dam had gone to fetch. They had taken us in when Jose Ignacio had started to feel unwell. I pushed the thought away and said to Jack:

"If you want we can stop, you can tell me the rest tomorrow.

"No, no, I would rather tell you all of it, I will feel more liberated," and he continued.

Little by little, in only a couple of hours, poor Peter passed through all the stages one passes when one knows death is near: denial, anger, bargaining, depression and resignation. He asked me to climb Everest for him and to leave the mouthpiece of his saxophone on the summit. He gave me messages for his family and friends. He then asked me to help him die. But I couldn't do anything to help, only descend down the crack again and try to comfort him. He then told me to leave, to save myself. Well into the night, I had to leave him and climb up again, to the top of the damned crevice.

We had been in silence for various hours. What could we say? I was so exhausted I couldn't feel the time pass, I didn't suffer nor

117

worry anymore; I think I even passed out at times. Maybe he did as well. I woke up when I heard the weak sound of his weeps, carried up from the depths of his prison. This made me more and more anxious. I despaired of not being able to do anything. We had tried everything possible. Suddenly, at around two in the morning, he started to sing. His voice, an overwhelming sound, clear and much more powerful than expected from someone having been trapped for ten hours, was amplified by the walls of ice:

"O say, can you see, by the dawn's early light..."

Our national anthem rose in the night, from those jaws of ice that trapped him. And I, a useless witness, without being able to save him.

"Whose broad stripes and bright stars, through the perilous fight..."

His voice faded. He tried again, but it was an incoherent sound. That was the last I heard from him. And up there, that starry sky to whom he was singing, impassive! As if God didn't exist...Then, silence. I knelt near the edge and screamed:

"Peter, my friend" I howled.

I howled against the mountain, against the sky, against myself. I think I stayed there for a couple of hours, screaming and crying, completely beside myself. Afterwards, I suppose I got up and started walking in the darkness. When the sun rose, I realised that I didn't have my bag, nor my sleeping bag. But I didn't care, and I continued walking, walking...I don't remember anything else."

In the meantime, the sun had set. The jagged line of the peaks drew enormous fangs against the orange sky, between shreds of dark clouds while the temperatures decreased rapidly. One could hear, again and again, the prolonged cry of a jackal.

VIII

What power holds the female flesh!
Round and white like the Moon,
which they say, raises the sea.
José Luis Sampedro
The Etruscan Smile

I had plenty of time to ruminate on the happenings of my past, prostrated at the entrance of the tent or lying down in its interior. This depended on the state of the weather: whether it was snowing or a strong wind was blowing, if it was sunny or covered, or if it was night time or during the day, while Jack continued sleeping. Flowing memories, which entered my mind unasked for. One isn't where the physical body is, but where one's dreams fly. In the same way, home is not where you are born or have spent your childhood even though you have it anchored deeply in your heart. The concept of home grows and widens as life passes, as new people and new experiences enter your life. You grow roots somewhere else and join other lives with yours. And so, while I scrutinised the skies trying to foresee a change in the weather and searched the broken horizons trying to spot the help that wasn't coming, I thought about you, Ursula. You were or had been a vital part of my life.

I re-read your letter that I had received in Kathmandu a few months ago:

Francisco: How much I waited for your letter! Now I finally

119

know that you are all right, in an environment where I suppose you will reach the essentials of life more easily. I am not happy, but I do not feel that deeply vulnerable sorrow. I can't afford to as there is no one to help me out of that deep well. You neither, as for that there is the need for complete commitment and dedication, something we didn't have, nor wanted, and I know that when you return, in three or five months, we won't re-take our common path again like couples who are in love would do. You will come to Munich to visit me and there we will lead the artificial life we have led other times. I can't continue with my daily chores and duties because you have none here; so we have to behave like tourists, always "doing" something so we don't have to deal with the incompatibility between the circumstances and what we each want. We can't simply be together, each one dedicated to his own project and telling each other about them afterwards, conscious of a strong union, spiritual and physical.

I don't want to hug you for a couple of weeks and then lead an entirely different existence in my university environment. It is a huge shock which takes too much out of me. I don't want the freedom of being with a lot of men anymore; I want to experience the world through only one. Francisco, I was different before, I know, but I have developed. I am mature enough now to measure myself with only one person and independent to fight next to another for the common path. I don't see a chance for this between us. I understand that you can't, that you don't want to live in Germany, the same as I don't want to live in Paris or Spain without being independent financially. Maybe, we are also of a different nature, too different to be able to give ourselves to each other. You, search for solitude, and far away horizons; I search for people, for what moves them, the conscious analysis of ideas and things.

But I am not sad, how lovely it would be to see the light at the

120

end of the tunnel. I am depressed, nearly sick, my work barely moves forward. I am sorry that I can't write happier things to you. I am sure you are not surprised though, if you have thought about me and what happened to me last year. Moreover, you know I am lucky to know how to save myself from despair. As for you, I need not fear, you knew what cards you were playing, what you wanted to do. It is not the first time that you leave, and I was very clear about what would happen. You have chosen consciously, as I knew you would, the mountain, the solitary life. Understand that I don't want to ruin your trip. It is you and above all your subconscious who pushed you into going on this second journey. Exotic places appeal to you, places away from civilisation, with naïve, simple and happy people. And I can't follow you in that world; for me, it is a dreamlike world; I live in a corrupt, alienated one; this is the one that interests me because I live in it and I understand it, I even like it. I still love you, with the reserves that allow me to survive. I am not, and I don't want to be your Ophelia.

"Oh, Ursula, your letter moves me. I am not seeking your pain but my freedom. I continue loving you as well. You have been, or were, I don't know anymore, the most important woman in my life. We have spoken about it many times: our relationship has no future."

"When you return I don't think I will be waiting for you. You will be very far away and for a very long time, and I need to feel you near", you told me before I left. "But we barely see each other, you never have time, once every two months. Who cares if I am in Paris or on Everest," I would answer amazed. "It is not the same. Munich and Paris are practically the same; we are an hour away by plane or one night on the train. On the other hand…the Himalayas!" you sighed. "I am sorry, Ursula; let me fulfil my project. I have been thinking about it and preparing it for a while now. Four months pass by fast".

121

The truth was that, in those days, the call of the "Virgin Lands" was more attractive to me than my relationship, often stagnant, with you. Moreover, it annoyed me that now that I had decided to be more independent of you – you had always been more independent of me –, you were blackmailing me. So I left, "without looking back." As the saying goes. From time to time I was worried: "Do I love her? Does she wait for me?" And now, in the solitude of the snows of the Nanda Devi and its acolytes, I felt that anxiety more. And also your absence.

I had brought several of your letters, and others I remembered, with the intention of trying to understand you better, of guessing our future. In letters, one expresses feelings which are not said out loud. When one writes, it seems one feels freer, more inspired, shows love not only to the loved person but to love itself. Maybe you were also thinking of me at that exact instant. Your gaze fixed in the distance, beyond the trees that adorn the park in front of your house. You could feel my remote absence, and you were jealous that I was fulfilling my dreams, but maybe you did not understand my desire for those solitary nights in a tent set up in the depths of the Himalayas. If it weren't like that, maybe you would have been able to renounce your career for a while and be here with me.

It could also be that in consequence of me being far away you were even more dedicated to your studies and investigations. Or maybe, on the contrary, you were more sociable and saw your friends more, and bestowed them with your charming smile in the gatherings and debates in the cafés of Schwabing and in the student residence's parties. Thinking about it, it was better that you had not come with me: it would have been difficult for you later to return to your world of intellectualism and academia. Here, where I find myself, reside these mountains and these people that attract me; and there, between books and obligations, you, for years the goddess of my dreams. Everybody sees the world differently. If we were here together, your eyes would not see what my eyes contemplate, and your heart would not beat to the emotions that move me. How far away was Edinburgh, where we had first met.

It was a late afternoon, a wet street due to a recent summer downpour, grey and red facades on either side, the sky in shreds of lead and silver, and you walking uphill towards the Castle. Medium height heels, white stockings up to your knees, slightly tanned thighs, short chequered skirt, blue jacket, white shirt, short blonde hair, straight and light like that of a woman from the north, long decided steps, tall and statuesque. That is how I imagined Valkyries to be like. I had spotted you as I had arrived at the Royal Mile, after leaving the Scottish National Gallery where I had sought cover due to the rain.

We had met that same morning in the main office of the University of Edinburgh when we were both signing up for the English summer course for foreigners. Already then I had admired your appearance. You, however, appeared not to notice anybody. Distracted, perhaps shy, a little arrogant as well.

And so, I followed you for those ten minutes, at a safe distance under the aegis of the houses, from medieval to Victorian, while my gaze drifted from your locks down to the visible part of your thighs until we got to the square in front of the castle. You exchanged some words with the guard and, after a moment of hesitation which I observed after slowing down my footsteps, you turned back on yours. I decided to approach you.

"Can't one go in?" I asked with a controlled smile. Already then I thought you were not a spontaneous woman and I didn't want to seem pushy.

You looked at me with the friendliness of a polite person to a stranger, while my gaze hung on your light blue eyes and delighted them on the contemplation of your cleavage. Do women know how much that warm groove, similar to a smile, arouses our interest? I recovered in time to hear your words.

"No, they are rehearsing for tonight's concert," you answered in your very academic English, "I wanted a ticket for the concert of Claudio Abbado."

I had walked past the ticket office for the Festival and had stopped for a second to read the programme. I remembered having read the name of that conductor, until then unknown to me, so I took advantage of it and acted as if I knew who she was talking about.

"A promising concert and a good combination, an Italian conducting the London Symphonic Orchestra. But…" I searched for the adequate words in English while you looked at me patiently, "the tickets are bought in the offices down there," I continued as I pointed in the right direction.

"Oh! Thank you," you answered, ready to continue on your way.

But I was not ready to lose the chance of getting to know you.

"If one can't go in, I'll head back to University then. I saw you there this morning."

You didn't react, but we started walking down the street together. Walking next to you, your discrete perfume stimulated my senses. We introduced ourselves. I asked, and you answered. You were studying in Heidelberg: History of Art and Spanish. What a surprise! But I was only able to get a few Spanish words out of you, something which would have been in my favour as I would have been able to express myself with ease and so give you a better image of myself. With this reluctance to speak Spanish, you also showed what a perfectionist you were. We got to the crossing with North Bridge, and you insinuated a farewell. I let you continue alone, but I was not at all disappointed. I could picture in you an elegant and discrete personality, reflecting the beauty of your physique.

However, my hopes of becoming friends were not fulfilled. It took a few days until I saw you again. Obviously, we weren't in the same class; you were taking the Advanced one; I was in Elementary. We ran into each other a couple of times and spoke during the coffee breaks and in the canteen, but always in group conversations with other students. I saw you a few times afterwards, accompanied by one of your compatriots who seemed friendly and relaxed, I must admit, in his way of dressing and his manners. I accepted it without becoming very disappointed. I said goodbye to you on the last day and, even though it was not done in Anglo-Saxon environments in those days, I, determined and provocative, planted a couple of kisses on your healthy cheeks. You looked at me, mockingly and surprised at the same time. Your friend, not less determined than I, when I offered him my hand to shake he took it, drew me to him and planted two kisses on my cheeks as well. What a nerve. You laughed, entertained, but I didn't really mind. Anyway, I was not going to see you again,

Half a year went by. I guess I had forgotten your existence, when a Saturday in February, on the ski slopes of Navacerrada, specifically in Cotos, while I waited for my turn in the queue for the ski lift, I spotted you descending down the slopes in wide curves over the snow. I recognised your tall figure, somewhat majestic: black skiing trousers, tight red anorak and multi-coloured woolly hat covering your platinum blonde locks. I waited for you next to the ski lift. You also recognised me, although, true to yourself and to your difficulty of being spontaneous, you barely showed any surprise. I invited you for lunch at the old inn

Marcelino, next to the road; pure Castilian food: white beans from La Granja and suckling pig. Already on that occasion, you showed me your great appetite.

You were studying an advanced course on Spanish Culture at the Complutense University in Madrid. It was clear that you were really taking advantage of it, your Spanish was quite fluent and very precise. You were not satisfied with just any word, you would interrupt your discourse until you found the right one. In the afternoon we went skiing again, this time together and later on we returned to Madrid in my MG convertible: the young intellectual and the international executive.

Our next date was at La Bola. You loved its flavour of a cultured nineteenth-century tavern as well as the steak with peppers. I continued my conquest by alternating the classic Madrid nightlife with the liberal and cultural places. From Casa Paco to El Amparo, from El Botín to Pepe "the communist", from the Gijón to El Commercial, and from El Cock to Casa Patas. Neither discotheques nor bars for snobs. They weren't your thing, nor mine. You would talk to me about Plato and Nietzsche, the backwardness of the Spanish university and about ecology, until then something completely unknown to the rest of the Spanish population and, of course, me. And I talked to you about Serrat and Cecilia; about the magazine *Triunfo*, about Ramon J. Sender, about the novel *Tiempo de Silencio* of Martín-Santos and its importance in the literature of the time, and of Pío Baroja, my favourite author from the generation of the 98. I listened to you, I admired you, and I didn't dare to desire you.

At Easter break, we went to Formigal. Before arriving, in Sabiñánigo, we left the main road to go and visit some of the Mozarabic churches of Serrablo. You were seduced especially by the one of Saint Peter of Lárrede, isolated by the foot of a mountain, with its curved façade and its slender tower. On our way back to the car, next to the parapet of the old stone bridge over the Gállego river, obnubilated as you were by such art so pure and simple, I lit your lips with our first kisses.

In the Hotel Formigal, I had booked two separate rooms, taking into account our lack of intimacy up to that point. And even though I assume I insinuated something concerning this, you did not seem to be prepared yet to move from the dalliances to the final encounter. So we spent a few days of skiing down the slopes, snuggling up together and having drinks next to the chimney, accompanied by the desires of not wanting to separate myself from you when midnight struck. It was not until a few weeks later, on a trip to Santiago de Compostela, that I experienced the glory I had been waiting for. We had taken advantage of the free days due to the festivities of the Ascension and, after spending the night protected by the spectacular plateresque façade of the Parador of San Marcos de León, I went to find you to go for breakfast together.

They had given you one of the big antique rooms, with a bed with a baldachin, silver coated mirrors, chests lined with silk and lamps mounted on Baroque angels. When I pushed the heavy carved wooden door, you were already waiting for me, fresh and gorgeous, dressed in a light white dress. You were on the balcony looking over the square. You turned around and came to my encounter. The light from the balcony illuminated you from behind, and the fabric of your dress became translucent, shaping your body and lighting up your hair over which I believed I saw a halo of white flowers. Ophelia, I thought, coming to Hamlet's encounter. Although I, at that moment, did not feel undecided as did the Shakespeare hero.

I think I didn't even say good morning. I took you by the waist with my right arm, searched your mouth that was already waiting for me and we enticed ourselves with kisses, while I explored with my left hand the origin of your breasts. Like this, we reached the bed, and I lay you down on it without any resistance from your part. I had been waiting for so long! So much accumulated desire! Why had I not taken the step before? I thought.

I began to unbutton your blouse that closed the passage to your breasts; I slid my hand between your thighs. I slid it up again and down. You helped me to take off your dress. I did not need your help to rid myself of my clothes. Broken words, caresses and whispers in the dim lights of a spring morning in the alcove. What does it have that it makes us talk in whispers? Lying next to each other, on top of each other, entwined in yearning and pleasures; a growing desire, a fire of uncontrollable flames which become red embers and, finally, ashes of appetite, before chimeric and now satisfied. A silence afterwards, embracing one another, which expressed everything. Falling in love and blissfulness, liberation and purity, as one feels authentically in the encounter with the predestined woman. Or that is what I thought at the time.

In June you returned to Germany, and closely after that, you went to New York with your parents and to Chicago to visit your brother, married to a lively young woman of colour, head of the cabin Services at United Airlines, or was it Delta? I preserve your postcards, one from The Cloisters, *"Can you imagine that these marvels of medieval architecture are also Manhattan?"* you wrote; and another one of Chicago: A Picasso sculpture facing the Civic Centre, *"The only sign of culture in this city."*

When you returned from the States, you had a Lufthansa ticket to Madrid waiting for you at home. What a fabulous week we spent together! I showed you Cuenca and its hanging houses, the Enchanted City and the mountains of the area, Albarracín, its old fortifications and the prehistoric paintings hidden in its forests. You would later write to me: *"I recall a beautiful week which deepened our friendship, even more, a week full of tender moments, of happiness and comfort. I remember having breakfast together, kissing me in the lift, wouldn't you like to live in a skyscraper? Taking my hand or looking at me fleetingly while you drove...Showing me your affection. I feel your absence, and I will feel it even more at night time when I go to bed. You have left something of you in me, a feeling that you have given me."*

Oh, Ursula! The inspiration of my life, you made me think of Nabokov and his Lolita, fire of my waist, rapture of my senses. Ur-su-la: my lips like the beginning of a kiss, they then open to receive yours and finish open, mouth against mouth. Ur-su-la.

That summer of 72 you went to work at the Olympic Games: *"Yes, Munich has received me with open arms, like a Madrid sun and a southern life in the night time streets of Schwabing...When you come, on my free days, we could go to the lakes at the foothills of the Alps, to Baroque castles or, if we get up early, even to the Alps. Would you like that? Come soon. I am waiting for you."*

How would I not! I remembered you, so loving, trusting, and hanging on my arm, so soft in your caresses and so receptive of mine. But I met another side of your character. I arrived in Munich excited and full of desires. You were waiting for me at the airport. But not like I had imagined, in the front row after the barrier facing the exit doors after the customs control. I didn't even see you at first while around me friends and couples, mothers and sons, hugged each other jubilantly. Then I did. There you were, twenty metres away from me, leaning on a column and concentrated on reading the newspaper, the *Süddeutsche Zeitung*. I went up to you, confused.

"Oh! Hello, you are here already?" you said as if we had just seen each other just the day before.

I didn't even know how to answer to that. Where was the hug, where was I to deposit that passionate kissing that burned my lips?

"I haven't brought the car because it has no petrol. We can take the underground. It's new. You can try it out," you added with the same apparent passivity.

You and your Citroën 2CV; one of those super economic cars built with the French peasants in mind, but which the French liberals had adopted. Your father had bought it for you when you turned twenty-one. As you had very little money, it spent most of the time parked rather than running. So we went by underground, strangers in the crowd. You kept quiet, indifferent. I would slowly learn with time that that was always your first attitude when we met in Germany. A character that went in accordance to the cold ambience of the country. Then, little by little, you would slowly open up, getting used to my presence, my spontaneity and carefree Latin character; but I never got used to yours. Afterwards, instead of a cute hotel, you had reserved a room for me in the same student residence where you were staying, but two floors and a large corridor separating me from your room. Not romantic at all. My expectations continued disintegrating.

I remember you, Ursula, with your Olympic Games Hostess uniform. Every morning you left early. They were preparing you for the event, to be the hosts of the delegations and athletes. You needed to know every inch of the facilities, the characteristics of each country competing, and understand each sport. You arrived every evening late and exhausted. Sometimes, you had a dinner organised with your colleagues and you, always devoted to making a good impression, would not miss any commitment. I, without speaking German, felt left out and killed time by visiting the museums, walking up and down Leopoldstrasse or strolling between the lawns and flower gardens of the Englischer Garten.

Disappointed at seeing you so little, and when I did, feeling you so far away from me. Alone, every night waiting for your possible visit in my Spartan room, I decided after four days to take a train to Prague. I found a grey city, sombre, squashed by the claw of Moscow after the hopeful "Prague Spring" which had happened four years ago. Resilient people, stealthy looks, blackened facades and blackened statues observing me on the Charles Bridge, a gigantic castle crowning the city and still closed to tourists who would soon start visiting the country. My first contact with a communist country while my hopes and yearning were still fixed on you. I didn't understand that our relationship didn't seem that important anymore after our beautiful letters and the usual loving encounters between us.

Therefore, I didn't enjoy my stay at the Czech capital much. Its sinister ambience, the lack of spontaneity in the limited contacts I had with the local people with whom I had the chance of exchanging a few words in English or French increased my disappointment. In that state of mind, it was not surprising that tears came to my eyes on my visit to the old Jewish cemetery as I read the history of the ghetto. How, for centuries, and even before the Nazis had come, Jews had already been persecuted and forced to live in subhuman conditions which extended after their deaths, buried one on top of the other, up to twelve layers of bodies.

The only positive memory I have of those days was the surprising and cheerful receptionist from the Grand Hotel Europa where I was staying. Located in Wenceslas Square, it was a beautiful Art Nouveau hotel with sumptuous but shabby decorations and rooms furnished in Louis XIV style furniture on the verge of collapse. The receptionist, who was around forty years old, stocky figure, blond hair gathered in a bun and generous well-exposed breasts, due to the Czech national outfit which she wore, received me with a broad smile every time I approached the reception desk, and with some friendly words of her Spanish learnt in Cuba. From the second day, her plea was: "take me to Spain. I love the happiness of the Spaniards. I want to visit Sevilla" and would hold on to my hand as she looked at me straight in the eye while she gave me or received my room key.

Back in Munich, the games were about to begin. However, you Ursula, had thought it over, felt my departure and this time you received me with open arms, although still far from what I was hoping for. I then understood that you were absorbed by your task and your great sense of responsibility and so, two days later, I left.

When I arrived in Madrid I received a letter from you: "*Even though they very often seem hidden, Francisco please, do not forget that my feelings are authentic. And, to close the circle, I believe like Siddhartha – you had just read the book by Hermann Hesse – that love, patience and perseverance are the most important.*"

But I had already written you my frustrations before receiving your letter: "*I don't understand that someone can hide and repress their feelings, and not show them for fear of feeling weakened. Is that what happens to you?*"

And you answered: "*I have felt very hurt by your words on feeling humiliated and disappointed. Believe that I am ashamed and regret very much having acted so inconsiderate and selfishly. You know I am a difficult person. Inside me, two opposite characters clash, one is simple, cheerful, easy-going; but the other moves with steps of autumn is melancholic, self-absorbed, closed, vehement and shy. I need to learn, like a good Olympic referee, to coordinate these two factions better.*"

And so you were, and so we were over the years that our

relationship lasted. Difficult but always exciting, complicated but prodigal in feelings, misfortunes and rewards.

IX

Since life may summon us at every age,
Be ready, heart, for parting, new endeavor.
Be ready bravely and without remorse
to find new light that old ties cannot give.
In all beginnings dwell a magic force
for guarding us and helping us to live.

Hermann Hesse

Ursula, I liked thinking about you. I could see you in your short white dress, untouchable and tempting, walking in front of me through the narrow, deserted and dark streets of Chefchaouen. We had gone on a mystical walk up to the springs of Ras al-Ma to admire its small waterfalls and the views over the picturesque city, whitewashed houses and red rooftops, hanging from the buttress of the Rif. We had been so ecstatic with both the views and our embraces that when we got back to the first houses the night had caught up with us. You walked calm and carefree, wrapped in the soft and warm temperature of the early autumn and the penetrating scent of the wallflowers, the spices and the *tagines* that cooked in the homes. I walked behind you because the narrowness of the streets did not allow for us to walk next to each other as I would have liked, with my arm over your shoulders and yours on my waist. You walked so lightly and upright that I desired to come close to you without a sound, take you by the waist and whisper something simple in your ear, maybe something silly and affectionate. I followed you fearfully. I expected a pair of hands to emerge from the mysterious depths of one of the houses at any moment, and grab your appetising figure to drag you into the unknown shadows of the interior. You seemed so fragile to me that I wanted to defend you from everything and remain alone with you. Moments of our most intimate life shone like stars in my memory.

You were the one that suggested going to Morocco, the October after the Olympic Games in Munich. At that time, no Spaniard, I included, would have thought of such a destination. In our selves remained the atavistic rejection to this land and its people, the Moors, our ancestral enemies of seven centuries of "Reconquista", of the wars of the Rif, and the disaster of the Annual. But you proved to be so persistent in your desire that I, generally convinced by your good ideas and, desiring to please you, overcame my prejudice and there we went.

A Friday afternoon we embarked the MG in the express from Madrid to Algeciras and as soon as we got there, the next morning, the boat to Ceuta. Our first stage on Moroccan soil was Chefchaouen, where we stayed in the then only lodging of the city: The Parador, a vestige of the Spanish protectorate over the region. No one kidnapped you on our visit through the little town, and a couple of days later we found ourselves in the religious and intellectual city of Fez. We enjoyed its labyrinthic Medina, its mosques and madrassas, and the colourful but smelly dyers souk. I remember that, unlike Marrakesh which we visited a few days later, people in this city were discrete and the men, loyal to their pure Islamic belief, barely looked at you.

On our way to Meknes, another of the imperial cities, although with much less character than Fez, we visited the Roman ruins of

Volubilis, very evocative and emotional in their abandonment of centuries. Your face would light up before each discovery: the mosaic of Orpheus with its lyre, the Corinthian capitals of a temple and the medallions of the house of Venus. I learned with your explanations the foundations of classical architecture and the secrets to the strengths of the columns, arches and vaults due to a combination of Greek and Etruscan construction techniques which the Romans had merged.

We then continued our trip crossing the Atlas Mountains. Green, humid and wooded on its Atlantic side, rocky, inhospitable and deserted in its heights. And the descent towards the Sahara between sweet Palm groves at the bottom of the winding valley of the Ziz, its deep limestone gorges and the miraculous blue fountain of Meski. There, we went for an improvised swim in its springs between Palm trees, before the curiosity of shepherds and veiled women, preface to the encounter with the real and idealised dessert.

I remember you Ursula, barefoot like me, excitedly climbing the hot dunes of Merzouga, violet rather than golden by the sunlight at sunset.

"Do you realise? We are in the Sahara!" I shouted, "the legendary Sahara exists!

"Yes, and we are walking on it! " You accompanied me by shouting even louder.

"And it is thanks to you. I have never been interested in visiting more dry and deserted places; I have enough at home.

"Come, let's climb to the top," you said, pointing to the highest dune.

From there, we contemplated the vast desert extended in silence before us, indifferent and endless. But also attractive in its mystery made of legends, readings, feelings of freedom, of infinite doubts formed by the winds that sing with them; of oasis, elixirs of the soul to comfort the traveller. Its monotony hid secrets ready to reveal themselves to the intrepid adventurer that dared to penetrate it trusting and defenceless. But we didn't go further. We were happy just to descend over and over again, rolling down the hill while we felt the warm sand flowing down our backs and chest. I took off my shirt; you, your dress. Afterwards, we lay on the ground where we would have stayed, entwined looking up at the sky, feeling the desert on our skin. At that hour, sweet and soft, it even felt welcoming. But we admitted, very Cartesian, that night time in that place scared us and we decided to return.

We went back in our car, not at all designed for these roads of earth and sand, and remembering how we had nearly got stuck on our way to the desert in the crossing of the *oueds*[18], dry at that time of the year. After a few minutes, we found the first one of them. We crossed it to get to the other side, but the road had disappeared. We got out of the car; you went one way, I went the other, looking until, despite the limited light, you found it. Further along, the road divided into two. We took the one on the right, but at the next junction, we wondered if it was the correct way.

It was already dark. I had enough petrol to get to Erfoud, where a hotel which boasted a petrol station was waiting for us, but not enough to roam around that inhospitable terrain. We would end up lost, forced to spend the night wrapped in the cold and maybe without petrol to continue the next day when the rising of the sun would show us the way. You proved your strength.

---

[18]Valley, gully, or streambed in northern Africa that remains dry except during t he rainy season.

"Don't worry about me," you said, "we can continue a bit down the road in front of us, it looks like it climbs up that hill and maybe from there we will be able to see some lights."

So we did, but we couldn't see anything. The darkness was nearly complete. We could only perceive an undulating plain that blended into the night sky. I turned my gaze upwards, to the stars that already populated it. It was like a spark. I remembered *"Lover of the Ursa Major"*, the novel that had thrilled me during my youth: the adventures of a smuggler on the frontier lands between Poland and the URSS a bit before the Second World War. *"We lived like royalty. We drank like Cossacks. Women loved us. We spent money foolishly. We paid for vodka, music and everything else with gold and silver. We paid love with love, hate with hate,"* started his tale, full of adventures: clashes with the frontier guards, hideaways and escapes between the forests and hills, debauchery and disputes with his colleagues and clandestine love encounters.

When the hero got lost in those wild territories, he would look up to the sky and look for the Ursa Major, the Big Dipper, for guidance. And yes, there she was, with its seven stars well positioned in the sky and thousand fabulous shines, willing to guide me as well. I redid the procedure that I had learned from the smuggler. I searched for the two stars at its base and prolonged the distance that separated them five more times, following the straight line that they formed. It shone less brightly than its peers, but it was the one I was looking for, the Polar star, always immobile indicating the North.

"I didn't know you were an astronomer," you said with a hint of irony.

I explained. We spread out the map, situated our goal in relation to the star and this way we oriented ourselves. We repeated the operation at each intersection until we spotted the small city and, a little while later, we rewarded ourselves with a tasty couscous.

Embraces, words and silences, whispers from heart to heart in the autumnal gloom of the alcove. Stars shine brighter in the desert. They shone through the window to caress us, lying one next to the other under the sheets, half naked, while we remembered the twilight, red embers in a calm fire, shared mysteries in the African sands. My mouth roamed your skin and your mouth my skin. When we reached the hotel, there had been no water left, so we had not been able to shower. And so, my tongue tasted the sand stuck to your skin, collected the grains on your breasts and returned them to the interior of your thighs. Yours returned my caresses and, when both found each other, we exchanged the taste of sand with the taste of kisses. And our enjoyment was elated in the thoughts which stated everything; they were the whole life of each one of us resuscitating, rebuilding and needing the other one to complete themselves; our existence, embraced in a future of longings and hopes.

After that night of worrying and loving, we continued on the route of the Kasbahs, where the children with one hand asked for sweets and with the other rejected our presence with a mixture of shyness and terror of the foreign devils. Between villages of mud walls, rivers of stones and snowy peaks, we arrived at the fascinating Marrakesch. Its souks and its medina seduced us, the hustle and bustle of the Jemaa El Efna square, constant fair and daily carnival with its water bearers, its story tellers, its Qur'anic reciters, its musicians and jugglers and snake-charmers, its monkey trainers and fire breathers, its crawling beggars, the tourist tricksters and itinerant kitchens, turned into two-minute improvised restaurants as soon as night started to fall. We discovered the pigeon pastille, the mint tea, the Bohemian cosmopolitan around the writer Goytisolo on the terrace of the Argana and the "Thousand and one nights" of the Hotel La Mamounia, where we were staying.

It was in Marrakesh where we had our only small conflict. You continued to dress as you normally did in Europe, dresses and short skirts, although not mini-skirts, and blouses with short sleeves and summer necklines. While in the towns we had crossed before the people had only looked at you from afar and sideways and in the devout Fez, they hadn't even looked at you (or if they had it was with discreet reproachfulness) in Marrakesh many men observed you brazenly and commented. Some even dared to touch your buttocks, while we stood in the square watching the acrobats or story tellers, and then disappearing in the flurry of people, so we were not able to identify them. This annoyed you and made my blood boil.

So, on the morning of the second day of our stay and before leaving the hotel room I said to you:

"Couldn't you wear something more discreet?'"

"I don't have anything else."

"We should respect the local customs. In every place, one should dress trying to adapt to its customs," I ventured in a cautious tone.

"If they oppress their women I am not going to bend to it, don't you think?" you answered.

"There is always a middle point, try to be more flexible," I insisted.

"I have already told you I don't have anything else," your voice sounded impatient as you went towards the door.

I feared, by previous experiences, that the small row would lead to another day of us barely talking to each other. I reached out at you.

"Ok, let's not create a drama out of it," I said as I hugged you. "Let's not ruin such a lovely trip, " I caressed your cheek with my hands and kissed your eyes.

"Ok, I will wear one of your shirts, the light blue one," you gave in.

"And some long trousers?

"It is boiling, don't push it. They are not that short; they are fine."

As soon as we left the hotel and one after the other, guides started to approach us, some official and some fake, vendors of jewels and crafts, one said he didn't know how to read a letter he had received from France and needed help, and there were some who even invited us for lunch at their homes. We had already been warned at the hotel that these invitations always ended up in a jewellery store or a carpet dealer where we would feel harassed and pressured to buy at very high prices. We rejected all of them, walked along the square and the souks and bought some souvenirs. Night caught up with us well settled on the terrace of the first floor of the Café de France, looking onto the square, already becoming dark and dimly lit by the carbon lamps of the food stalls and souvenir shops, and with the silhouette of the Kutubia profiled against the starry sky.

"What a good idea to have come to Morocco," I commented.

"Yes, I have also enjoyed it very much. Thank you, one day I will be able to compensate you for everything you do for me."

"You are my love, you compensate me every day," I lifted your hand to my lips and kissed it, "with your tenderness, your affection, your kisses. We are different," I continued, "It is normal that we clash in some things. And I would not like it if you were the typical submissive woman."

141

"And I hope never to be," and then you added while you looked at me teasingly, "but you Spanish are half Moorish. You like them like that, don't you?"

"Of course not, it must be because of my French education, I looked at your eyes and continued, "I love you Ursula, you know that, even though it might be in a selfish way."

"Why are you saying this now? Why are you becoming so serious?

"You are complicated, too much for me. I think, and I suffer when we are separated, you in Heidelberg and I in Madrid. I need to be by your side, "I continued. "I am not able to trust our relationship. You write to me, and I am satisfied for a few days, but then time passes without us talking, and I can't help but go over everything in my head."

"I also miss you, you know I love you, and I tell you so in my letters."

"And you prove it when we are together. Well, not always."

"Can you please forget Munich?" your voice was affectionate.

"Yes, I will try, I am sorry. I need to understand that we are different."

We remained in silence for a while. A thought had been roaming around my head for a while now, and at that moment, it hit me heavily. In two days we would be separated again.

"When will we be able to live together Ursula?" It came out spontaneously.

"But we barely know each other! And I am in the middle of my studies," you exclaimed, while you looked at me, surprised but weary at the same time.

"You are right, it was just a thought," I gave in.

"Francisco, I am happy spending these days with you. You are happy with me too. Don't you think? It is wonderful that we are together here and now. Don't you think it is enough?"

We returned to Madrid refreshed and happy. The next day I dropped you off at Barajas airport, returning to your student life in Heidelberg. And we said goodbye, once again!

X

That anxiety, that wound that only finds solace in her eyes, in her arms.

Gonzalo Suárez

Don Juan en los infiernos.

The nights in the tent were silent, cold and lonely. There was a peculiar anonymity to being isolated, wrapped in tarpaulin. A feeling of being in a place completely off the map, which could be anywhere in the world but where, at the same time, you felt a sense of security and comfort enveloped in your sleeping bag. Even though inside it and next to you, but being careful not to touch it, was a lunch box full of snow with the purpose of melting it with the heat of your body. Afterwards, you would add some sugar and a little salt, and you had prepared a hydrating drink. In the mornings, it took a lot of effort and willpower to leave the sleeping bag to light the small gas stove and warm up the water to make tea or to unzip the tent's entrance and take a look at what the day would bring. Not to mention when, in the middle of the night, one had to get up and move a few feet away from the tent to attend to biological needs.

It was also at night time when the inner voice of everything inside me came back, without invitation. It is well known; love darkens the ideas and shortens the nights. Maybe that was why I returned to my thoughts of you, Ursula, and my life in Madrid.

144

We wrote to each other, although not as much as I would have liked. I was willing and did so nearly every night, as compensation for my permanent and unreachable desire to hug your pale body, give myself, bury myself in it. I would write to you every evening, when I returned from my office located next to Cuzco Square, two hundred meters from my apartment, in the neighbourhood of the new multinational companies. You would write to me once a week, at least, busy as you were with the tasks of a responsible and good student, one who also had to work every weekend to pay the bills, in a Biergarten or in some flea market.

If days passed without receiving a letter from you, I would rack my brains and question myself: "What is she doing, so far away from me? Why isn't she answering my letters? Has she forgotten about me? Has she fallen in love with someone else? Has she had a car accident? Did the Baader-Meinhof terrorist group kidnap her? Or even worse…Has she joined them?" But I had learnt from previous experience: love does not mean happiness. I hated calling you on your dorms' phone. No one bothered to pick up unless they were accidentally walking past it. And if finally, someone did pick up and summoned you to the phone, I was incapable of hiding the reproach in my voice of feeling neglected. So I ended up even more frustrated than before calling you.

But when they did arrive, your letters were wonderful, sensitive, tender, funny: with your excellent Spanish, and with a sometimes unorthodox syntax, but always with very well thought ideas. You would often include poems that you found in your study books: "*Habrá un silencio verde todo hecho de guitarras destrenzadas. La guitarra es un pozo con viento en vez de agua.*"[19] And you would add: *I miss you. Isn't it terrible? Because it goes against my ideals.*

[19] *"There will be a green silence made of unmanned guitars. The guitar is a well filled with wind instead of water."*

And I would answer: *We can't change. It is always the same cycle. You soothe me, I feel like your worshipper, and then, you disappear. This cycle destroys me. All my hopes are placed on you. I have nothing left for anything else. I should not say it because it is not a good feeling, but I am glad that you miss me. Why terrible? On the contrary, I find it wonderful.*

However, we rarely spent more than four or six weeks apart. I would take advantage of my business trips to the headquarters in Paris to present results or attend some commercial meeting, current annual budgets or some other motive that multinationals always make up to make themselves feel dynamic and modern. I would try and make these trips coincide with the beginning or end of the week to be able to run off to Frankfurt, where you would wait for me at the airport with your peculiar Citroen 2 CV. In Heidelberg, we would climb up to the castle or go for walks on the Philosophenweg or "Walk of the Philosophers", imitating the University teachers from the past and, like them, talk about the divine and the human, before seeking refuge in one of the taverns full of students, before us a delicious ham joint with Sauerkraut and a bottle of white wine from the Rhine or from the Franken area.

But again, we must remember, Ursula, that my visits to Germany did not always end in harmony. It was hard for you to be spontaneous, to get used to me, and I would become impatient, I felt neglected, and we ended up arguing. On the other hand, not being able to speak the language did not allow me to integrate myself and I felt stupid when we were with your fellow classmates, or you left me to attend to your obligations. In the end, we ended up distant from each other and hurt. We would separate again, we would think about it, miss each other, write, apologise and the rivers of love would return to their banks.

I am not sure if it was the verses of Gerardo Diego or those of Garcia Lorca: *"La guitarra hace llorar a los sueños. El sollozo de las almas perdidas..."*[20] The fact was that you longed to own a guitar. And in one of the trips where you accompanied me to Barcelona, we bought a beautiful Spanish guitar in the "Lutier Estruch", near the Ramblas. From then on, you rarely let go of it. You told me that for hours on end you would forget your studies and books, me, and everything else, and would concentrate on Joaquín Rodrigo, in Tárrega or in Albéniz.

Do you remember when, in one of my visits during those years, when you were already living in Munich, that we were lucky to be able to attend a Paco de Lucia concert and another one of Andrés Segovia? How lovingly did the elderly master hug his old instrument while he made it sing. What a contrast between the rectilinear shape and the serious face of the young Andalusian player and his overflowing music, "flowing like water." I also keep a drawing that I made of you one morning in my apartment in Paris. You had just woken up and were sitting on one of the big cushions that served as a sofa, with your body only covered by your guitar, and you were delighting me with the beautiful melody *Forbidden Games*, rescued by Narciso Yepes. What happened to you to write that letter?

Francisco, I write to you today for the first time. The previous days I had something like a "black out"; I think I was trying to suppress your existence. When, in uncontrolled moments, the memories of those days together came to me, it hurt...It hurt so badly that, now, it has become happiness because I feel and appreciate and notice your absence. They were moments which I turned off thinking about our periods of misunderstandings. How few times where we only "you and me" intimately! Now, the heart

[20] *"The guitar makes the dreams cry. The sob of lost souls ..."*

has won over reason. I don't know what you were the thinking on your return. I love you more than I am sometimes aware of.

I was very disappointed, but afterwards, when I thought it over, I thought that I had been too harsh, too idealistic, maybe even egocentric. How can I forget that love is also selfish? I don't know how you feel, hurt and mistreated? Are you angry? Forgive me. Are you not also easily irritable due to the lack of motivation you have when going to work?

Yes, it was the time I was suffering from depression, full of dark thoughts occasioned by the zero motivation I had towards my job and going to the office every day, and the feeling of guilt deriving from this because I was the general manager of the company. An unhappiness which a few months later pushed me to leave the company and go to Fontainebleau, looking to leave that part of my life behind me and with the excitement of attaining a Masters degree. Or was the real reason behind this a primordial desire to be free?

A feeling that, curiously, I had been aware of, albeit in a vague way, in Edinburgh that summer when we met. Each afternoon, while returning from the city centre to the University campus in a junction and next to two pubs facing each other on their respective corners, there were three or four tramps of relatively good looks due to their physique and their dress that, pint in hand, joked around and laughed without forgetting to ask for some spare change from passers-by. I surprised myself by thinking. "What happy men! No obligations, they can come and go as they please."

Jack interrupted my thoughts. He was very agitated that night, at times thrashing around like a chained animal. He spoke in a loud voice, complaining. He asked for water every so often. During the day he had seemed to me quite recovered, both from having shared his story of the ascent of the peak and the horrific death of his partner. I was also uncomfortable. I was lying down in a rigid, twisted position. My neck hurt. That small space for both of us and my scarce belongings was a torture every night. Irregular breathing, snoring. Complaints and finally silences. Why were the nights so long? Is that why they were so prone to bringing back memories?

A few days later you came to Madrid to spend the weekend with me. Already at home, I gave you a present, the music album *La Bohème* which I had just bought, with a passionate interpretation of a young Mirella Freni and Luciano Pavarotti, directed by Herbert von Karajan. As I expected, the music, the voices and the sentiment opened you up to our intimacy easier than other times. You were wearing one of your simple white shirts between which the first open buttons the birth of your breasts smiled at me. I adored them, white, smooth, with the perfect feel, the perfect balance of softness and hardness. I could spend hours caressing them, running my tongue over the pink aureolas in which they culminated, while I felt the excitement of my sex, anticipating the sovereign pleasure in the stimulating humidity of your most intimate organ. And your kisses. Your mouth was always the same, but your kisses always tasted new to me.

We went for dinner to La Bola. Afterwards, we strolled down the street until we reached the small square in front of the façade of the Convent of La Encarnacion. Humble in the simplicity of its brick walls and the severe austerity of its stone façade, but with the mysterious beauty of four hundred years of barely unaltered existence, one of the most intimate corners in Madrid. Between the shadows of the trees we shared hugs and kisses while Lope de Vega, untouchable on his pedestal observed us thinking that, maybe, we would be a good subject for one of his dramas.

We sat down on a bench in the neighbouring Plaza de Oriente, between a pair of giant statues of white stone and with the view of the Royal Palace on the horizon. The figures depicted medieval kings of ancient names with descriptions of unknown deeds adorning them. There, we had a long and profound conversation which, having already gone over various times in my head, I remember quite well. I explained to you the thoughts which for some time now had been worrying me:

"I have thought about what you said in one of our last phone conversations when I talked to you about the future, if what led me to you and to a life together was the fact that I felt alone," I told you. "It troubles me that you think like that, even if it is only occasionally. That is why I wanted to get to the bottom of it". I paused for a second, while I told myself that I had to be convincing and stay calm. "You and I are deep thinkers and will never be convinced of anything. We have now a certain maturity, and we don't find people that `complete us´ easily, that motivate us and make us feel fully alive. Therefore, in your absence, I actually do feel lonely and more so than I felt before meeting you when my feelings had still not woken up, and I hadn't really been aware of them."

I took your hands to show you my affection and in some way counteract the tone of my voice and the serious words I was pronouncing, while you looked at me with a slightly worried look: Where does he want to get to, you seemed to be thinking. But I continued.

"I think that it is serious that you can even think, as you insinuated in one of your previous letters, that my personality is so poor that I need to give it away because I can't sustain it myself," it looked as if, with the increase in the tone of my voice, I was getting angry. "Anyway, if you love me you should accept me as I am, despite the risks it might entail and convinced that they are worth it. I prefer to be with you with conflicts than without you, blissfully settled in a life without surprises."

I waited, expectantly. You had listened to me without interrupting, you were courteous as always.

"You are gravely mistaken if you think that I, having reached maybe, the bottom of you and our relationship, am seeking new motivations," you answered with amazement in your eyes. "I have not reached your depths, and I would never dare such arrogance, claiming that I know a person completely. No, I love you, I love and care for you. Even though it is not always self-evident at first, it is my own love that wants to communicate with you, but when I am far from you, it seems as if it were locked up in a castle and, if they attempt to escape slightly, they encounter the walls of your fortress. Do you understand? My feelings are not combative warriors, they are very peaceful and will wait patiently for the drawbridge to be lowered freely."

"Yes, I know. I know what you are like," I answered and continued with the metaphor. "However, by now, those two castles could maintain good relations and build an underground tunnel between both of them, don't you think?"

I let go of your hands, they had remained intertwined during the conversation, and put my arm around your shoulders and tried to draw you to me to kiss you; but you became rigid and leaned backwards, you wanted to make something clear without letting yourself be led astray by feelings.

"I think we are, or at least I am, on the threshold that leads from our beautiful friendship to a more intense and conscious love that wants to be more active," you answered. "It looks as if you are still not sure where I am going with this. It is straightforward and

151

natural. A love relationship needs to have two fundamental components: the sexual relationship and the intellectual one. Between us, up to now, I think the sexual one has had preponderance, and we have neglected, because it isn't very obvious, the intellectual one. In the eternal path towards the ideal love, I don't want there to be only these two distant parts, without intercommunication, I want them to always be united. One without the other has no value because the engine of sexual love is the intellect and vice versa. Do you agree with me?

"How can I not," I said as now, yes, you allowed yourself to be hugged, "and I admit that I want to go faster than you, I know, but I can't help it."

You responded to my touch. I felt we had come to an understanding, we stayed there for a while, enjoying our harmony in the silence of the night and we returned home happy, hopeful, loving…

And we met again, and we understood each other, hugged each other and then separated again, months, years, both happy and unhappy. Couldn't we have a quiet and serene love? Was it then that it wasn't love?

However, I often still had mixed feelings. An open wound, raw, which still bled. I could not mitigate the pain. I desired you with such a love that it overwhelmed me. I felt lonely, and you were the women I longed for: intelligent, complex and lovely. Your letters were beautiful and sensitive, but it was like reading Anna Karenina and imagining that she was in love with me. I needed daily contact, a life in common. The imprint of your body on my bed and the smell of your locks on my pillow were not enough. Is she as beautiful and tender as I remember her? I would ask myself. Will I manage to convince her to come and live with me? I would look for a larger flat for both of us to have more space. I wouldn't spend so many hours in the office; we would alternate dinners at home with good restaurants. We would go out during the weekend to the mountains of Guadarrama, or the villages of Segovia...We would have children, two, a boy and a girl.

I then admitted to myself that that idea was impossible, at least for the moment, and tried to console myself. "Love is also pain. Don't be dramatic," I would tell myself. "It is only love, not an arm or a leg. How long will you revel in your suffering, when will you stop being so sensitive?" I felt depressed, frustrated, and helpless and did not know the answer. And then summer arrived once again.

I remember you, Ursula, at the helm of the boat or changing the orientation of the sails, always in deep concentration, attentive to the wind, always ready, perfectionist, the best of the crew and, of course, the most beautiful, a mermaid, "white and round like the Moon that raises the sea ". Oh, that wonderful summer that we spent discovering a great part of Italy and ended in the seas of the north of Sardinia, on a sailing course!

We lived on the tiny island of Caprera, near the house and the tomb of Garibaldi, the Unifier - perhaps his spirit helped us then - in a small hut made of wood and reeds at the edge of a semi-deserted beach, in a state of semi-wildness and semi-conscious love. We lived on the shell fish we found in the sand, small fish that we caught with our net, *spaghettis al Pomodoro* and sun and kisses. We only dressed to go out in the evening to drink a Vernaccia white wine or a red Montepulciano at the village tavern. I have not forgotten that scene where you showed the firmness of your character and your sense of righteousness.

We had thought of crossing over to the neighbouring Sardinia for a day, to go for a walk in some of its villages and landscapes. So we went to the jetty one afternoon and bought a couple of tickets for the boat that made the crossing between the two islands. The following morning, we were there a few a minutes before 9.00, the ship's departing time. There was a notice on the ticket booth where the tickets were issued: "Due to a technical problem, the boat will leave at 12.00 o'clock."

"We'll have to wait, let's go for a walk, and come back later," I said, wanting to take the mishap philosophically so as not to ruin our happy days.

"No, we can't. We will arrive at one or later, and the return boat is at four o'clock. It's not worth it; we will not have time to see anything."

"You are right, let's change the tickets for tomorrow," I suggested.

"No, we can't tomorrow either. We have the tour around the island. It will be beautiful all day sailing, the wind filling the sails la, la, la" you danced for a few steps around the dock. "And getting tanned" you added, while your eyes glittered in anticipation of a day you were looking forward to. "Let's go and ask for our money back."

We approached the ticket counter. Behind it, the same presumptuous character in his blue-striped white T-shirt, his red Garibaldi revolutionary scarf around his neck, his well-groomed moustache, his glossy black hair and a toothpick between his teeth.

"*Bongiorno*," I said, " *no e possible prendere la nave a las dodici. Prego"* that was the end of my Italian. "Can you give us back the money?" I said as I held out the tickets.

"*Ma no è posible. Cambio biglietti para domani*" the man replied.

"*Domani no posible per noi,"* I said. "We want the money, las quatro mille lire," I insisted.

154

"*Ma no. Lire no, solo cambio bigletti. Prego,*" He gestured to me to make up my mind, while pointing behind me.

In the meanwhile, three or four more passengers had arrived and were waiting patiently behind us. I was about to give up, but you, Ursula, took over. With a great calm you placed your elbows on the counter and informed the man:

"We won't move until you give us back the money."

The guy stared in amazement at that calm and determined blonde, "this is going to ruin my day," he must have thought. He hesitated for a moment. He looked at those that were waiting behind us, prepared four notes of one thousand liras and offered his hand to receive the tickets. When he had them, he gave you the money back. You turned towards me, smiling, and I loved you for your courage.

It was the summer in which I had left my company in Madrid and had became a student for a year in the INSEAD Business School of Fontainebleau. We spent four happy weeks, with no worries, full of sun, sea and sand. But, Alas! "*Nessun maggio dolore che ricordarsi del tempo felice nella miseria,*"[21] as Dante wrote. Because misery came back a few months later.

---

[21] "*There is not a greater pain than to remember the happy times in times of misery,*"

XI

*Only those who will risk going too far
can possibly find out how far one can go.*
T. S. Elliot

When I woke up, bright daylight was filtering through the canvas walls of the tent and illuminated the messy interior of our shelter. The clouds had disappeared, and the sun was shining in a practically clear sky. So began our fifth day of waiting. Perhaps this afternoon they would come to rescue us. Jack felt quite energetic and excited. So, with our morale high, we decided to go and fetch water from a torrent about an hour from our camping site. This way we would stretch our legs, after so much inactivity, and check out his state of recovery.

It was wonderful to walk again through that wild and lonely landscape of tremendous peaks and deep gorges, now all white. In front of us stood the Betartholi Himal, its foot, immaculate, the inviting lap just below its jagged summit; to its left, the Trisul, the trident of Shiva, with its three peaks crowning its western slope. More to the left, dominating with her presence, almost a thousand meters above all her acolytes, stood guarding that paradise, the Nanda Devi, the sacred goddess, the unreachable subject of my desires. And behind us, very close, the Dunagiri, with its twin peaks like two old fortresses at the ends of the curve of its summit ridge; with its edges and cracks, Peter's recent tomb.

At a point, Jack turned and looked at it for a long time.

"That's the one, the damned Dunagiri. Its beauty and the pride of having summited it no longer matter to me. I'm sick of it," he said, clenching his fist and raising it threateningly. "I hate it now, for its cruelty, for killing Peter. Having climbed it was stupid. I do not think I would be able to do it again; neither here, nor in any other mountains."

"You did everything you could. Unfortunately, he is dead and you, alive," I said as I put my arm around his shoulder and he placed his around my back: a hug in memory of his friend. "If you allow me to say, I think you have to have things clear when you go home and face the inevitable criticisms and questions. Only when you accept what happened, will you be able to explain it to the others," I added.

"They will never accept what has happened; they will never understand how I have felt and how I feel. I wonder if I will be able to articulate the necessary words. I was able to tell you, but you were a stranger," he said, pressing his hand to my back. "And by doing so, it has helped me."

"The healing process has begun, but I fear it will be long," I replied.

"And you, why don't you climb mountains, why are not you a climber?" He asked me, "don't you have the feeling that you're just halfway there?"

"Not really. What drives me, above all, is to see and to discover, the curiosity, the contemplation of the landscape and the joy of feeling it. Like now," I said, opening my arms as if I wanted to cover everything before me. "You walk, you climb, you come to a hill, and a new world opens before you. And you start again. However, the summit is an end. I suppose it is a feeling of triumph, being able to overcome all difficulties and having suffered to achieve it."

"Exactly, that's why it's worth it."

"Yes, I understand. But apart from that, you also have to return. But with the hill or the pass you cross, and then you continue. You have a kind of vertigo of the endless as you contemplate the new scene in front of you. You either decide to move forward or return; there is no triumph or defeat. I have summited some peaks, but only those that do not need a great deal of preparation or technique nor means to climb it. I'm satisfied with that and, besides, you do not need strings, crampons or ice axes ... You can go up the mountain, like one would say, with your hands in your pockets.

"And without having to plan months in advance. That's pure freedom, you're right," he conceded.

We continued our walk. We crossed the small herd of bharals which were descending to the bottom of the valley in search of pastures and watched the circular flights of a pair of eagles. I took some good pictures of both species. Not many, since I only had two rolls of film left until we returned to New Delhi. I had no doubt we would make it. The good weather and the ease with which we moved through the hard snow brought our optimism back. We reached the stream. Water flowed between the rocks below the ice sheet. We broke it, filled our water bottles and the pot, and started back. Jack stared at the last trees in the forest that rose from the gorge up to two hundred yards below us on the slope where we stood. He looked at me.

"Are you sure they're coming to get us?"

"You must be joking. Of course, they are, I trust Pemba," I replied," and I believe that the people from the village, apart from being very generous people, will be extremely interested in the reward for doing so."

"Well, regardless if they come or they don't, since we have those trees there we´ll cut some branches and make some walking sticks. We'll sharpen them, and they will serve as support and make our walk in the hard snow and even on the ice safer." They will be almost like piolets."

"You think that if they do not come soon, in a couple of days let's say, we should try to go back alone," I stated as the thought entered my head. "Yes, there is no doubt, that's what we'll have to do."

We went down to the forest and used my knife to cut the four branches which seemed the most suitable, not without difficulty as the knife which I had bought in Srinagar was handmade. On our way back, the snow had already softened, and I noticed Jack was taking longer than me. I slowed the pace. "He is not as recovered as I thought," I told myself, "but let's be optimistic, it's fine weather, and maybe our rescuers will be waiting for us when we arrive at the tent."

But we didn't have that good a fortune. Quite the opposite, when we arrived and wanted to make a broth to warm us up, we realised that we had no gas left. The last gas can we had opened for breakfast that morning and which had to last us three or four days, was empty. No doubt the flame had gone out after heating the water to make coffee, and we had not noticed. We were left without hot drinks, without being able to cook rice, or make soups. "Well, it's not that terrible," I thought. "This afternoon or tomorrow they will come to rescue us. We could also get firewood and dry it at night inside the tent. Yes, we will do that tomorrow if they do not arrive today."

In the idleness of waiting the memories returned. As a young man, in my student days, I was quite lazy. I spent the mornings when I had class, at the School of Engineers, although we skipped one or two to go to the park for walks or play rabbi or poker at a bar near the school. At home, after lunch, my usual occupation was to accommodate myself on one of the armchairs located in the dining room – we regularly ate in the living room - and doze off listening to music. I usually listened to classical music or Zarzuela, coming from the Philco radio, housed in a huge cabinet with a speaker of at least fifteen inches, inherited from my grandfather. My mother had to come to wake me up and get me to study. But at eight o'clock in the evening, I would find an excuse to go for a walk with my friend Mario down Independencia Avenue or, better still, under the shelter of the gigantic trees of the then-called Paseo General Mola, less crowded and more select, to flirt with the girls.

But that indolence of my character changed as soon as I finished my degree and I started focusing on developing a career. Apart from that, difficulties motivated me. The decision of going to Paris that month of June, having just finished the last year, to do a traineeship, was a decision that determined not only the future of my professional career but also that of my whole life. It was there that the first shock between the education imposed on me by the priests and the society in which I grew up and my instincts clashed. Among the ideas that imbued me, and what I read in the books, I learned from other people and life in a very free society which was the Parisian one.

Years later, at thirty-six, I decided to leave the company, I was working with, for one year, in order to take a master's of business management at the INSEAD of Fontainebleau, the European equivalent of Harvard Business School. I was at that point the director of C.H Spain, which I had helped to found in Spain seven years earlier, and which was growing successfully, but I was also

160

quite bored with my work, even becoming depressed a couple of times. My mood was also affected by my continued anxiety caused by the irregularity of my relationship with Ursula, more than two years at that time, always thinking about her letters, whether they would arrive or not, and on our meetings, sometimes fruitful, sometimes disappointing.

Going back to getting tired of my professional life, I was not thinking of abandoning it altogether, but of taking a break and taking the opportunity to train in those aspects of business management I did not know: finance, administration and human resources. This would allow me to aspire in the future to more important positions.

One day in April I sent my application accompanied by my C.V. and the letter of recommendation of my former boss in C. H. Europe, then the president of the French Chapter of Engineering Companies. I also had to attach the quite good result of the admission test for American business schools: three hours in a classroom of the Spanish-American base of Torrejón de Ardoz to complete one hundred questions in English of a questionnaire of multiple solutions to arithmetic problems, logical reasoning and sentence structure. I waited for their answer with optimism, given my excellent record, but I got the following letter that said:

"Dear Sir, we acknowledge the receipt of your INSEAD admission dossier for the next course. Unfortunately, as you will see in the enclosed brochure, our students have an age limit of 24-30 years with some exceptions up to 32. However, we have 2/4 week seminars for those who, like you, are older than that and have more professional experience. If this interests you, you can contact ... We return your cheque accordingly. Sincerely".

But I did not want a course of a mere few weeks, but really a long break that would open new horizons and new challenges. At least, that is what I told myself, without admitting yet that the usual life of a business manager did not satisfy me. The beginning of this process had begun a few weeks earlier in London.

Executives, when they feel depressed, buy a tie. On that day, I bought myself a suit as well. But not a standard suit, but a suit of natural wool with a soft shine, light cream colour and a double breasted jacket. And not in any store, but in Boggi on Kings Road. I also bought shoes to match. In total I spent 900 pounds. "Bah," I thought," four-days salary." I must point out in my defence that we were in the middle of spring and that Saturday afternoon was unusually warm and sunny for the British capital.

I had spent the Friday at the annual branch managers meeting at the company's European headquarters in the Docklands. Another monotonous meeting, predictable and sterile. Results, accounts and marketing plans. I had come to the first one, four years ago, full of hopes and with a slight fear due to my mediocre English level. As time had passed, my English had improved proportionally inverse to my hopes; which, at that time, were almost null. I had no more goals to achieve. I was suffocating in my own life, and that was the reason for my depressions. What was I going to do? There was nothing worth making an effort for.

Neither the economic incentives, nor a larger office with windows to Paseo de la Castellana, nor three service managers and fifty people under my supervision made me feel as fulfilled as I should. Maybe I did not know how to enjoy my brilliant situation. After all, I was "a winner." And to become one, I had studied and prepared for years. So that afternoon I bought my suit and matching shoes to show myself that at thirty-six, I was where I wanted to be. I also decided to take better care of my look. Back in Madrid, I went to the barbers in Salamanca neighbourhood, and I allowed him cut my hair at his discretion. I also got a moustache:

fine and well groomed.

A few days later I went to Zaragoza for the family lunch that, one Sunday a month, would gather the whole family at the paternal house. I arrived a little late when everyone was already seated at the table, dressed in my new suit, showing off my new moustache and my most satisfied smile:

"How strange you look; I don't like it" my mother whispered to me as I bent down to kiss her. My father looked at me perplexed. My sister, always radical, snapped at me:

"You look like a snob from Serrano."

But my younger brother and brother-in-law encouraged me somewhat by admiring my attire, while my young sister-in-law, mockingly and provocatively, threw at me:

"Yes sir, no complexes."

The atmosphere returned to normal, and we had a pleasant and fun lunch, with occasional jokes between siblings, comments on the economic and political situation, my father's wise words to appease the moods when they seemed to overflow and the compliments of both in-laws to the culinary arts of my mother. I did not contribute to the general conversation as much as on other occasions, but when, after coffee and cognac, the conversations became calm and affectionate, I felt very comforted.

I left the house full of good memories. Instead of taking the car and going straight to Madrid I stopped for a while in the park, scene of my first love and student parties with some drunkenness included. "Did I have goals and dreams then?" I asked myself. For I was not sure if the ones I had had were entirely mine or imposed by education, the post-war environment and the implicit eagerness to carve oneself a future. I was quite happy. I did what I was supposed to do. I studied, some years more, others less, always the minimum to pass and with some unexpected exemplary grades, and carried the standard existence of the young middle-class boy of the time.

My professional life had gone too fast. From Zaragoza to Paris; from there, back to my hometown for a couple of years, to help my father in his business and, at the same time, work as a regional delegate of a Catalan company that manufactured the same type of apparatus as the Telemecanique. Then Bilbao, another two years with this last company, who had come searching for me in Zaragoza when taking control of its Spanish subsidiary and, finally, Madrid with the Americans. I had never been afraid of change. I had ridden on the meteoric economic development of Spain at the time. My bosses cherished and promoted me from one job to the next with regular salary increases. I was the first one surprised by my successes. I wondered if triumph and happiness had anything in common. I answered myself with a no. Although you cannot give up something if you have not achieved it yet. Nor can one feel happy if one lives at odds with himself.

So I continued reflecting during the more than three hours of the journey home. My mind suspended in my thoughts as I searched for the right moment to overtake the trucks at the passes before arriving at Calatayud, in the curves of Arcos de Jalón, with the road encased next to the river, or on the plains of Guadalajara, with the remains of the trenches of the civil war a few meters from the asphalt. I arrived at night, changed my clothes, put the suit away in the back of the wardrobe and went to the bathroom to shave off my moustache. Then I went to see my neighbour and friend Dominique, a Frenchman who had been living in Spain for some years and who, a few days before, had told me of his intention to leave the following year to INSEAD. He gave me an application form.

The rejection of my application, weeks later, seemed unfair to me. Not admitting me because of my age. Unacceptable! I was not going to accept it and give up. I telephoned Santiago Fernández, a former student of the INSEAD, senior manager of Saint-Gobain in Spain and a kind of ambassador of the School in Spain. We made an appointment. Dominique accompanied me. He had not been admitted for the same reason as me, he was a year younger.

"Perfect timing," said Santiago, as soon as we entered his huge office in a modern building on the Paseo de la Castellana. "Gilbert Sauvage, one of the members of the admission committee, is coming next week, he is scheduled to give a lecture. I'll arrange a meeting with him. For you, Francisco, there is a bigger chance, because they have very few Spaniards," he continued. "With you, Dominique, I fear it more challenging because they receive many requests from Frenchmen, it is where the School is best known, and they limit the quota to twenty-five percent of the students. They want to remain a very international school."

And that's how it went. Professor Sauvage welcomed us in a small room of the Hotel Fénix, next to the Plaza de Colón. With Dominique, he excused himself: "We have too many Frenchmen. As for you, I won't say no. I think you are a person who keeps himself young and dynamic, your French is excellent, and I hope your English too; I'm going to see with my colleagues what can be done."

A few days later I received a letter from him: "If you want to continue with the process, come to Fontainebleau to have an interview with Mr Gareth Dyas, Director of Admissions, and take the language tests here: English, French and German." This last thing I did not expect. I had trusted on taking the tests here in Madrid and that Santiago would turn a blind eye to my English and especially with my little German. But I couldn't back down now.

So one afternoon in May, I left the office a little earlier than usual, took the plane to Orly and from there, a train to Fontainebleau. The station was at one end of the village and the hotel I had booked, on the other, a couple of miles away but close to INSEAD. It was a beautiful day, and I only carried a light bag with me, so I walked.

I loved the small town. Well-kept houses of two or three floors, several cafés, well-dressed and quiet people, little traffic and a grandiose palace, half renaissance, half Napoleonic, in front of a park Versailles style, with its ponds and its avenues lined with statues of mythological characters and centenary trees.

The next morning, I showed up in Mr Dyas's office. He turned out to be an Englishman of my age, friendly, easy-going and with abundant curly hair. He looked more like a former Beatle than a scrutinising chief of admissions. In addition, he was eager to talk about Spain, which he had discovered by auto-stop after finishing college and where he had had a great time, as he told me. He spoke more than me so I could hide my imperfections in English fairly well.

I then proceeded to the language lab to take the corresponding tests. They consisted of listening to a tape in French and then doing a summary in English and vice versa. The young woman, who was in charge of the tests, after explaining what I had to do, left me alone. I took advantage of this to rewind the tape in English as many times as I wanted until I fully understood the content. As for German, they explained to me that, if I did not consider myself fit to pass the test, it did not matter, I would have the chance to learn it better while studying for the Masters degree. Moreover, they considered Spanish important enough to be the third language that was needed in the INSEAD. I waited for half an hour for the language teacher to correct the test. In the meantime, Dyas had spoken to Sauvage, and both came to give me the good news. "We will expect you next September."

On my return to Madrid, I announced my resignation to my American bosses, from June 30, and my departure to my colleagues and subordinates in the company. The president of the company answered with a very affectionate letter in which he regretted my departure, wished me many successes in the future and asked me to contact them, once the course had finished, for they could surely offer me an exciting position in Europe or the USA. I sold my MG convertible and bought a modest R-5. Afterwards, already in July, I left on holiday with Ursula, as I remembered yesterday, to Italy and all the way to Sardinia. At the beginning of September, I left to INSEAD with my heart and mind as free as eager for the novelties that awaited me.

XII

Hold infinity in the palm of your hand
and eternity in an hour.
He who binds to himself a joy
Does the winged life destroy;
But he who kisses the joy as it flies
Lives in eternity's sun rise.
William Blake

Yesterday, after our morning walk in search of water, the unhappy surprise of finding ourselves with no gas left upon arriving at the tent and my evocations of some of the stories of my youth and my professional life, the afternoon seemed to run without major upheavals until all of a sudden, the heavens covered up and a heavy snowfall began. This circumstance increased our concern about the difficulty our rescuers would have when crossing the pass as well as, later, on our journey back, due to the amount of snow that was accumulating from other snowfalls the previous days. How would that edge that "flew" over the cliff look now? I wondered. Would we get out of there? I liked difficulty, but I hated danger.

At night time, the weather changed again. The clouds opened up and from the northern lands, the Tibetan plateau, the wind came. It grew as the darkness advanced and became an incessant hurricane that bellowed all night. The small tent swayed with the force of the wind to the rhythm of its gusts, while we noticed how the snow was accumulating against its weak walls. At times it seemed that it was going to yank it from its hooks and hurtle it down the slope to the bottom of her gorge.

How long would it last? I heard its loud whistle and the repeated sound of the snow crystals against the tarp of the tent. The wind caught them from the top of the mountains and carried them from one place to another. Not only did they come from the sky, but they were transported from here to there. I was awake, attentive to the gusts of wind: as long as the sound didn't change it meant that it was bringing snow. I would have liked to have a very hot tea, but I had to settle for a few sips of cold water.

We lay tight against each other in our little space, the American and the European, both alone with our thoughts. He, like me, was feeling, intangible and definitive, the proximity of death and, consequently, the beauty of life. Neither he nor I wanted to abandon it. In vain I tried to channel my ideas, to think of the people who were dear to me; I could not do it. I felt Jack's proximity, and I was glad I was not alone. After a while, I noticed that he had fallen asleep.

The walls of the ridge tent swelled and crushed to the beat of the winds. Around midnight, to inspect its fastenings, I unzipped the flap and stuck out my head. The hurricane hit me straight in the face, so strongly it made my eyes water, but I had to resist. The double-roof was beating, desperate to fly away. It had already ripped off one of the pegs that held it to the snow. I wondered how, as when I tried to nail it to the ground again, the snow was so hard that I only managed to do so by hitting it with a lot of patience with one of my boots, while suffering Eolo's cruel lashes.

I returned inside, but the incessant roar and the concern for our security due to the aggressive swaying of the canvas prevented me from sleeping. It finally occurred to me to make a slit in the ceiling – I must have read it somewhere – so that the wind would find less resistance. And so it was. This eased the tent´s movements significantly. "On the other hand, the hurricane will have at least cleaned the edge of the pass quite a bit and so will have swept away a good amount of the accumulated snow," I told myself. And sleep overcame me.

I woke up with a heavy head. I had fallen asleep very late, and then I had dreamt of Ursula. I remembered her in her white, vaporous dress with a crown of flowers on her hair like that morning in the Hostel of San Marcos where she had seemed like Ofelia to me. I could not catch her. I followed her, and when I was close, I tried to hug her. Impossible. She escaped like a spirit. Of course, that's what she was! And so, over and over again. During all those years I had thought of her too much. I was fascinated. Was it because I did not manage to understand her? Was I rather fascinated than in love?

I must admit, Ursula, that my new life at Fontainebleau changed my perspectives. I did not need you that much anymore. Going back to student life at thirty-something - one of the eldest at the course - and with many lessons already learned and suffered, was like a gastronomic tour of the best restaurants in France or like a few weeks of safari with a Hemingway heroine across the hills of Africa.

The campus, three or four functional buildings with lots of glass and only two floors between gardens, spread surrounded by forests in front of the small town, located 70 km south of Paris and famous for its lavish château built by Francis I and enlarged by Napoleon. The course was made up of more than two hundred students from thirty different nationalities, from Brazil to Japan, with many

French, German, British and few Spaniards. Of all of them, only nine women. I lived with twenty classmates in a small hotel, of rural charm, on the other side of the great palace park. I bought a bicycle, and every morning I crossed through the park with its ponds, its gardens and its courtly trees to go to class. My spirit liberated. Optimism in abundance. My Madrid depressions forgotten.

I was no longer so much on top of you, but our epistolary relationship was perfect. At Christmas, we did not see each other. We each wanted and had to spend it with our respective families. You in Nuremberg, I in Zaragoza. And afterwards, you had to work until the semester started again, to earn some money to support yourself. You suggested I go to Frankfurt, where you had found a job at a stand in a fair, but I refused. I feared, as I knew from past experiences, this situation where I would be waiting for you all day, you would be bothered by my null integration in German life and, moreover, a cold and dark winter, which would only bring us frustration and conflict. I explained this to you, but you did not accept it willingly. So the first week of January I went skiing in the Alps with some friends from INSEAD. You did not like this very much.

You do not trust me; don't you understand that it is better to leave it for later, for when you are freer? If not, you know what happens ... I wrote to you. You took several days to answer. Cold. You wrote about your daily life and talked about newspaper news. A firewall was needed.

February arrived. The academic year was well underway, without the pressure of the first trimester, where at the end, and after the corresponding exams, I had convinced myself to be no more foolish than the average of my colleagues and, therefore, to look with optimism at obtaining my Master's degree. You had just

171

worked for a few well-paid days at the Frankfurt Book Fair, and we could see each other. We both wanted to. So I took my little R5, and I went to pick you up for a tour of Alsace.

Blonde as its beer, fresh as its wines, beautiful towns and cities, vine-covered hillsides and fields lined with flowers in that explosive spring. We looked up, and there were the Vosges and their forests. The scenario certainly contributed to our reconciliation. We were sitting on a terrace of the market square in Obernai, in front of the typical half-timbered houses with their windows full of geraniums, while we tasted a Gewurztraminer.

"This wine is glorious, how delicious it is," I said, as I lifted my glass to the candle to admire its golden colour after bringing it close to my nose to smell it.

You raised your glass too. Your gaze, after a day of smiles and discreet caresses, while visiting wineries, museums and churches, became serious.

"I am astonished, Francisco, how easy it has been to meet up again," you said to me, "a look, a smile do more than a hundred thoughts or a thousand words."

"Yes, perhaps we should not have written the previous letters."

"The situation has changed, it has been good to see each other, we have fortified a common foundation. Don't you think?" We put down our wine glasses and held each other's hands as you continued. "I, for my part, have taken a step forward, I will try to give you more trust, more affection, and show you my inner self."

"Yes, Ursula, please try to open yourself a little more. Understand it positively, our relationship is strong, we have met again, to love each other without anguish or haste, but we must turn it into a constant fire" I almost begged.

You brought your chair closer to mine and rested your head on

172

my shoulder. I remembered the night before, the first one together for weeks. We had regained, without problems, our passionate love from before. And this, I thought, thanks to that young man, not more than twenty years of age, the guide to one of the wineries of what was called the Wine Route in Riquewihr. We had met at noon at the station on the arrival of your train from Heidelberg, and it was the third and last winery we visited that afternoon. During the whole tour the little Frenchman had not been able to take his eyes off you; for him, you were the only person in the group. And during the wine tasting, standing before us, he looked more at your cleavage than at the wines he was talking about. You, polite and interested as always in learning new things, followed his explanations without, apparently, noticing his fixation for your person.

The interest of the boy ignited my feelings: jealousy, on the one hand, the pride that you were my girl on the other, and desire. So, as soon as we reached the hotel room, while you were standing with your back to me, unpacking your suitcase, I wrapped my arms around your waist. My hands moved up to cover your breasts; my mouth reached for your neck, I pressed my body to yours and the bottom part of my torso to where your back became two welcoming hemispheres. An inconsiderate fervour grew which ignited my organ without misgivings, I opened the buttons, and found your white and round flesh, you searched for my lips, we moved to the bed and, once again, we coincided: it is the place where lovers best understand each other.

After our conversation in Obernai Square, we went for dinner: Sauerkraut, various cheeses and Riesling wine. We returned to the hotel. That night you wanted us to go slow, not to rush, not like the night before. For me, everything that you asked when it came to making love was good. So we loved each other without embarrassment or haste.

Back in Heidelberg, you wrote to me.

I am amazed and even frightened of the strong ties that unite us. Any conflict, even if it seems important to me, disappears before the feelings of belonging to one another that already feels natural to me. And this, at the same time that it consoles me, scares me. Have we already lost some of our independence? Is my body already synchronised with yours, to its existence? What will become of me if that symbiosis is broken, if you leave me or I leave you? Will we be able to live without the other half?

I believe in you. Maybe, sometimes, I believe less in myself. The difficult thing for me in our encounters and after them as well is that here in Heidelberg, I live a very different life to the one I live when I am with you in France or elsewhere. As soon as I come back here, I become more intellectual, dominated by books, especially now. With you I am not, I can not be; I'm just a person. So for me, it is a break when we say goodbye - or when we are reunited - because it almost seems like a change in my persona, which is a little harder than changing my dress. I would like one day to combine, in a natural way, both characters.

How could I not love you, Ursula, with those beautiful letters you wrote to me! And maybe from this came some of our problems. You raised so many expectations in me that I saw you "like the moon that raises the sea," but when days of silence followed or I called you and you seemed distant, or I would see you and found you prudent and cold, surprised by my outbursts of speech and action, there my hopes would shatter. I phoned you one night in early May.

"You're invited to a fantastic party in one of the most beautiful palaces in France," I announced.

"Oh! Really? Where?"

174

"In the Château de Vaux le Vicomte, near here, on the twentieth; it is a Saturday."

"But I ..." your voice sounded doubtful in response to my enthusiasm.

"Does the date not suit you?" I asked in alarm.

"No, that's not it. But I can't go."

"What do you mean you can't come? Do not be antisocial. You know many of my classmates. Has something happened? Are you okay?" I continued, alarmed.

"I have nothing to wear to such a place. I don't have a dress."

"Please, Ursula, don't come up with such excuses, you can't leave me all dressed up and with no girlfriend," I said, not daring to offer you the money to buy one.

"Why don't you go with another girl, with one of your friend's sisters, with Isabelle for example.

"Why would you say that! I just want to go with you."

"But I can't go," you insisted.

I hung up extremely angry. "Why did I have to fall in love with such a strange woman?"

"She seems so natural and far from the social conventions, and here we are again with the story that she has nothing to wear, like that night in Marrakesh," I remembered. I told my friends in class the next morning. By mid- afternoon I already had three candidates. But I realised that I just wanted to go with Ursula. She called me two days later.

"I'm making myself a dress. I found some lovely fabric in the Ludwig Beck fabric section. A friend is going to lend me a pearl necklace, and I have the shoes you gave me for my birthday the last time you came." And you added jokingly, "so you can now harness the horses and prepare the chariot to take me to the castle."

"But I have found another dance partner," I answered, as joy flooded through me.

"What an amazing girl I have!" I thought. And, days later, that night, I felt very proud. With your blue dress of a soft sheen and a simple and classic cut, you were the most beautiful of the party. I do not remember much. I think we got a little drunk, stimulated by the free flowing champagne, courtesy of one of my classmates, the son of a family with wine cellars in Reims. Chords of waltzes, some tango, a lot of twist and rock and roll in the grand oval bright hall, Baroque decorations and caryatids holding the great dome, where even Louis XIV and his wife Maria Teresa had danced.

You leant lightly on my arm as we walked through the beautiful gardens to the entrance gate. We had to wait a few minutes for the bus that would take us back to the hotel. I was proud of your beauty and felt happy to be with you. You pressed your body closer to rest it against mine and the body contact produced in me an uncontrollable attack of desire. You answered with a mischievous look in your bright eyes, your smile, your soft kisses on my neck. Our encounter had to wait until we reached the room.

The next day in the evening you returned to University on a night express. We spent the afternoon in Paris. You wanted to visit the Louvre again. We strolled for more than two hours from room to room; you were especially interested in the paintings, hardly speaking. I followed you. We went past many paintings without looking at them. In front of others, you stopped, and you remained absorbed. At points, it was inexplicable to me. You focused your attention on the portraits, the expression on the faces of the characters; you immersed yourself in them, without perceiving my presence.

"I'm sorry Francisco," you answered the first time I pointed it out. "I was thinking of something else.

I followed your steps and your gaze. A young marmoreal, a bearded nobleman, a party in the midst of nature, a dying man in his bed. Who were all these people? What succession of random events had led them to gather under these ceilings? You gazed at a lady, and I gazed at you. There was an instant where I felt disappointed. Why? Last night so united and loving, and today so distant. But it was normally like this when we were in a museum or an art gallery. Towards the end of the visit, suddenly, you seemed to appreciate my company. You had been standing for a while now, in front of the "Girl in the Mirror" by Titian. It represented a young woman combing her hair before a man and two mirrors.

"This is a complex matter. It allows for several interpretations; it is not known whether it is a double portrait, a genre scene or an allegory" you started without looking at me, sure that I was next to you. "I interpret it as an allegory of Beauty, boasting of it and, at the same time, lamenting the ephemeral of its existence."

You stood for a few seconds while I, surprised that you had spoken to me and admiring your explanation of the scene, changed my gaze from you to the painting and vice versa.

"It has also been suggested that perhaps it transcribes Petrarch's sonnet that speaks of the triangle between beloved, mirror and lover, and how the man is envious of the mirror as it is receiving the gaze of the woman.

"Maybe it's all much simpler," I said. "The woman wants to be sure of her beauty to seduce her beloved, I would say."

"It's not a bad interpretation," you conceded.

And I felt satisfied and happy until it was time to say goodbye in the midst of the hustle and bustle of the platforms of the Gare de l'Est. Again we parted. And each separation would absorb a piece of my being.

After your departure, the job interviews began. The international companies came searching for us, the new INSEAD graduates, for positions in their headquarters or subsidiaries all over the world. They placed their offers on the boards prepared for this purpose in the hall, and we left our C.V. tailored to them in the office designated for that same purpose. I was interested in an oil company to be its director in Indonesia, in one specialised in machinery in Mexico, another in Egypt ... I wanted something new, outside of Spain, in virgin territory for me. I told you so in my letters.

You answered:

I think of us I think of what lies before us. You will look for a new job and will go away, wherever you like. It makes me sad. It's an intense pain I have. Already I feel that you are separating from me. So far you've been away, but always close. I think about the summer, where will you be? It hurts so much. Is the farewell beginning already? I know there's no reason for it, nor to be here crying. But I am weak; I must become strong. And I will be, I will not tell you to stay. My sadness will give me joy; my weakness, strength. You give me sadness and joy. I think you've never understood me. My weakness forces me to be strong to survive and only from such sadness can a deep joy be born. I'll feel better tomorrow. Each one of us is expelled into the world alone, in the most intimate and most complex manner, and has to walk during his life with a body he cannot abandon, like a snail. Everything seems fleeting, yet it is a circle; Can we get out of it? May the Holy Spirit enlighten us! Or, profanely, intuition.

I felt selfish, just thinking about myself and what I wanted. Willing to jeopardise or obviate our relationship. No, you were still the most beautiful woman in the world, the most tender, the most intelligent and, above all, the most complex. I never got to understand you and, therefore, to possess you. Is that why you attracted me so much?

I was in the middle of the exam period, but I took a train, and the morning after I received your letter I was knocking at your door in Heidelberg. Remember? We spent the day together wandering along the banks of the Neckar and then in the intimate Cafe Burkhardt, except for the one hour where you had a very important class. You were then more calm and realistic again.

"Let's think about a country, a city that attracts us both, and in a year we can live together, the year you need to get your doctorate," I said.

"It is not easy to think of a place without knowing it. Finish, I do not finish in a year.

"How come?"

"Yes, I've been thinking about going to Venice after finishing my doctorate."

"And why Venice? I would not find any interesting work there.

"I can get a scholarship. There is a residence of the Goethe-Institut. I already have the theme: The Venetian Settecento."

"Fantastic" but I remained pensive and disappointed. "And then?" I added.

"How can we know where we will feel comfortable and both find a job that will satisfy us? And why not Germany?" You asked me one more time.

"You know that my German is very poor and, besides, I do not feel comfortable here, I don't like the discipline, nor the people's serious faces, "I answered, once again.

We had Paris left. I had just received an offer from my old company to be marketing director at the European headquarters in the French capital, but I had not thought of considering it. You did not say yes or no. You accompanied me to the station to spend another night on the train, and we said goodbye, more confident but with our future as open, as unknown, as before.

XIII

A life without music is a wrong life.

Anne Sophie Mutter

And a life without love is a lost life.

Popular wisdom

I would have continued navigating through my memories, but Jack, in high spirits, decided and rightfully so, that we should go and fetch water and even make two trips because the day was calm and we had to take advantage of it. At that altitude, it was essential that we maintained ourselves properly hydrated. And so, we went to the stream again at mid-morning, but despite our high hopes, when we returned to the tent, our saviours had still not arrived. So, after emptying the water, we had brought in a plastic bag and hanging it from the tent's ceiling, at mid afternoon we set off again. We had to wait until that time because I was the only one with glacier sunglasses and we could not risk being exposed to the snow for long during midday. The reflection of the ultraviolet rays blinded the one who did not wear them, and would even burn our face if we did not wear a handkerchief tied around it and our hats down to our eyebrows.

When we started back, the sun had disappeared behind the peaks to the west, over Kamet and Nilkanta, and the air suddenly became chilly. From one moment to the other, our environment changed as if we had magically appeared elsewhere. Until a few minutes before, every fold of the Nanda Devi had been inviting, shining brightly basked in sunlight; now it looked dark, cold and gloomy. Every inch of it was now menacing. It made me feel tiny and fragile. Never before had I felt the dark power of the Himalayas that surrounded us. I was afraid. And Jack looked no less frightened. His voice encouraged me, and I regained rationality.

"We'd better hurry up. Otherwise, we won´t find the tent in the dark."

We could not walk very fast because the snow had already become hard. The light was rapidly diminishing, and the shadow of the night began to surround us. Just like the previous days, the clouds from the valley began to rise. We realised the danger we were in, but there was nothing we could do but keep walking hoping that we would find the tent before the fog enveloped us. But we didn't succeed. Little by little, it crept up on us. We knew that not only would we not find the tent but that there was also a big chance we would get lost, maybe even fall off a precipice, and that we would have to spend the night out in the open, soaked by the humidity that the fog gave off. We decided to climb to escape it.

The mountainside became steeper and more treacherous as we climbed, and at times it felt like my heart would burst out of my chest. Jack was suffering as much or maybe even more than I, but we couldn't give up. After an hour of tenacious efforts in the dark, we managed to reach a safe spot and leave the now stabilised clouds behind. We decided to spend the night there. We had no tools to dig into the hard snow and try to build an igloo, and it would have been impossible to do it with our hands. So we had to settle for the shelter of some rocks.

The sky was strewn with stars that shone so brightly they were even reflected in the snow. There was no moon, but we could make out all the peaks around us. Below, however, the fog thickened in the gorge and the distant valleys and climbed all the way until it nearly reached our feet. It was a glorious sight. The mountains rose, as if by magic, from a sea of white foam. And there we were, in the centre of all those giants. We could admire them or feel their terrible threat: an avalanche coming from one of the ones behind us could sweep us away in an instant.

But we were not in the mood for admiring the landscape. We had nothing to eat, and the cold paralysed us. Every gust of wind would make us shiver uncontrollably. We pressed ourselves against each other and tried to reduce as much as possible the contact of our bodies with the snow which had already transformed into ice and on which we were sitting. We could not sleep. If we did, we would risk freezing to death. How stupidly we had put ourselves in danger. We talked and encouraged each other to stay awake. What a never-ending night! But it is amazing how powerful the will to survive is.

At midnight the wind decreased, and after a few more hours of suffering, dawn broke at last. We set out, anxious to reach our tent. We descended about three hundred meters diagonally, surpassed a ridge and, incredible! There it was, only two hundred meters from where we had started to climb when the fog had covered us. We rushed towards it in search of shelter and comfort, of something to eat, of the sleeping bag for one, and the survival blanket for the other. When we arrived, as sullen as we were, we did something worthy of passing to the annals of mountaineering: we both jumped into the same sleeping bag! Well, Jack could only fit into it up to his waist and had to cover his torso with the survival blanket. When we woke up, we were sweaty and hungry. And remembering the avatars of the previous night we told ourselves that if we had

183

passed that test, we were destined to survive and save ourselves. While Jack prepared somehow something to eat, I returned to my relationship with Ursula.

I continue thinking about you. What a woman! At the age twenty-five you wrote to me about old age:

Is it old age what makes me more in need of the presence of a friend who can care for me in my different moods? Or is it a disempowerment instead of due emancipation? Is it maturity? The freedom that I so need only exists if one is committed to all its consequences and if it has to do with love, with all its inconsistencies. Or has my love reached its deep end before falling apart according to the laws of nature? "For the beautiful is but the beginning of the terrible." It is, it will be all of that. For me, love has always been painful and very beautiful, very personal, now addressed to you and awake to all the senses. Bye. Kisses.

What could I even answer? You were impregnated with Rilke and his elegies, floating melancholically in the spaces of the subconscious, while I felt earthly. You made me see you as superior, intelligent, beautiful and terrible when I just wanted to feel you like a simple and loving companion, jovial and carefree, as I aspired then to be. The reality is that I felt then a resigned acceptance of our differences and told myself that we had to live with them and continue our relationship that seemed, despite everything, certain. Now that I think of it, I also did not want to keep imagining things about us and suffering more from it. I wanted to be practical.

It was the summer in which you had finished your studies in Heidelberg and were going to move to Munich for a more specialised course. I, from my side, had completed the master's degree and had accepted the offer from my old company for the management post in Paris starting in September. Partly because I liked the mission they entrusted me with, to direct marketing and sales for the whole of Europe and, in part, because we would be closer and who knows! Maybe, in the end, you would decide to come and live with me. In the meantime, I wanted us to spend the month of August together and hoped that, as in our previous summer in Italy, a whole month together would be definitive in consolidating our relationship and define our future. But here it was that you wrote to me:

I have finally found work for August. It is in a "Gasthof" in a village in the south of Bavaria. It will be hard work, ten to twelve hours a day, but I hope to earn two thousand Marks for the whole month, most of it in tips. Don't you want to get to know this part of the Bavarian Alps? It's beautiful. Write to me, tell me what you are doing and what you think.

On the one hand, I understood that you needed the money, but on the other, I felt disappointed that we wouldn't go on holidays together as August presented itself with nothing motivating or attractive and I would begin my new employment right afterwards.

"I'll lend you the money, and you can just give it back to me whenever you can," I suggested while talking on the phone.

"When and how will I give it back to you? I never have any spare money. "

"In a year, when you've finished your degree and have a job."

"Thank you for your good intentions, as I thank you for everything you do for me, the travelling, the expensive meals ... but you know I want to be financially independent, and I will always want to be."

"It will only be a loan as if a bank was giving it to you" I insisted.

"Don't insist" was your final answer.

But I did not despair. It was typical. I insisted again by letter. I tried to be kind, sympathetic, reasonable, while I kept hoping you would accept my offer. But no, you stood your ground.

Francisco: How difficult it is to write to you. On the one hand, I feel love, on the other, sadness, misunderstanding, even anger. On the one hand, you write such a funny and affectionate letter; on the other, the feeling of our last telephone conversation was so destructive; I felt so much aggression in your voice. You did not want to show even a little understanding because of my economic situation that forces me to work. Do you believe that the value of our friendship depends on whether or not we go on vacation in August, regardless of the consequences? And the fact that you do not want to come to Germany to spend a few days together disappoints me terribly.

September arrived. I joined my new team in my office on the twenty-fourth floor of a tower in "La Defense." And you did not come to Paris as promised: *I thought of visiting you after the Book Fair, but I have to go to Munich to register and talk to the teachers and people in my study group.*

After days of silence, I decided to call you. I spoke to you softly and affectionately, and you responded in the same way. We talked about what we had been up to and felt close to each other. There were deep silences and whispers of desire. I wanted to say, "Oh! That yearning, that wound that only finds comfort in your eyes and in your arms. Tell me if you still think of me when your feelings sink into your memories. Tell me if you still long for the touch of my hands on your skin and the taste of my lips, the game of our mouths united, say if ..."

Francisco: Your call this afternoon has awoken so many emotions. I am such a coward and so stupid! I longed to see you, to

186

talk to you, but I could not tell you. How easily we hurt each other. Have we no basis for understanding ourselves intuitively? When will we make the sun shine through so many clouds?

I will come to Paris to be with you for a couple of weeks, in early October. I will uncover my heart and its creases, which it also has. Why do we have to clear our shared path of obstacles that seem to accumulate because of our very different lives? Yes, it is not new, I know. But are we still stagnant in our relationship? I do not think so; I feel more and more emotionally attached to you. I think a lot about you, and for that, I have no fixed schedule.

We returned to our cordial and loving relationship but I still felt that I had been materialistic, clumsy, mean. Many things had happened between us since the beginning of summer, so much tension and unforeseen hopes, so to have you in my arms again was something which I never wanted to end. I would make sure your stay in Paris was unforgettable. Maybe you would even convince yourself to come and live with me permanently. I was sure that you would love my apartment with a garden out front and two balconies looking out upon the Forest of Bologna.

I waited for you impatiently. The last weeks had been for me, times of that endless solitude which only the great cities can cause. And in that state of mind, a few days before your arrival, I went to a concert at the Concert Hall Pleyel: concerts for violin numbers 3 and 5 by Mozart. The soloist was Anne Sophie Mutter. I told you about it later.

A beautiful young woman on stage, an unknown violinist. A virtuous one. I close my eyes, and I can see her again: she plays the sounds precisely, the vibrato and the tremolo. During the slow melodies, the strings of her bow never seemed to stop. The violin, a lively and sensual Tononi - or perhaps she already has a Stradivarius - prolongs her body, which stretches and ripples like her blond hair to the beat of the music. She must have made a mysterious pact with beauty. It feels supernatural. In each note, she gives her soul. Her feeling captures me. No musical instrument expresses as much mystery as the violin: This is why romantic musicians identify it often with the devil.

As I watched her, I could imagine her inner self. Devoted to art and the pursuit of beauty and feeling. Like you. How many struggles, how much effort she must have made and will continue to make to reach her goals. "Now I understand you," I told myself. "I love music, and it was you, Ursula, with your knowledge and your passion, who taught me to love it as well. I must compensate you for all our previous disagreements and misunderstandings. So I have planned a special night for the day of your arrival. I'm going to seduce you forever. "

I picked you up that afternoon at the Gare de L'Est. You had been on that train for nine hours all the way from Munich, but you got out of the carriage fresh and giggling as it was usual with you. We were both thinking the same, the enjoyment of the near future. We went home. You loved it:

"How lucky you are!" How nice! You will now have a guest for a long while" you said, looking at me mockingly.

"Until death do us part or nothing," I added.

"Do you know what Thomas Mann said about death?"

"No, nor do I want to. Don't start," I cut you off as I hugged you.

"Please, get ready, we're going out for dinner and after there is a surprise," I added.

We went for dinner to Le Monde des Chimères, a small and intimate bistro, candles, flower bouquets, mirrors and a lot of wood, which two young graduates in Hispanic literature had just opened on the island of Saint-Louis. The perfect setting to meet again, to exchange caressing looks over the table, to join our knees under it, to extend your hand and me to receive it, to talk about our lives of the previous weeks with gestures and words, and to promise each other love and suggest pleasures with silences.

And all this while we tasted a *foie de Landes*, the best *Coquilles Saint-Jacques* we had ever eaten, accompanied by a fresh *Sancerre* and, finally, a passion fruit soufflé. After a romantic walk along the river, between the shadows of the night, the faltering lanterns and the lime trees on the banks of the Seine, with the well-lit images of the ethereal apsis of Notre Dame on one side and the elaborate Renaissance facades of the "Hotel de Ville" on the other . I led you to the stage I had prepared. The importance of our encounter deserved an exceptional frame: the Coco Chanel suite at the Hotel Ritz in the aristocratic Place Vêndome.

Baroque mirrors and Coromandel lacquer of the furniture reflected the lights of the Baccarat crystal chandeliers, while the silk drapes dialogued with the Aubusson tapestries and the sofas dressed in the famous padded work of the *Grande Mademoiselle*. On the living room table, a bottle of Cristal Roederer from 1972, the year we met, and a tray of Lady Godiva chocolates. It didn't take long before your feminine soul appeared from beneath your frugal nature, and you felt spoilt and content. You changed into an elated, smiling and suggestive woman. We looked at each other. Your aquamarine blue eyes gleamed, your delicate breast palpitating as I approached you. We toasted. We kissed. You became provocative. You played with the bows on your shoulders, and your dress slid to the carpet.

I had recorded a music tape to enwrap you, Ursula, in adages and allegrettos, in scales and arpeggios. Music is more important than speech. Music is passion and passion can be music. And it has so much force, as much as the explosion of a star in its desire to be part of the Universe.

It was Mozart, to begin with, Piano Concerto n° 7. How well it suited you! Cheerful and fun. A music piece without messages. Mozart only sings and dreams. And there we were, naked and longing. Your body was a pure melody, cadence and rhythm, a palpable music. You felt proud of it, and you showed it by giving it to me. I adored those sublime breasts, and you seemed to adore the most secret part of my anatomy. The pianist's fingers were delicate and playful, like mine as I traced your beautiful back.

The waltz of the women's choir of Beethoven's King Stephen followed. Floating and light that it didn't really sound like the great and deep Ludwig. The music became distant, submerged as we were in the pleasure of our united bodies. Can you remember what we did to the rhythm of that melody until we reached ecstasy? We rested. More champagne, smiles of delight and looks of complacency. Händel's moment came with a fragment of his Messiah, a song tribute to the union of people. Then, yes, we felt enveloped by the triumphant harmony of sounds and voices. Hallelujah! Hallelujah! Sang the chorus. And so we told ourselves: let us praise love, sex and the gods of all religions.

Astor Piazzolla. One of his slow tangos, a nostalgic oblivion in that sad elegance that so well defines the violin and the accordion, sometimes in accompanying each other, sometimes in an antagonistic rivalry. A rhythm made for the changes in rhythm. And so led we resumed our dialogue, and our senses changed the enjoyments of music to those of the touch. Now I hold you, now I slide down your body, you kiss me, and you kiss me, I kiss you, I kiss you...... My tongue ran gently over your body, savouring the most secret corners, now with intensity and passion, now with tenderness and delight. You rewarded me a thousand fold. Again inside you to the chords of a ballad of Salvador Bacarisse: pianos, violins and six-string guitar. The agility of the instruments, vivacity, passion ... A melody of immemorial resonances. Sensations of time without measure.

Après un rêve of Gabriel Fauré: *Tu m'appelais et je quittais la terre pour m'enfuir avec toi vers la lumière.*[22] Yes, I was summoned by your clear eyes, iridescent of emeralds, to flee together from this earth in a long farewell until we reached the light of ecstasy and pleasure. We listened in silence until the lively fandango of Rodrigo's Madrigal Concert awoke us from our reverie. Rhythm and change. The relevance of the soloist and contrast of instruments. And of organs that seek to be found! Until they come together and dissolve into one another. Then Wagner sounded: The Sundown of the Gods. Very evocative and appropriate for the end of a battle, even a love one.

The hours had passed. It seemed that our time of ecstasy granted by the gods was finished. I let go of your arms. I stood up and started getting ready to go to sleep. You rested in bed. A dreamy look and the last champagne in the glass. Relaxed, beautiful. So beautiful that I could only love you. You looked at me, you beckoned me towards you, and you kissed me. We seemed to read each other's minds. "This cannot end already." More music. Mozart was played again. I got lost in your eyes, your breasts, your skin and your lips.

I close mine now and remember that last scene: You on top of me. I feel all the heat of your being. The intensity of your embrace transmutes me; I perceive myself, leaving my body and ascending to the heavens. That must be how a mystical experience feels like. Oh, the music, the only love that does not make you suffer!

---

[22] *"You called me and I left the earth to flee with you to the light."*

XIV

Every man wants to live at the top of the mountain, without realizing that true happiness comes when climbing its slopes.

Gabriel G. Marquez

It was already our seventh day. It was snowing again, but without much force, and with absolute indifference to our hopes. This forced us to spend the majority of the day stuck in the tent trying to grind rice to then dilute it in water, drinking cold milk with coffee, telling each other stories of our lives and the reason for our wanderings in these lands. Jack had recovered and was eager to talk. It looked as if he wanted to make up for the days of silence that we had spent together. He told me that he was married and had a three-year-old son. His wife had not been pleased with his new departure to the Himalayas. Two years earlier, on his return from the Makalu, he had promised her that he would only climb in North America, but he had not been able to resist the temptation and had come again.

When, in turn, I told him of my intention of reaching the inner sanctuary of the Nanda Devi, he looked at me with certain astonishment and exclaimed:

"But, I think that is very dangerous. I thought you only wanted to reach the cave."

"Man, it's far less dangerous than climbing the Dunagiri," I said. "Look at the result," nearly escaped my lips. "Yes, I have read about it," I continued, "crossing the gorges of the Rishi Ganga is not easy; towards the end, one has to climb some tough walls although, according to Pemba, there are fixed ropes left by some Czechoslovakians last year."

"Well, I did not mean that. Have you not heard the story of the plutonium? All that area and in particular the river must be contaminated. Did you not know anything?"

"What are you talking about? I had no idea," I stared at him in amazement.

"A friend who works at the American embassy in New Delhi told me. And it seems to be common knowledge in the power circles in India. They have recently dealt with the matter in Parliament, and it has been said that they are going to close the whole region."

"Well, tell me all, I'm all ears," I said with some disbelief.

"Do you remember the" cold war "?

"Yes, of course, in the sixties, the Russians and you, the Americans"

"Exactly. But it was no joke. In 1964, the tension was at its peak" Jack began his story. "Communist China exploded its first atomic bomb in the deserts of Xinjiang, north of Tibet. Then, the CIA decided to install a spying station on the heights of the Himalayas to monitor Chinese nuclear testing and contacted the Indian government to allow it."

"And the Indians were delighted, of course," I interrupted. "If I remember correctly, there had just been a war between the two of them over the control of some regions of the borders."

"Therefore, no plan was considered unheard of, and any investment was justified by the need to protect the West from the evil intentions of the Red East. So they trained the best North American and Indian mountaineers and chose the top of the Nanda Devi to deposit the artefact.

"The Indians are such hypocrites!" I exclaimed. "For them, well, for the Hindus, the Nanda Devi is one of the most sacred mountains. How could they accept?

"Yes, but the CIA needed it. From there, they could intercept the radio signals between the Chinese missiles and their control stations on the ground. And then a transmitter would send the data to the agency's listening stations. The system was very high tech, but on paper, it seemed as simple as it was effective."

"I do not know whether to believe you; it sounds like a movie."

"At the end of the winter of 1965," he continued, ignoring my words, "they established a base camp at the foot of the mountain. They needed hundreds of porters and even a couple of helicopters. After equipping several high altitude camps, they transferred all the material to the last camp at only five hundred meters from the summit, and there it was that the tragedy occurred. An avalanche caused by a massive storm buried several men, dragged all the technical equipment until God knows where and forced both Indians and Americans to abandon the project. The bad thing was that the spy station was powered by plutonium batteries, a highly radioactive material as you probably know."

"No, I had not worried about the bloody plutonium until now. And what happened to the batteries, where did they end up?

"The whereabouts are unknown" he shrugged his shoulders and continued. "Several expeditions were sent the following years to recover the material, but they found nothing. The batteries must be buried somewhere in the glacier and their contamination, carried by the water, may have even reached the Ganges."

"Damn! Now I'm scared. I don't know what to think. The other day I drank from those waters and Pemba as well. He did not say they were dangerous. And we used it to cook."

"I suppose this whole thing has not yet reached these people's ears," Jack reasoned, "and I would not worry, almost twenty years have passed, and if there was any actual contamination, it's in the Indian Ocean by now."

"Ok, I won't worry; for the moment our problem is to get out of here," I thought out loud. "By the way, I have heard and read that the waters of the Ganges have a certain radioactivity and this counteracts its contamination and so prevents the latter from affecting all those millions of people who drink and bathe in them. Varanasi for example."

"Anyway," my companion continued, "as we prepared our expedition in Joshimath, bought food and hired the porters, we talked to the people who live here. They believe that the goddess Nanda jealously protects her domains and punishes all those who dare to disgrace her by putting a foot in her residence. Please, pass me the coffee, and I'll tell you more."

"Another science fiction story?" I teased as I held out the jar.

"No, this is more tragic and romantic than you can imagine and seems to confirm the supernatural power the goddess has over life and death in this area. Where do I begin? I'll start with her: Nanda Devi Unsoeld. In fact, it was her story that drew Peter and me to these places. Before, this area was unknown even among the mountaineering circles most in contact with the Himalayas. The events she starred in, not without regret, place these mountains on the mountaineering map."

"Well, Devi, as they called her, was the typical Californian girl, like we see them, with long blonde hair, athletic body and a generous and enthusiastic character. She was twenty-two years old when she arrived here in 1976, as a member of an American expedition that wanted to celebrate the 40th anniversary of the first ascent of this mountain by placing their feet back on the summit. Her father and leader of the expedition, Willi Unsoeld, was a well known and expert mountaineer who had achieved in 1963, along with Tom Hornbein, one of the greatest prowess of the history of the Himalayas: the first ascent of Everest by the very difficult West Ridge and the subsequent crossing to descend from the summit down the south side of the mountain."

"Yes, Pemba told me about the father and his daughter. He was one of the porters of that expedition. What he could not explain was why the girl was called like the mountain."

"Several years before, in 1949, when young Willi was a member of the Peace Corps in India and Nepal ..."

"Of what?"

"The Peace Corps, a volunteer program run by the United States government," he explained. "As I was saying, this Willi had then seen the Nanda Devi from afar and had been captivated by its hidden and wild beauty. He promised to name his first daughter like the mountain. He returned home, and five years later he was able to keep his promise. And so, there were a father and a daughter ready to fulfil a dream, a journey as spiritual as it was an adventure. For Devi, crowning the mountain from where her name came from, felt like fulfilling part of her destiny, while sharing with her father the attraction of entering a sanctuary so sacred."

At that point, I stuck my head out of the tent and saw that it had stopped snowing.

196

"Let's see if the good weather continues and we have Pemba here by tomorrow," I said. "Why don't we go outside for a little while and you can keep telling me the story?" I added.

So we did and stood in the snow with our cups of cold coffee in our hands, while my friend continued with the story.

"Well, soon after it started, the expedition was shaken by internal quarrels, which would make the tragedy of Devi's death even more painful. In recent years, as you know, many mountain expeditions to the Himalayas are formed by a large number of people, compared to those in the Alps or other mountain ranges, due to their geographical scale and the need to transport a great amount of food and materials. This makes you lose the atmosphere of comradeship and even scientific interest of the 50s and before. On this expedition to the Nanda Devi, there was a strong feeling that one part of the group, the ones that were mountaineers exclusively, were using the others as "pack mules" to carry supplies to the last camp."

"Yes, and so be able to "climb on their shoulders" as they say, for the final ascent," I said.

"Indeed. The idea of the "summit climbers" was not new, but until then the process by which they were chosen had been more democratic. Those who, after a similar effort in the tasks of establishing and provisioning the successive high-altitude camps, were in best shape. This was the case, for example, of Hillary and Tensing in Everest or Herzog and Lachenal in Annapurna."

The clouds had slowly receded, and we could now see some peaks and the top end of the meadow where we were standing. There, a hundred meters from us the group of bharals that we saw every day appeared. Their bluish wool stood out more on the white of the snow. They stared at us for a moment, and then began to nibble at the branches of the shrubs and plants that protruded from

197

the layer of snow as if we did not exist. Jack went on with his story.

"Well in this case and from the very beginning, there was a group led by the egocentric John Roskelley, who only thought about reaching the summit quickly and who put pressure on others like Devi who he thought were not as strong as him. In fact, Devi was probably the best person in the group, the most cheerful and generous. She had lived in Nepal for a few years as an aid-worker, had gained experience in the mountains, studied the Hindu religion and was attracted by its most transcendental ideas."

"Exactly. Pemba told me," I said. "He pointed out that it was she who took care of the other woman in the group when she fell ill during the approximation trek, who finally was evacuated by helicopter. He also told me that it was Devi who got on the best with the porters."

"Yes, it's obvious that she was a great woman... Anyway, as I was saying, Roskelley reached the summit with two other companions. Upon returning to the advanced camp, they found Devi next to her father and another young mountaineer, Andy Harvard, to whom Devi had just got engaged. The girl was suffering severely from the altitude and complications from a strange disease she had. Roskelley and his companions continued their descent without offering any help. Devi died right there without her father and boyfriend being able to do anything to help her.

We were silent for a while. We looked at the mountain. There it was, white and cold.

"What a pig that Roskelley and company. They could have perhaps carried her down", I said.

"Well. I guess after summiting they would have been exhausted and were just thinking of going down as soon as possible. In the mountain, there are times when every man is for himself."

We were quiet again. The bharals, half a dozen, had come closer, around 30 feet from us, and were busy feeding, but when I tried to approach one of them, it lifted its head in a gesture of rejection, and they all went away. Meanwhile, the clouds had completely disappeared. The sun came out. But its last rays hardly reached us. Soon the shadows took hold of the mountain side where we were and climbed up the mountain slopes. The summits of the Dunagiri, the Trisul and especially that of the cruel queen, the goddess Nanda, shone of an intense pink for a while longer.

"And what did the poor things do? What a tragedy!"

"Because it happened at the height of more than seven thousand meters, it was impossible to bring the body back down. So they put her in her sleeping bag and dropped her down a cliff in what the desperate Willi described as "committing her to the deep."

"Jack, what do you think of all these deaths caused by climbing impossible mountains?"

"Look, many reasons have been sought to explain and even blame for the death of Devi Unsoeld. The fact is that the "tragic expedition Nanda Devi 1976", as it is known, joined the blacklist of others who were also terribly tragic. All of them with a higher number of deaths. Remember, up to twenty-six, between German mountaineers and Sherpas, at Nanga Parbat in 1934 and 1937." Jack paused, then pondered aloud.

"What makes Devi's death different, I think, is the circumstances in which it occurred. Apart from her excellent physical and technical conditions as a climber, she sympathised with the local population and was exemplary in her relations with the other members of the group, a quality that stood out against the nasty character and selfishness of some of her companions. She wanted to unite spiritually with the mountain from which she bore the name. She longed to reach the summit as she saw it as a spiritual beacon in this corrupt world. Her intentions were truly pure; her attitude, detached and yet the mountain-goddess cruelly took her life."

"Yes, but the mountain neither thinks nor suffers. It is entirely indifferent, a pure geographical accident. The story that it is a goddess that does not allow anyone to put their feet on her is pure fantasy, a mere religious belief of primitive people. Strictly speaking, religions are born in antiquity from not understanding the natural phenomena."

"But the truth is that this damn mountain has a halo of tragedy."

"Of course, like all of those very difficult for man to conquer. The more people attempt it, the higher the number of deaths. Look at Everest or Nanga Parbat like you've said before."

"Yes," Jack agreed. "Let me finish telling you the end of the story," he went on. "An extract from Devi's diary is inscribed on the monolith that was erected a few years later in her memory in the prairies of the base camp. It says, "I stand upon a wind-swept ridge at night with the stars bright above and I am no longer alone but I waver and merge with all the shadows that surround me. I am part of the whole and I am content. "

Inevitably the personality of the deceased girl brought to me the memory of Monique. They were comparable in their idealism, but while the Californian girl had had a stable childhood and adolescence, surrounded by a happy family, the French girl had suffered sorrows and hardship, solitude and misunderstandings. I got myself together and answered.

"I would have really liked to go there now, into the Sanctuary to see the monolith. Of course, I would not have understood what it meant without knowing the complete story." I continued as I felt the memories veiled my eyes. "It is always the best people who die. And, poor father; baptises his daughter with the name of the mountain as a tribute to the goddess and seals her fate. How can he live with it?"

"Well," answered Jack, "a journalist once asked him at his house, where a large picture of Devi presides over the fireplace in the living room, how he could continue climbing mountains after losing his daughter to one of them. And Willi replied, "How do you want me to die? From a heart attack by drinking beer and eating chips while watching a golf tournament on TV?"

"I don't know, maybe he's right, but this is a frightening example of what can happen when the dream of a sanctuary, one of the most mythical symbols of humanity, collides with the reality of wanting to reach it."

"But not because of it do men stop wanting to achieve goals and ideals."

Jack's last words sealed the story. We were silent as I thought about what I had just heard. If I had met that girl, now I would feel terrible, I thought. I could not help but think of Monique again. The same primitive innocence, the same fervour for a dream. Would it lead to her death too? Suddenly night was upon us and the wind re-appeared. Like a Cyclops in heat.[23]

---

[23] The Sanctuary of the Nanda Devi and its surrounding areas were closed to any human presence, including the exploitation of its pastures and mountain expeditions, between 1982 and 2000.

XV

Everest rises, not so much a peak as a prodigious mountain mass. There is no complication for the eye. The highest of the world's great mountains, it seems, has to make but a single gesture of magnificence to be lord of all, vast in unchallenged and isolated supremacy.

George Leigh Mallory.
(vanished near its summit in 1923)

After hearing Jack's stories on the Nanda Devi - always there, guardian of our anguish or inspiring our hopes - the difficulties of my trekking to Everest Base Camp filled my memory.

At last. There I was. Light, euphoric, breathless, gasping to fill my lungs with oxygen. Standing on the summit of Kala Patar, 5,650 meters high, face to face with Everest: Chomo Lungma or Goddess Mother of the Earth, as the Tibetans have always called it. Or Sagarmatha, as it had recently been baptised by the Nepalese to show that the peak also belonged to them. Only five kilometres separated me from its summit at bird's flight. Powerful, domineering. The roof of the earth! The object of desire of all climbers.

At my feet, base camp. Blue, orange, green tents and drums,

clothes, plastics and piles of garbage abandoned by successive expeditions. The famous curve of the *seracs* (ice pinnacles) and the icy waterfall of the Khumbu glacier, biting upwards along the western face of the great peak, on its way to the South Col and the summit. Also in front of me, slightly to the right and even closer and therefore more impressive, the abysmal and frosty facade, completely white, of the Nuptse and, just behind, another giant, this one black and white, the Lhotse, the fourth highest mountain on Earth. From the summit of Everest, came a permanent whirlwind of snow powder.

"Namaste," I said, putting my palms together in front of my chest.

A woman was squatting between the rocks and the blanket of snow. I had seen her the night before in the hut at Gorak Shep where we had both slept. I recognised her anorak stamped with daisies. She must have been American, I thought. Her cap well fitted and her glacier glasses made her face barely visible. But I remembered that her blue eyes were very light but sad. I had not seen her in the morning. But I had come across the Sherpa who accompanied her a while ago, as I had begun the ascent. She must have woken up and started her day before me, very tired as I was of the previous day's march.

"Hi," she replied and greeted me by raising her hand slightly.

"What a view, how incredible. We have made it."

"Yes, of course. Forgive me; I am not feeling very communicative."

Her accent was pure British, no doubt about that. I respected her silence. I took some photos, first with the 28 mm. in horizontal to capture the biggest panorama possible. Then I switched the polarising filter to 50 mm, and I took with it some vertical photos with the Nuptse in the foreground. Then I zoomed in and took closer shots which showed the details of the slopes, the ice and the peaks. In all of them overexposing one or two diaphragms to compensate for the luminosity of the snow. The day was very clear, but the wind lashed out with strength in this place without any protection.

"My husband is up there," the woman told me when I finished taking the pictures.

"Is he climbing Everest?"

"No. He disappeared there." She gestured towards the summit, lifting her chin and nodding towards it. "Last spring. That's all he cared about. A crazy man ... damn crazy," she added. "He promised me it was the last time. He always did. And this time..."

"I'm sorry," I muttered, not knowing what else to say.

"I came to see where and, also, to try to understand ... to know."

"I'm so sorry," I muttered again. "Would you like me to leave you alone?"

"No, don't go. You haven't come all the way up here for just two minutes, have you? Like me, you must have been walking for days and days, suffering these slopes." She took off her glasses and uncovered her eyes, damp with tears. I took mine off too. "Did you get to Lukla by plane? What an experience, wasn't it? Landing on a hillside in the middle of the Himalayas."

"Yes, it was. Very exciting. But it is even more so when taking off, I already experienced it last year, and it feels like you'll fall into the void. It's my second time here. But this is my limit," I added.

"You are not a mountaineer then; you can't explain to me why they do it."

"Well, that's the big question: the attraction of the mountains, its conquest, testing oneself. They say it's like a drug. Some of them look to break the record of climbing the most mountains or dangerous things such as who will climb the highest, who will be the fastest. But for me, that's not loving the mountains. In love towards nature or a woman, speed is the least important thing.

The sun hid behind a cloud. We noticed, it suddenly grew colder. She shuddered. She looked at me again with her blue eyes. In the light of day, they were even lighter. But they seemed less sad and in them shone a gesture of friendship.

"You can sit by my side if you like. In the mountains, we are all equal, and there are no bad people."

I obeyed and introduced myself.

"I'm Francisco, from Spain."

"Elizabeth, English."

"So, how did it happen?"

"It's not very clear. It was during the descent. We do not know if he fell off a precipice or could not continue and died of exhaustion. We don't know either if he ever reached the summit." Her voice broke for a moment but then continued. "You know, there is a mountaineering saying which says "reaching the summit is only half the way." Most accidents occur during descent. People are already exhausted after twelve, fourteen or more hours of struggle against the topography, the winds and the fight with themselves to reach the summit. That is what I have read and what I have been told."

"Was he alone?"

"Yes. His companion turned back before he reached the South Summit. His oxygen flask wasn't working, and he had no strength left. William continued, but it was already quite late. The night caught up with him, and he was not able to return to camp IV." She paused, bowed her head and shook it sadly. "If only I could see his body. It has not yet been found. I can't believe it until I see it," she added.

"I understand."

I shouldn't have said that. How could I know what this woman felt? We were silent. The sun returned to mitigate the cold atmosphere. We heard the dull rumble of an avalanche and watched as the corresponding cloud of powdered snow plummeted from the icefall and fell between the *seracs*, five hundred meters before reaching base camp. She pulled out some binoculars from under her anorak and began to scrutinise the face of the mountain with them.

"There are a Polish and a Japanese expedition trying to make the summit," she said, "although I do not see anyone. Just a couple of tents up there, under the pass."

"Let's hope they're lucky and that the good weather accompanies them," I said. "They say that the ascension itself is not the most complicated, compared to Annapurna or K2; But of course, the weather..."

"Yes, that's what they hope for. And they only think of climbing and conquering, they don't care about taking risks, and I understand that. My husband said that the mountain is not a gamble, it's a feeling; but the suffering! I think they enjoy it. However, they don't think of who they are leaving behind: women, children, parents, girlfriends, friends." She gestured helplessly. "And so, over and over again. Until they do not come back."

She was right. We always hear about and mourn the death of mountaineers stripped from the heights, lost in the ice. We read about it in the newspapers, on TV and in the books. But nobody describes the suffering of those who remain, of so many lives shattered by the absence. It seemed useless for me to express it. Elisabeth, a sad and broken widow, understood it better than I did.

We stayed for a long while, contemplating the magnificent setting. Both, of course, seeing it with very different eyes and thoughts. I told myself, selfishly, that I had to seize the moment and take more pictures; one does not witness such a spectacle every day. The day had begun to draw to a close. A few clouds rose from the valley and submerged it in the shade, but the sun was still high in the dark blue sky, and all the gigantic peaks glowed, even more gently, with a hidden flame as if a fire illuminated them from within through the rocks and the ice.

The clouds continued their ascent, they approached the base of the mountains, and it seemed as if they were no longer born from the ground, they did not touch the earth but hung weightlessly from the celestial vault. Ah, my flying mountains! I remembered a reflection from Albert Camus: "There is no sun without shadow, and it is essential to know the night."

I had started my trek fifteen days earlier from Lukla's high-road, a precarious track hanging from the slope of a mountain at 2,500 meters high, after a short flight in a small propeller plane from Kathmandu. In the Nepalese capital, I had waited a couple of days for the optimal atmospheric conditions which would allow the plane to land and therefore make the flight possible. Once in Lukla, right on the runway, I chose a jovial Sherpa named Dhama among the several who were waiting, to carry my thirty pound backpack, and with my whole life ahead of me as I told myself, I took the first steps toward the Everest massif. According to a repeated Chinese proverb, every great journey can begin only with a first step.

But I wasn't fortunate, to begin with. The first night we slept in Phakding after only three hours of walking, in a house with an adjacent orchard and owned by a Japanese who had just moved there with the purpose of giving food and floor space for the trekkers' sleeping bags. I don't know whether it was the dinner or breakfast that did it, but the next day at mid-morning, on the way up to Namche Bazar, the "capital" of the Sherpa country and just after having crossed a deep gorge by a precarious bridge made of planks and ropes that swayed at every step and under which the Dudh Kosi thundered, I began to feel a severe gastric discomfort.

I thought I recognised the symptoms of giardiasis since I had already had it once during the previous year in Kathmandu on the return of my first trekking. At that time, the friendly owner of the Hotel Shakti, where I was staying, had called a doctor. After the due analysis, he had determined the presence of those annoying parasites in my intestines. The solution, a few days of bed rest and two tablets of Flagyl every twelve hours for eight days. So, I thought I knew the solution to this evil, but did not know how to carry it out in these wild territories where I found myself. Perhaps in Namche Bazaar I would find the medication and a bed where to wait for the parasite's death, because I didn't think that some simple insects could lead me to mine.

But after eight hours' march, instead of the five that I would have required in a normal situation, we arrived at the said village – very picturesque with its houses of stone and slate, in a semicircle on a hill at more than three thousand meters of altitude, on an opening of the valley which brings the waters of Everest and other giants– there was no doctor or pharmacy. However, we were told that in the village further up, Khumjung, there was a small clinic which Sir Edmund Hillary-the lanky New Zealander and the first man to tread Everest's summit - had donated to the Sherpa people in appreciation for the help they gave to all the mountaineers who passed through and, in particular, to him.

An hour and a half more of an agonising uphill trek and I was in front of the young Japanese doctor who ran the clinic.

"Yes, it must be a giardiasis," he said. "You have two solutions, eight days of rest and Flagyl, here it is," he continued as he reached for his medicine box, "or, take twelve pills tonight and another twelve tomorrow night, and all the parasites will be dead." "Between this samurai and the one in the village below who gave me the bugs in the first place, they want to kill me," I told myself, "but at the end of the day, what else is there to do! It is a prevalent infection in these places, so I guess this kind man knows what he is talking about."

We found shelter in a local house. I took the first dozen pills mixed with rice and got into my sleeping bag to rest, lying over the yaks and the goats that, sheltered in the lower floor, provided natural heating to the house's residents. The next morning I felt much better and, on top of that, it was beautiful weather, so we continued our trip. We passed Syangboche, a runway for small planes with a simple hotel next to it. This is where the wealthy tourists stay, those who come all the way from Kathmandu for one night, enough to admire Everest and its acolytes. Needless to say, plugged into oxygen bottles the whole time! The hotel was empty but on its terrace was a handsome Sherpa sewing on an old Singer. He, in the foreground, with his raven hair held back and braided with a red ribbon decorating his face and the beautiful Ama Dablam in the background was a perfect motif for a beautiful photo.

From here we descended, five hundred meters to the Dudh Kosi and its enormous prayer-mills in the name of Buddha and driven by the turbulent descending waters. We then ascended another eight hundred meters to the famous monastery of Tyangboche: a perfect Shangri-La located at 3,800 meters and surrounded by the last pines and rhododendrons. At that time, it was the highest inhabited monastery in the world, as well as the one with the most spectacular scenario, the sharp peaks of Ama Dablam, Kantenga and Thamserku framing its white and red facade.

We were received by the chants, cymbals and trumpets of the monks - it was time for the evening prayers. We then heard the good news that in ten days, just before we expected to be back, the Mani Rindu celebration was going to be held including the traditional dances of monks turned into demons. And moreover, my friend Patrice was there, one of my companions in my first trekking in Nepal the previous year. Patrice was French and an architect. This time he was accompanied by his girlfriend and, like me, aspired to reach Everest base camp.

Patrice was a sybarite as well. They had arrived three days ago from Paris and were well prepared for the rigours of the trekker. In addition to the delicious sausages from Lyon and the cans of squid and mussels from Brittany, they had also brought a bottle of Remy Martin and several bars of Belgian chocolate. However, mixing the dose of Flagyl with the sublime food was not one of my brightest ideas I must say. Especially with chocolate and cognac. Its fight against the parasites lasted all night although finally, it was the medicine which triumphed. The final act occurred the following morning when, after barely an hour's march, I found myself leaning against a giant rock vomiting mussels, sausage and chocolate in a morsel of indescribable smells under the eyes of the descending yaks, who were coming from the fields laden with potatoes, and my astonished Sherpa who wondered how such a weak man dared to walk those paths.

I had decided not to follow the usual route to Everest from Tyangboche, as I had already done it the previous year, but had chosen a less travelled one, to the West, which led to the Gokyo lakes at the foot of Cho Oyu and from there, through a pass at more than five thousand meters, cross over to the Everest glacier. I trusted that there would be no ice or much snow. So, after receiving the blessing of the chief lama, in exchange for a ten-rupee bill wrapped in the traditional white gauze handkerchief, we continued our ascent following the narrow valley of Dudh Kosi towards Maccherma, the next stage of the trek.

Maccherma was a small group of shepherd's huts, at more than four thousand meters altitude, where the shepherds stayed when it wasn't snow season, and the yaks could graze in those pastures. Its name was well-known between the "explorers of the impossible" and the lovers of mysteries. It was here that, on July 11th, 1974, the most spectacular appearance of the Yeti had taken place.

Lakpa Domani, an eighteen-year-old Sherpani, told the story like this: "I was near the cabin when I heard a muffled growl behind me. I turned and found myself in front of a giant monkey with dark red fur, sunken eyes and protruding cheekbones. The animal grabbed me and dragged me to the stream. There he threw me to the ground. He went towards the yaks and attacked them." The police report from Namche Bazaar said: "We have found the remains of three yaks; two seemed to have been beaten to death with a large stone or with a club; the third had a broken neck. "

During the previous years, there had been other signs of the yeti's existence in the Himalayas such as unclassifiable footprints found in the snow, blurry photos and some sightings from a far distance. The result of all of this was that, for the experts, there was not enough proof to either affirm the existence of the supposed hominid nor to deny it. An alleged scalp, which I had seen in the nearby monastery of Pangboche, had been examined by an American university and it had been concluded that it was made of goatskin.

It had to be the place where the Yeti had killed those yaks and attacked the young woman, where I was to act as his antithesis. It was not Lakpa Domani who gave lodgings to us that night, but another young Sherpani named Pasang Lhamo, a name whose meaning, as Dhama explained to me, was that of "beautiful goddess." I did not realise at that point how appropriate the name for that cheerful young woman would be. She was quite pretty with expressive eyes of a light brown and well-drawn features. Like all those of her ethnic group, she wore her hair in two braids adorned with coloured ribbons and held together on the top of her head. She must have been around twenty-five years old. Her husband was a porter in a mountain expedition. It is an ancient custom among the Sherpa people that when a man marries he must bring with him a younger brother to live in the new home with them for the purpose of caring for it, wife and children included, during periods in which the husband is absent, nowadays on a mountain expeditions or before in one of the caravans between Nepal and Tibet before China closed the border crossings. Polyandry is common amongst the Sherpas, and the woman is by no means subdued by her husband. She occupies the main bed and receives, alternately, one husband or another. This was not the case during my visit. It was only Pasang Lhamo and her child living in the hut.

The little boy, around two or three years old, was very happy and excited by our arrival and did not stop running around showing me all his rough wooden and tin toys, with long explanations which I did not understand at all, while I unpacked my bag and spread my sleeping bag in the corner of the cabin in front of the fireplace. So, when I finished this task, and with unexpected and spontaneous joy, I entertained myself playing with him. He had no cars, no planes, no trains, he had probably never seen any. Only a pair of animal reproductions which looked like a yak and a kind of monkey, perhaps a Yeti? As well as a drum and a sort of trumpet, similar to those that the monks in the temples played but much smaller. It had been a long time since I'd played with a little boy like that. His enthusiasm amazed and touched me. It reminded me of my little nephews back at home.

Meanwhile, his mother was busy preparing dinner. I saw her rush out with a hoe in her hand. She crossed the road, rolled up her heavy skirts and leapt like a gazelle over the wall that bordered the adjacent field. In a blink of an eye, she dug up some potatoes and returned with a basketful. The agile and powerful leap of Pasang had left me so astonished that when, a few minutes later, she rolled up her skirts to her hips and climbed onto a stool next to where I was to reach for a tin of onions from a shelf, I could not help but feel her thigh with my right hand to make sure that it had no wings and was made only of skin, muscle and flesh. She turned towards me and laughed loudly as her eyes shone more mischievously than surprised. I did not foresee the consequences that my innocent act was going to carry.

After a dinner consisting of potatoes with onions and a piece of cheese I retired to my corner, put on my pyjamas and got into my sleeping bag. It is much easier to wash some pyjamas than a good feather sleeping bag. Outside it was already night time. I watched as, by the light of the fire, still burning vigorously , the young Sherpa tidied her belongings at the other end of the room. The boy had been sleeping for a long time. I felt too warm, so I got out of the sleeping bag, covered myself with it, and immediately fell asleep.

After a while, I thought I was dreaming. Someone had taken my arm and guided my hand over soft, warm, and curvilinear territory. I felt a sudden thrill as well as a slight shock. I felt insecure, not in control of the situation. I was still half asleep. I could hear her fast breathing next to me. Desire overcame my fears; it overwhelmed me at first and then flooded me with pleasure.

The room was dark; I could only see outlines. Apart from our breathing, silence. Searching, caressing, abandonment. No other language was needed. Our hands and bodies spoke for us. I searched for her mouth, she replied, pressing her lips against mine. It reminded me of those teenage kisses, but she soon understood what pleasure we could give each other. She wanted me to penetrate her; I think it had more to do with her thinking it was the appropriate thing to do, rather than due to an uncontained passion; but I taught her to wait. Her hands, her skin and her legs were rough; however, the skin of her intimate area was as soft as rose petals. I noticed due to the smell of soap that she had washed before coming to look for me. I thanked her with more caresses, and when we climaxed, she stayed huddled next to me for a short while. She then wanted to leave, but I didn't let her, and we began all over again.

When I woke up, she was already making breakfast. The boy was running around naked in the embraces of the cold dawn. "You wanted a simple life? In Nepal you have it, "I thought. Here there is adventure, beauty and emotions. But after a breakfast of porridge and the salty tea with yak butter, I gathered my things to leave. Pasang watched me calmly and with a certain flirtation in her eyes. We could not communicate now; we only had the common language of caresses and gestures. There were mutual smiles of gratitude and affection. When we left, she stood in the doorway. One last look, clear and straightforward. Maybe she thought we'd meet again on my way back, but I knew I would follow another path.

Two days later, proud and satisfied, we reached Gokyo. I had walked as if Pasang had lent me the wings of her feet. It was late afternoon and the last climb over the rocks of the glacier's moraine, to whose side one found the lake, had been rather tiring. As we approached the shore, I admired the landscape of rocks, snow, towering mountains and hanging glaciers. "This is the end of the world," I thought. We had not seen any white men in the last four days. And low and behold, at five thousand meters and seated on folding canvas chairs, I found two old ladies drinking tea and eating pastries while they waited for the sun to set.

"But, who are you?" I asked them, stupefied.

"We are bird-watchers," they replied as if it were the most normal thing to do in this part of the world.

Then, they invited me to have tea with them as they continued to watch the Mandarin ducks flying over the water. The encounter showed me that my proposed challenge was not that great, although I found out later that they were just over sixty years old and were travelling with a legion of porters who had carried them for the last few kilometres.

Dhama and I stayed in a new shepherd's hut occupied, likewise, by a young mother with her son who was a couple of years old and who every morning ran around naked in the snow. "That way he gets used to the cold," Dhama said. He, of course, had no interest in walking anymore, so for the next couple of days, and with great precautions, of course, I had to go exploring alone, immerse myself in the immense landscape and take photographs of the high mountains and their surroundings.

In a bookstore, in Kathmandu, I had found the very coveted map, at least among the mountaineers, of E. Schneider "Khumbu Himal 1: 50,000" the region of Everest in the 1978 edition. I could see that following the western margin of Ngozumba glacier there were a couple of peaks, the nearest one slightly more than five thousand meters high and the second one of around five hundred

215

meters more, from where I could obtain good perspectives of Cho Oyu (8,201 meters), the easiest eight thousander, or so they say. To its right, the Gyachung Kang or Young Snow Prince, thus baptised by the locals. An imposing peak and ignored by mountaineers as it doesn't quite reach eight thousand meters, just falling short of forty. Moreover, it offers greater technical difficulties than its neighbour.

The first morning I walked along the lake shore with the intention of climbing to the first summit, but after a few hours of walking, an imposing rock wall cut my aspirations. So on the second day, I followed the western moraine of the glacier and managed to ascend to the highest peak. To my surprise, from the second watchtower, in addition to the above mentioned peaks, I found that Everest stood majestically above the mountains that enclosed the valley where I found myself on the eastern side. I caught a very original, barely known, vision of the "mother goddess of the mountains", with her head clearly protruding above the peaks surrounding her.

The next day was quite difficult but, with the assistance of an Italian expedition, who well equipped with piolets and crampons helped us to cross the pass, we finally arrived at the top of the Everest valley. The next day I climbed up to Kala Patar and met Elizabeth the Englishwoman for the first time.

Upon returning, I veered eastward from Periche to the Khumbu glacier to get a new perspective of the peaks around Everest. That night, once again, I slept in a shepherd's hut in company of a Sherpani with her young son. The photograph of mother and child sitting at the entrance of the house, while she peels potatoes and he plays, is probably one of the most beautiful of the trip. The next morning, I ascended for a couple of hours the west side of the glacier, facing the Lotshe and in search of good views. I was very careful because I was completely alone in this huge circle of mountains. My Sherpa, again, was not interested in walking more than was necessary, and he gladly declined my invitation. Since I was not taking my backpack, why should he come? He must have thought.

I sat on the ice, small and overwhelmed by the magnitude of the spectacle, surrounded by white walls and ice pinnacles, erect and in search of the overhead blue. While I focused the camera lens, changed targets and fitted one filter or another in order to get either more natural or intense colours, I had some silly thoughts: "that if I stayed there, no one would come looking for me and if one day someone did pass, I would have become a new ice pinnacle ..." But I also thought about how my life had changed and how far I had come. Something unimaginable a few years before.

I had discovered the great mountains and worshipped them. A feeling that does not come suddenly but with slow steps, with experiences like this, in solitude, far from the influences of the outside world. These landscapes are endless, mysterious and, at the same time, a refuge, amplifier of the spirit. Home of dreams, therefore unreal; of elusive temptations in whose quiet depth lies the subtlety. Here, among the mountains, the feeling is pure emotion and fills the soul better than any other reflection learned in the books or born out of intellect.

On my way back, with wings on my feet for it was downhill now, on our way to Tyangboche's Tibetan monastery I felt reborn. These days of walking, healthy diet and nights of ascetic - the night with Pasang belonged to the world of the unreal - I had purified the body and turned my soul upside down. Just looking at the summits, the stars, the flora, the eagles, the simple daily life of the inhabitants of these mountains, and, above all, savouring the freedom of the walker, made me see a new way of approaching the world. Aesthetic contemplations and the rediscovery of the value of the elemental in the face of the tyranny of our civilisation of development and consumption.

We arrived at the monastery the evening before the November full moon, just in time to see, the next day, the dances of the Mani Rindu. The monks, disguised as deities and demons and wearing masks or hats adorned with small skulls, depict for three days the rituals and scenes of Tibetan Buddhism, a religion that incorporates Buddha's teachings with the old animist beliefs. It was here that I had the good fortune of seeing Elizabeth again, who, a few days later, would help me with Monique.

XVI

Happiness is in the search, not in the achievements.

The night was quite calm, but I couldn't fall asleep. I was worried about the Satkula pass, those seven dangerous gorges where I had witnessed the tragic death of the porter falling off the cliff. Then it had been dry and without snow, so what would it be like now? I was also worried about the pass which followed. We were silent, wrapped in our respective covers and ready to sleep when, unexpectedly, Jack began to talk.

"I'm afraid my marriage is over ... There's something I've not told you."

"What do you mean?" I said after a few seconds, surprised that after so many days together he wanted to make a sort of confession.

"Daisy, my wife was convinced that something was going to happen to us and was very much against us coming.

"Well, that is something wives and mothers always think of when we leave on a trip, and even more so if it's to distant mountains.

It seemed as if Jack had not heard me and went on:

"One evening, early this summer, we were sitting on the porch of our house, enjoying the coolness of the night air."

"I think I'm going back to the Himalayas," I said.

"Do you want to go back to Makalu after such a bad experience?" she replied.

"No, this time we're going to go to an easier mountain, a much easier one, and it will only be Peter and me, a light expedition."

She looked at me with a mixture of worry and sadness.

"I don't think you should go," she said. I guess my surprise must have shown on my face because she had never said anything like that to me before.

"I have a bad feeling this time," she added.

"What are you talking about? In Makalu, we had bad weather, where we are going now the weather is more stable, and we will need only a couple of weeks to reach the Mountain, summit it and return back down," I said. She shook her head, and a few strands of blond hair covered her eyes. She did not tie them back up; I think she didn't want me to see that she was worried.

"But Peter doesn't have much experience. I still have a bad feeling about this."

At that moment we heard Jimmy call for his mother through the open window.

"And you have a son, if he has woken up now, it is because he also can sense something. You don't want to leave him an orphan, do you!" She added.

"Don't be so tragic," I said.

Jimmy appeared at the door, and we stopped the conversation. But later on, with Jimmy back in bed, we resumed it.

"You promised me that you would not go back to the Himalayas, or the Andes, that you would just climb near home," she reminded me.

"Calm down, you worry about nothing. It is not a dangerous mountain."

"And what mountain is it?"

"Dunagiri," I replied.

"I've never heard of it, and I really have a bad feeling," she insisted.

She said to me, with a tone of irritation in her voice, that it was the first time that she had asked me not to go somewhere. I answered that she was being ridiculous. I had some photos and a map of the area and showed them to her.

"Don't go," she whispered in defeat.

I started to lose my patience. I went into the house and went to the studio to study the maps and photos I had prepared for the expedition. During the two months before my departure, we argued about it from time to time. She kept begging me not to go, going as far as to tell me that she dreamt about an accident. In her dreams, one of our ropes broke, and we fell off a cliff, in another an avalanche would bury us alive. But I would not listen. I was set on going, and besides, Peter was dying to go and impatient. He called me every day or came to see me. But I'm not going to blame him, of course. "

Jack remained silent for a long time. When he spoke again, he seemed to be thinking aloud.

"In love, you should not do things halfway. If you love a woman, you have to value her and love her completely. It is something I have failed to do, and I am aware of it. The mountains, always thinking of them, have made me into a solitary and selfish person. I believed that I loved them above all else and that that was the reason I had never been able to love a woman completely, or at least that's what I told myself. For many of us, mountaineering is a way of channelling those desires of struggle and fight which have always nested in the heart of the human being. Today's life does not facilitate the fulfilment of those desires. Sometimes I think that had I been born three or four centuries ago I would have been a soldier or a pirate. But the passing of the years, the deaths of some companions and a few disappointments changed me. And then I found Daisy. Now I know that I love her completely and I am about to lose her if it hasn't happened already.

In the meantime, I had sat up, and half sitting on the floor, with my torso out of the sleeping bag, looked at him by the light from the torch I had lit and hung from the ceiling. He had tears in his eyes and let out a deep sigh.

"Listen, my friend," I said, "all that is in the past. You have made your wife suffer a great deal. And even more now without any news of your whereabouts. She probably thinks you're dead. But as soon as you call her in a few days she'll be happy. What is certain, "I continued," is that you will not be able to leave again. Or at least not in the next few years."

"Do you think so? Will she forgive me? And will she understand and forgive my promise to take the mouthpiece of his saxophone to the top of Everest."

"You'll have to get someone else to do it. Come on, cheer up! You've already been through the worst. Stop worrying, your wife will not leave you. Let's go to sleep," I said and wrapped myself up to my ears in my sleeping bag.

I would have liked to sleep until I forgot I was hungry; to eat until I was sleepy, to be hot and not cold, and think about simple things so I wouldn't think so much about the past, but I had to admit it, the memory of Monique made my heart beat faster. And

222

so I returned to it.

As soon as I got to Kathmandu, back from the paths of Everest, I went to Jean Pierre's house with the intention of learning about Monique whereabouts. First, we shook hands, very French; then I gave him a hug, very Spanish. In those days I was prone to embrace everyone.

"The man of the snow is back," he said, "and you are skin and bones."

"Yes, I have not shaved or washed in a month. The Himalayas are not prepared for tourism "de luxe", there is no hot water nor soap at this altitude" we laughed "there are no good restaurants either, but I feel great."

He offered me some tea, and we sat down on the large red and purple cushions that, under the vigilant eyes of a dozen bronze gods and Buddha's, covered half the floor of the room. I did not wait long and immediately asked if Monique was still at Jang's house.

"I went there a few days after our visit together, and she was still there, and still seemed happy enough," my friend told me. "She asked me why you had not come as well. She now she remembers you, that you were a great guy and that the other day she had not paid much attention to you because she was a little gone. She seemed to feel sorry..."

"And how did she look?" I interrupted.

"Well, I thought she looked ok. But don't get too excited," continued Jean Pierre, "I went back last week, and she was gone. It seems that Cindy got jealous, Jang preferred her, and sweet Monique had to leave. At least that's what he told me."

"What a piece of shit! So she must have been here and there for a couple of weeks now. That is if she has not returned to France," I said.

"Well, it's not easy to leave here, look at me!" he replied.

There were noises followed by a long yawn in the adjoining room. The door opened, and Caesar appeared half-naked and drowsy. He waved at me and headed for the bathroom.

"Returning to Monique, I think she's still around," Jean Pierre told me.

"How do you know that?"

"Have you not learned yet that I am aware of everything happening in Kathmandu?" he replied with his usual irony. "Someone told me that he had spoken to her in one of the coffee houses on Freak Street."

"Bad news then, that is the meeting place of junkies."

"What do you expect? This paradise is like this. Either you become a yogi, or you become an addict.

I sat up and punched myself in the palm of my left hand.

"I have to find her."

"And you're going to save her?"

"Yes, I'll try. She's a good girl. She was very down when she came here and desperate in a way, running away from home. She was an easy prey."

"You're a romantic," Jean Pierre said, "but I'll help you as much as I can."

Caesar returned and went into his room. A moment later, a thin girl with untidy blonde hair came out. She was dressed in a long skirt and a pretty white blouse and had some twenty rupee notes in her hand.

"Hi!" She said with a sad smile and disappeared through the door and down the stairs.

Caesar returned again.

"You see? You give them a few rupees to buy some weed or share a trip with someone, and they are happy."

"Don't tell me you are the one who's seen, Monique?" I said alarmed.

"Don't worry, the girlfriends of my friends are sacred to me," he replied.

But I did not like the way he said it.

I said goodbye to both of them and went out. For the rest of the day, I walked the streets and squares in the hope of finding her. I asked all the westerners I stumbled upon. I went into the Oriental Lodge and the Eden to investigate. In vain, no trace of her. Night fell and with it came the animation of the squares and markets. The people returned to their homes in the villages around the city, the merchants packed up their stands or closed the wooden shutters of their modest shops, and the lights of the temples extinguished one by one. An Italian couple, both rather filthy, their hair intertwined with leaves and covered with tattered long shirts, amulets and necklaces led me to a place at the end of the so-called Freak Street. The place was barely lit and occupied by a long table flanked by wooden benches where other young people of similar appearance were waiting for someone to come in with money to pay for their dinner. That night, the one who paid was me.

For a handful of rupees, the Indian who ran the place put a large bowl of white rice on the table; another one, smaller, with the usual lentil soup, plates, spoons and glasses for water. Some took good advantage of the food offered to them. Others, despite their

225

starving appearance, settled for two or three spoonfuls. They did not seem to want anything other than a shot of heroin. I looked at them. What a shame, they had given in. And in this country, far away from their home, far from their own country, it would not be easy for them to find help to get out of the addiction that poisoned them. I asked those who seemed more awake if they knew Monique. I only received lost looks, indifferent or negative gestures. The girls seemed more absent than the boys; on a more distant planet, more separated from the needs and obligations of life. I left in anguish, wondering if Monique would also have settled into one of those misty shores, transiting like a ghost through its unreal world and, therefore, near to approaching rock bottom.

Again outside, I waited for the two Italians. They had told me that in their hotel, the Ashok, there was a girl who could match Monique's description. I followed them down the dimly-lit streets. The hotel did not look very appealing. A narrow doorway between two souvenir shops gave access to a moonlit courtyard. In its centre, a stone god with a red-stained forehead knelt in front of a *lingam*.[24] A wooden gallery supported by sculpted columns surrounded the yard. Underneath were the rooms, with their doors open. From what I could see, in each of them, six or eight people were sitting on cots or lying on the floor. I smelt the potent aroma of hashish as I followed my guides to the one they occupied.

The room was poorly lit, by a candle placed in a hole in the wall between two bricks. At the forefront, a couple, both naked, had fallen asleep without barely detaching themselves from one another after making love. The Italian girl pointed at two other girls smoking on one of the cots. Both had dark, short hair, like

[24] A symbol of divine generative energy, especially a phallus or phallic object as a symbol of Shiva.

Monique, but the one that was the furthest away from me, by her size, could not be her. The other one turned her back to me. I touched her on the shoulder. She turned around with an "*Oui?*" a dreamy look and a forced smile that revealed teeth already deteriorated by hash and tobacco. I excused myself.

On my way back to my hotel, I told myself not to despair. She was somewhere, in or around Kathmandu. I was going to find her! I could give myself a few days to do so. It was what I wanted most. And I deserved a break after the battering I had given myself around Everest. But I had enjoyed it so much! I was proud of my deed. For a moment I felt guilty about my self-satisfaction. What if I never found her? It was impossible that I would not see her again.

The friendly Sherpa receptionist from the small hotel where I was staying distracted me with his questions about my trekking. He was thrilled when I explained how much I had liked his land. Once in bed, I started to feel anxious again. "Calm down," I would tell myself without fully managing it ... I insisted on being rational. "To hell with this, was I to stop living for a girl, barely a woman? Was she worth more than Ursula, than others? Was I starting to be stupid?"

When I woke up the next morning, I was still thinking about her. I decided that my destiny for the next few days in Kathmandu was to look for her. Although I couldn't abandon the photographic assignment for my future book. So after a proper breakfast to recover from my days of frugality in the mountains, I took to the streets, heading towards the south of the city, the pottery neighbourhood. In the streets, and piled up along the facades up to the ceiling, were the bowls, plates and pots, of a reddish and light brown colour. I reached a square presided over by an enormous fountain of five water pipes. A black pig and its half-dozen little piglets moved among the streams as they rummaged through the garbage with their snouts. Some women gathered water in their jars of shimmering brass, while others chatted and washed their clothes in the large basins of worn stone where the water collected.

In one of them, a young woman undid her black braid and dipped her long hair in the water for a long while. She then twisted it gently to remove the water. She then pulled up her sari and got into one of the basins with the water up to her knees. Turning her back to the rest, she undressed completely under her sari, wrapped her underwear in it and placed it on the wall of the fountain. Squatting, she washed from head to toe, with a total natural manner and decency, showing nothing of her intimate areas. The beauty of the moment seen through the passion of the photographer cleared my mind from any other thoughts which weren't taking the perfect picture.

When moving a little to the right to find a good frame, I suddenly saw Monique. She was lying on her back on the far wall of the fountain, her face turned towards me, but her hair had grown since I met her and covered her face. Her shirt was half-open, and her jeans were stained with mud. I rushed towards her. One of the piglets crossed my path, I tripped over it and fell on my left knee and elbow, but I was able to save the camera by raising my right arm to prevent it from hitting the ground. Forgetting the pain, I got up immediately and ran to Monique who was still asleep. I looked at her for a moment. Her mouth formed a strange expression, and her lips were almost white. I bit my own and closed my eyes for a moment, recovered, and pulled her hair back from her face. Disappointment and relief, it was not her!

The girl had the same body shape and the same hair colour, but her nose was long and straight. She stared at me, not reflecting in the depths of her drug-ridden eyes, any astonishment at all. I tried to help her get to her feet. She slipped through my arms. The women at the fountain laughed as they watched us. They then motioned me to leave her alone.

"Do you want something to eat?" I asked.

"Dollar ... dollar," she stammered.

She kept asking me for money. I felt sorry for her, but no, I wasn't going to give her money so she could get high.

I couldn't help her either. So I walked away very disappointed. But I shouldn't be discouraged. Perhaps she had found good friends and had gone trekking or visited countless interesting places in the valley, such as Patan, one of the ancient capitals of the kingdom of Nepal and, according to my guide book, the oldest Buddhist city in the world. I continued my walk, thinking of how much I would have liked to have Monique hanging on to my arm and feeling her happy next to me, forgetting the problems that had made her leave her home and free of false extra-terrestrial yearnings.

After slightly more than an hour and without having been able to overcome my longings I arrived at the small town "of the thousand golden roofs", as it is called. I discovered that its Royal Square was even more beautiful than the one in Kathmandu, wider, more homogeneous in the styles of its temple. Moreover, it was not invaded by shops, and there were scarcely any tourists. It was covered by no less than ten temples, with their pagoda roofs super imposed one over the other and statues of gods and kings perched on high columns in different prayer positions. And bordered with the old royal palace on one side. The spectacular panorama made me stop for a moment worrying about Monique.

I spent a good amount of time browsing and taking pictures of temples and statues until children pointed out the entrance to one of the courtyards of the palace. I wondered why, until they showed me two stunning, life-size golden bronze statues, two princesses, I guessed. But no, these were representations of goddesses of the two great rivers of India, Ganges and Yamuna. Both spring from the Himalayas and –as I would have liked to explain to Monique– join together, a hundred kilometres before Benares, in the also sacred city of Allahabad where they form, every twelve years, the background of the Kumbh Mela, the biggest pilgrimage in India.

I especially liked the statue of Yamuna. Standing on a turtle, the symbol of water, dressed as a Hindu dancer and in a dancing position, her right hand stretched out as if she wanted to receive an offering, while between the fingers of her left hand, raised with infinite grace, she held a ring. The artist who had sculpted her knew very well how to achieve the effect that her long skirt gave the feeling of transparency, hinting her legs through the material of her narrow trousers. Her breasts were abundant as required by the Hindu tradition, her eyes looked with complacency, and her mouth was drawn into a seductive smile.

While I was looking for the best angle to photograph her, a guy whom I seemed to recognise, approached me. I had seen him the previous night in the place where I had had dinner with the hippies and had also seen him lurking around the "piglet square."

"I can take you to where that French girl is. If you help me, of course."

He was skinny and of short stature, around thirty, black curly hair Afro style and with a moustache and goatee which made him look as if he were one of the Three Musketeers.

"And why didn't you tell me last night?" I answered, as anxious as I was suspicious.

"I didn't want the others to know," he said mysteriously. "Twenty dollars."

"If it's her, I'll give them to you."

We took a rickshaw, and he told me that she was in Thamel, a neighbourhood north of Kathmandu where, for the past few years, and thanks to the concentration of hotels and restaurants for Western travellers, most mountain climbers and trekkers hung around, as well as the majority of Tibetan refugees who had been arriving in Kathmandu since the 1960s, driven by the Chinese invasion of their country on the other side of the Himalayas.

In a little more than half an hour we arrived at a large old building, red brick and carved dark wooden windows, quite deteriorated but which must have been an old palace. On its three floors, dozens of Tibetan families were accommodated, renting rooms to some of the people coming from the West. Between its two wings, there was a large garden which was completely neglected. From the branches of its tall trees, among the leaves, hung black coloured "bags". I wondered if they were bird nests or some strange fruits.

"They are vampires," said my companion, who in the meantime had already told me that he was French and his name was Antoine. "Don't be scared, man," he continued to my look of astonishment, "they are a kind of bat; although they are quite large." Observing them, I could see that some were unfolding and retracting their wings from time to time while emitting a short squeal.

"They're waking up. It's starting to get dark. Now they will fly away and spend the night in the fields until dawn," he explained.

"As long as none fly through the window and wait for me in my room…!" I joked, as the animals began to leave the branches of the trees and melted into the sky.

I looked around the area. Young Americans, British, Germans, French and other nationalities, about a hundred, formed groups around small fires, smoking, talking, singing, dreaming or sleeping. Some made love in a dark corner or behind the statue of some god or tree. A pair of guitars accompanied the chants. It looked like the final day of a pilgrimage. But there was a lack of joy, a veil of abandonment and boredom drowned the sounds and lights, while a foul smell, a mixture of hashish and excrement, ascended to the treetops.

We started looking for Monique. He started from one side; I, from the other. I looked at all the girls. Some I had doubts whether they were girls or boys. Twilight had descended swiftly, and although I knew I was being somewhat rude, I began to illuminate with my flashlight the faces hidden in the shadows. But no one seemed to care. Groups of people who were far away, between the limits of life and eternal sleep, in other groups, sounds of a ballad or a folk song rose into the night mixed with cigarette smoke, pipes and joints passing from mouth to mouth.

From time to time I stumbled against a body lying on the floor accepting my blow without a sound. But this time, I stumbled across something more solid against which my leg re-bounced. I pointed my light towards it. It was a black god with a red and yellow elephant face. I pointed downwards, and the beam of light illuminated the face of a girl sitting at the foot of the image and leaning against it. She was alone and looked tired. I hesitated. Then she lifted her almond eyes toward me.

"Monique!"

My cry, a cry of resurrection, lit the night. I knelt down and shone the light on her face.

"Oh, it's you, Francisco! My Spanish friend, my best friend!"

It was no longer the flashlight that illuminated my face, but the light of the heavens in all their glory. We hugged each other while

232

a deep emotion almost choked me. She had recognised me. I felt tears streaming down my face. She noticed them and started to kiss my face all over. We cried and laughed.

When we finally stood up, I kept holding her, holding her whole being against me. I lowered my hands gently from her shoulders to her waist, feeling her fragile bones beneath the curves of her slender body. I continued hugging her wanting to lock her inside me, protect her, save her. I felt her weak, trembling and, at the same time, abandoned to my embrace. But in my happiness, suddenly, a slight concern came into my mind; I could not leave her there.

"Where do you live? Here?" I asked. "Come with me, to my hotel. You'll be much better."

"Yes, yes, of course ... but I have to wait for Steven," she said, "he's gone to the hospital to donate blood. And he will worry if I'm not here when he returns."

"The boys donate blood, and the girls prostitute themselves to be able to eat and get high." a voice next to me explained.

It was Antoine, the guy who had brought me here. I gave him the twenty dollars promised.

"You, on the other hand, know how to take advantage of the situation," I snapped.

"If I had known how much you cared for her, I would have asked you for fifty," he said. He turned and disappeared into the crowd.

"We'll wait for your friend," I said to Monique, "and you, why don't you donate blood as well?" "They don't want me, I'm too thin. Plus, I still have money left."

I experienced relief. I had imagined her, with a mixture of

jealousy and displeasure, passing from one man to another.

So we waited for Steven, sitting there at the foot of the statue of Ganesh, with my arm around her shoulders holding her against me. I felt so content, and she quite calm after her initial exaltation of happiness, that we barely spoke. We just savoured the moment.

Steven appeared after a long time. He was English. Compared with all the others that swarmed around us, he seemed quite awake and friendly.

"Monique has told me so many times that if only she had gone with you on your treks instead of coming here," he told me as soon as the introductions had been made.

"We can go on one now, can't we?" I said, turning to Monique rather than at him.

She smiled at me sadly. "I think I'm in no shape and Steven is leaving next week. He is saving money to buy the flight."

"You can get back in shape in a few days. I'm going to make sure you rest and eat properly. I am not leaving you now that easily," I replied as I looked into her eyes.

"Okay," she conceded.

At this point, Antoine reappeared. He took Steven to the side. Steven handed him a few dollars and received what I assumed was cocaine in return. He casually offered some to Monique. She hesitated, looked at me, and shook her head.

"Why don't you collect your things and we can leave? I have a room with two beds," I said.

"Ok, I'll go, wait for me," she said, kissing me on the cheek, and going towards one of the building's wings.

She returned after five minutes, dragging her backpack with

difficulty. I took it from her, strapped it to my back, and we left the building. My hotel was barely two hundred meters away, but we took a rickshaw. Monique was finding it hard to walk, but I felt optimistic and full of strength.

XVII

One day, love asked the affection:
Why do you exist if I am already here?
To which the affection replied:
Because I put on a smile where you left a tear.

And the waiting continued. We spent our time watching the clouds float by, and the snow fall. Darkness and silence are different in the mountains, they are exquisite and mysterious. Sometimes, the clouds would part, allowing for an absolute blue to shine like a smile on the peaks. And then, for a moment, these would gleam, until the clouds decided to hide them again. I still had hope, but Jack had started to doubt and to hint that, if the weather improved, we should start the trip back on our own.

"Let us trust in God," he said that morning, our eighth day of waiting.

"And that it doesn't snow anymore and Pemba comes soon," I answered.

"Don't you believe in God? Are you not a Christian?"

"I could be a Christian, but not a Catholic."

"I thought that all Spaniards were Catholics."

"There are many, too many actually. That's how we were brought up. Catholicism and other monotheistic religions refuse to allow you to be happy unless it is their way and you must follow

236

their rules. I am not up for that."

"My parents became Methodists, they said that Catholicism was corrupt after so many centuries and they liked the simple liturgy of the Methodists and their love for helping others. I'm not sure. In the States there are so many different churches…" he continued, a questioning in his eyes.

"The fact that there are so many churches in the world and that they all consider themselves the only true one proves that they are all false. For me, Churches are terrible, with their dogmas and prohibitions that petrify the soul. They hold society back, don't allow for intellectual development and scientific progress," I answered, convinced that he was interested in my opinion.

"Don't you believe in God?" He insisted.

"Instead of believing I would rather think. I can't say whether God does or does not exist. Not even science can confirm or deny his existence. And, if God does exist, you can't confine him into one creed or religion. Like nearly everybody, I like legends and stories of Gods and fairies, but they are not science. I want to understand, not just believe."

"And don't you think religion is necessary?" Jack replied.

"Yes, a lot of people do consider them necessary. I don't, religions divide people. They are the evolution of the old beliefs, and these come from ignorance. And it is precisely that by travelling through these regions where superstitions and stupid beliefs are still very much alive, one realises this. The religious man, defeated by life's adversities, seeks refuge in the faith of a divine world that awaits him," I continued, as Jack seemed eager to continue discussing the subject. "We are scared of the unknown, and this leads us to create this saviours image we call God. Nietzsche already said: It is not God who created man, but man who has created God."

"In my opinion, I don't think it's the right moment to discuss whether we believe or not, let's just let him help us," he answered, his eyes reflecting a certain confusion.

"Sorry, I went too far, I thought you wanted to know my opinion. You are right. It's not the moment to start doubting God nor let ourselves become bewildered by pessimism."

"There is nothing to forgive, Frank. Quite the opposite. I never thought that someone who didn't believe in God would risk his life to save someone else's. I am even more thankful now," he said as he took my right hand and held it between his.

The one in whom I continued to trust was in Pemba and, besides, I did not see myself without his help, crossing the passes and gorges with so much snow. We remained silent and returned to our usual chores. Well, not really chores, as they were limited to walks if the weather allowed, eating the bare minimum so we wouldn't exhaust our scarce resources – trying to hydrate the rice and lentils in cold water had proved to not be very efficient- and to tell each other the events and adventures of our lives. Sheltered in the tent, close to each other, together but isolated in our own thoughts, we tried to sleep. For me, every night I could see the mountains surrendering to the darkness, but I knew that the light would return, I could feel them so tall that they wouldn't let me see my loved ones, but I could remember them.

Monique spent the first two days after our reunion resting, with the help of a light tranquilliser. We barely spoke, enough to look after her in her daily needs. On the third day, I convinced her to go to the hospital. Jean Pierre recommended the United Mission in Patan, where there were a few western doctors and nurses. They checked her over with a stethoscope and did an electrocardiogram, as well as a blood and urine test. Her heart was slightly weaker than usual; she had anaemia and lack of iron, but nothing too serious.

They prescribed some vitamins and iron supplements, together with a healthy diet and daily walks.

"And a proper steak now and then," added the Swiss doctor who had seen us.

"But…I'm a vegetarian," Monique argued weakly.

"You have plenty of time to be one again in the future," concluded the doctor.

In the evening we went for dinner to the "Utse", a Tibetan restaurant in the neighbourhood of Thamel, near our hotel. Photographs of the Potala, the Dalai Lama and other prominent Lamas decorated the white walls. Over the windows and doors hung yellow decorations. We ordered *momos* and *cha*: dumplings filled with meat and Tibetan tea. I told her about some of my adventures since we had parted in Kolkata. And later, with the intention of encouraging her to tell me hers, I said:

"I didn't only look for you in Kathmandu these last days. More than a month ago, before finding you in Jang's house and then leaving for Everest, I spent a few days looking for you, around Patan and afterwards, another day, around the monasteries of Bodnath including Kopan."

"Yes, I was there."

"And you didn't like it," it was a statement, rather than a question.

"No, it wasn't like that," she answered and remained silent.

Her eyes welled up with tears. She wiped them away and

239

brought my hand to her cheek.

"I would rather not think about it. There was a man that hurt me very much. Not physically, but he disappointed me greatly. I never thought a lama could be like that."

She was silent again. I waited, hoping for a longer explanation, but she didn't seem very willing, and I understood. If she ever wanted to tell me the whole story, she would.

A week later, one afternoon, we attempted to go slowly up the hill of the Swayambunath temple. After a few stops, as the long uphill was still tiring for Monique, and after avoiding the monkeys that were milling around, we reached the great stupa. The monks from the neighbouring monastery, dressed in their burgundy robes and with the rosary of a hundred and eight sandalwood beads in their hand, recited the primordial mantra: *Oh mani padme um*, the jewel in the lotus floor – in its simplest meaning – while they walked around and around the white base of the monument. Below the seven gold-plated roofs, swollen with sunshine, Buddha's four pairs of blue eyes radiated in all four cardinal points, covering with his compassionate gaze the whole earth.

After completing the traditional circular clockwise walk around the stupa, as the Buddhist canon demands, we sat on the parapet, she leaning against me, my arms around her and we contemplated the city in silence. We looked like the typical tourist couple. No one could imagine the adventures we had been through the previous months. "But we are on the right track now," I thought. "I can devote my time to my book project, and take good photographs of the valley for the time being. In a few days, Monique will have recovered, and we will be able to travel together to the Annapurna circuit."

We returned to the "Utse". While we waited to be served, I noticed a couple who had just walked in and were looking for a free table to sit down. Surprise. It was Elizabeth and her Sherpa. I called them, waving to them to come over.

"How can this be? You are still here! How come you have not returned to England?" I asked her after a handshake which she turned into a hug.

I shook hands with Ang Rita and invited them to join us.

"I'm staying here, at least for a while," she announced with a broad smile as she happily looked over at her cautious companion. "We are living together," she added. "He is wonderful, I need him."

She told us how she was working in an NGO with abandoned children.

"They are marvellous, so natural, so in need of affection...I could adopt them all," she concluded with enthusiasm.

I introduced them to Monique and told them superficially how we had known each other and met again in Nepal. And as I did, I thought of how Elisabeth, with her kindness and experience in suffering, could help Monique. So they gave us their address, and we made plans to meet up again, visit the orphanage and bring something for the children.

The next afternoon I went to the library which had belonged to an old aristocrat, was situated in his palace and was now open to the public. I felt relaxed there, because even though there was nowhere to sit down, - the scarce visitors sat on the floor –, it contained the majority of all the books that had been printed in English about the Himalayas, India and Nepal since the beginning of the 20th century until mid 60's, date when the illustrious gentleman had passed away. All the subjects which were of principal interest to me at that point and which would be very useful for my travels and afterwards for my writing.

241

When I returned to the hotel, I found Monique wrapped in a towel and combing her hair in front of the small mirror in the bathroom. She had just taken a shower, and on her skin, the drops of water still shimmered.

"I'll have a shower while you finish getting ready and we can go for dinner," I proposed.

"I'm hungry again, even though we've been eating so well," she answered with one of those bright smiles that had captivated me so much when I had first met her.

As I stepped out of the shower, she was waiting for me with the towel in her hands to dry me. She started with my face, and continued down my chest, shoulders, belly and every time she removed the towel from the part of my body she had just dried, she showered it with kisses. I rejoiced and got excited wondering what would happen when she got to the more delicate parts of my anatomy. But she did not stop.

It was wonder, the unexpected, as incredible as, deep down, desired. There I was, close to her, against her, encircling her with my arms. I felt her all against me, from top to bottom, her mouth next to mine, her lips caressing mine, my tongue in her mouth and hers in mine. My hand reached for her small breast, caressed the sweet tip; I noticed it swell, getting excited with my caresses. I felt light, freed of a great weight. Our bodies already naked, skin to skin. I fed her with my heat, and she gave me back her own. Lying on the bed, the caresses continued. And I entered her slowly, with total desire but with an infinite delicacy, little by little, step by step, without haste, a moment of eternity. The moment longed for, dreamed of, hoped and never believed until now that I was in the very centre of my beloved.

I moved slowly inside her, open and closed again, and every movement made my flesh and bones melt. I felt her skin bare and

242

alive, and I felt her palpitation, both of us transformed into a state that had no name, nor memory, nor desire for it to end. I wanted her, sought her further, deeper, even further, still further and deeper, until she found the warm, burning, unmeasured sources of the oceans of pleasure.

And then it was as if with the end of my hard and soft, irresistible force, I had found the key to the padlock that closed all our yearnings. Anguishes were released, misgivings disappeared. All fears swept by pleasure and feeling of fullness to then give way to the great truth of surrender. I felt from the centre of my soul that the essence of Monique filled me to my last limits and closed a long and distressing as well as exciting episode of my life. Or was it a beginning?

One afternoon, Monique decided to go and see how her friend Steven was doing. I thought she would rather spend some time alone with him so I didn't offer to come along. I did ask her, however, not to come back late as we had decided we would get up early the next morning and walk all the way to Changu Narayan temple, the oldest one in the valley, sitting evocative and solitary at the top of a hill a few hours away from Kathmandu. When by ten o'clock in the evening she was not back, I decided to go and look for her.

When I got to the old park where I had found her a few weeks ago, it was half empty. Due to the late hour, the regulars had left. But Monique was there, together with Steven, sitting in a circle with half a dozen other boys and girls. Some were sleeping, others laughed stupidly. All of them, including Monique, looked high.

"I was going to leave now...Come, sit down for a while...I was waiting for Steven to walk me home," she stammered, while she smiled. I couldn't work out if her smile was fearful or just plain dumb.

I went towards her and took her by the arm to help her stand up. She leaned on me, muttered another excuse, and we returned back to the hotel, walking slowly and in silence. When we got there, she seemed to have woken up slightly. She had a shower and got into bed. She beckoned me towards her. I went to hug her. She kissed me softly. She nestled up to me and leaned her head against my shoulder. I felt her thin bony body and her tiny feet rubbing against my legs. I shuddered.

"When have you been the happiest?", she asked me.

"Now," I answered.

"And when have you been the least happy?"

"Now," I repeated.

"Why?" she asked, leaning away from me, surprise reflected in her eyes.

"Right now, I'm two people; one wants to hug you, the other rejects you."

"I'm sorry," she answered, "but hug me, I need you to make the fear go away. And forgive me, I sometimes miss that feeling of escaping from myself which I can experience through a little hashish."

We remained silent. I wasn't in the mood, but I held her in my arms until she fell asleep. I was worried about her again. My happiness was now mixed with fear and anguish. Thinking of the future, I had the feeling I was looking at a landscape covered in mist. When the haze lifted, it revealed the ditches and furrows and the river course that crossed it, with its clear waters and its muddy banks. There was more light, more details and it was these which moved and saddened me.

I had no experience with drugs, their attraction and addiction.

How was I going to liberate Monique of that ambience of quicksand in which so many young people of every part of the world, attracted by the promising songs of freedom, fraternity and free and generous love, sunk into the slavery of addiction and death?

The next morning, we decided not to go on our planned excursions and went to visit Elisabeth and her children instead. The orphanage had been built by an American NGO which had then left Nepal, and an English couple had taken over. It was made up of two buildings of one floor and a nearby terrain where a few bushes grew between the wild grass. In one of the buildings was the children's dormitory and a room which served as a school, dining room and play room; in the other building, the kitchen and the English couple's home. Both buildings were starting to fall to pieces.

Elisabeth introduced us to Kate and John. She was short, a curly brunette with lively black eyes, she looked more Latin than Anglo-Saxon. He, on the other hand, could not be any more British: tall, thin, with serene blue eyes and long blonde hair and beard.

"I think it is wonderful what you do," I said, "and not like all those that come to meditate and find their lost souls in the monasteries."

"The hands that help are nobler than the lips that pray," answered John softly.

Meanwhile, the children had stopped playing and had come over to us with curiosity and hoping, probably, that we would give them sweets or presents. But we, very conscious of Elisabeth's warnings, had brought them biscuits, a few children's books and some toys for the smaller children.

"We do what we can," said Kate when she saw me eyeing the

cracks in the wall. "With what our benefactors send from Great Britain we barely have enough to feed everybody. It 's hard to find people willing to help," she shrugged, with a gesture of helplessness. "We have no money to campaign."

Immediately, the marketing executive in me appeared.

"But you have so many possible donors right here!" I exclaimed.

They looked at me, puzzled.

"Why don't you go to the tourist agencies, the hotels, or you stand in front of the monuments and invite tourist to come and visit you to understand how a social project in this country works?" I added. "Once here, you offer them the typical book for them to leave a comment and sign. And after this, you suggest that they leave a donation.

They looked at each other.

"Great idea. Why don't you help us?" Elisabeth suggested.

And Monique added.

"Yes, it's true. Actually, we could all do it; I would help too."

"You've caught me," I thought. "But they do deserve it." So we began to plan what agencies and hotels to go to, to convince the general managers of the first ones to include the orphanage in their tours and the second ones so that they would allow us to convince their guests to do the same. Afterwards, while Monique entertained herself playing with the children, I took Elisabeth to one side.

"Monique is doing drugs again," I confessed. "Last night she was smoking with her old friends and who knows what else! While she was sleeping, I found some needle marks on her arm. This morning she assured me they were old ones.

"I'm sorry, I'm so sorry!" she answered with a gesture of despair. "She is such a sweet girl!"

"What can I do?"

I must have looked at her with such powerlessness, that she put her hand on my arm and squeezed it consolingly and answered.

"Not much more than what you are already doing. Don't leave her alone, give her affection but," and here she looked at me intensely, "try not to fall in love."

I shrugged my shoulders in resignation and smiled.

"You know that the heart is an organ made of fire. And when it lights, it's hard to extinguish."

XVIII

Serenely let us move to distant places and let no sentiments of home detain us. The Cosmic Spirit seeks not to restrain us, but lifts us stage by stage to wider spaces. If we accept a home of our own making, familiar habit makes for indolence. We must prepare for parting and leave-taking or else remain the slaves of permanence. Even the hour of our death may send us speeding on to fresh and newer spaces, and life may summon us to newer races. So be it, heart: bid farewell without end."

Hermann Hesse

The Glass Bead Game

Another afternoon had come to an end, and in a slow spiral, the silence and the clouds had risen from the far away valleys of the world to where we were, in our remote refuge. It came to talk with our souls directly, to plant its roots and stay, and shade our solitude with its luxuriant crown even more, and increase our anguish that the last rays of sunlight had not been able to disperse.

Pemba still had not returned, and I kept asking myself what could have happened. I remembered his honest look, cheerful, and engaging smile and trusted him completely. Maybe he had not been able to find anybody to accompany him. Or the passes and gorges had too much snow. I remembered his austerity, his care in not wasting water or food, like that afternoon when we had slept in the cave.

After a seven-hour trek to reach it, he had left to search for water. He knew where to find it, but it still took him an hour to return. I saw him coming with the water bottle in his left hand and the small saucepan full to the brim in his right. He advanced between the rocks with exquisite care to make sure he wouldn't spill a single drop. When I said that I had been worried that it had taken him so long, he explained that the spring was not far from where we were, but that he had spent most of the time filling both containers. The water fell very slowly, drop by drop, from the ceiling of a cave similar to the one where we had settled in.

For Jack and me, the situation had now become worrying. We had not been able to eat any warm food for days now, as we had run out of gas. We had a few biscuits left, a few pieces of chocolate, some powdered milk and a couple of tins of sardines, enough food left to last one more day and afterwards we would have to try to dissolve the soup packets and ground rice in cold water. This was not a problem for the time being, knowing that the stream was only an hour's walk away; but it might be in the future. We had also run out of anti-inflammatories, and Jack's shoulder was still bothering him. We weren't sure if he had broken a bone, but the fact was that, for the last few days, he had barely been able to sleep, which made him feel weak and depressed. Despite his good nature, I had already received a couple of abrupt answers. But I understood, and it didn't offend me. I was worried though that instead of improving he was getting worse again.

The weather, however, was reasonably good. It snowed sporadically, and there were plenty of hours of sun. Like previous days, we had gone to collect water and had done some exercises together. As we had decided, if by tomorrow no one had come to save us, we would have to try and reach the passes and cross the gorges by our own means and, from there, it would be easy as pie to descend down to the village and be saved.

The darkness and the freezing clouds kept us inside the tent. We had no light. The candle that I carried in one of the side pockets of my rucksack had already burnt out a few nights ago, and the batteries of our flashlight were empty. We each fell into our usual silence and tried to sleep. But I was worried. More solitude and waiting. I thought of Hildegard again, and how she had been, in a certain way, the reason for delaying my adventure towards the Nanda Devi and, consequently, finding myself in this situation. But because of this, I had found a dying Jack. For good or for worse. I had learned the real value of life, and of its lack of meaning without the closeness to death. In a few days, our situation would be decided and settled. And, thinking of Hildegard again, I decided I would go and visit her in Germany upon my return. I had her address in Karlsruhe. I was sure she would be happy to see me. Just like she had been happy to meet again in Kashmir even though those two villains that had tried to practically kidnap me. I saw myself again in that dark night.

The small headlamp of the motor-rickshaw lit only a few meters of asphalt of the narrow and lonely road in front of us and suggested the silhouette of the medium sized trees on its border. Ten minutes had already passed since we had left behind the last houses of Srinagar and I started to become suspicious and wonder where on earth these men were taking me. One of them drove while the other crouched next to him. They were both young, around twenty years old. They had approached me as soon as I got off the bus that had brought me from Jammu: twelve hours and more than three hundred kilometres of uphill, downhill and curves in the foothills of the Himalayas.

"Are you Francisco?" they had asked in unison with a deferential smile which should have already put me on guard.

I stared at them in surprise. How could they know my name in such a far away land?

"Your friend Hildegard is waiting for you. She is in our houseboat. Come, we'll take you," they continued.

I happily accepted. "Great! She remembered," I thought.

I had met Hildegard four days ago in New Delhi. I had arrived that same day from Kathmandu after saying goodbye to Monique, and in the afternoon had gone to visit one of the famous temples of the city, Humayun's Tomb, an immense mausoleum of Persian style with Indo-Muslim influences, built in the 16th century to house the tomb of the Mongol emperor of the same name. Surrounded by vast gardens, in which one can also find the tombs of his wife and other family members, is the architectural precedent of the famous Taj Mahal. But while this one is built exclusively of white marble, Humayun's Tomb alternates white with black marble and red brick.

I admired its perfectly balanced proportions as I approached it between the hedges and flowery bushes. I then climbed the stairs that led to its vast platform and penetrated inside its structure under its vaults until I reached the mortuary chamber: For a long while I was grateful for the cool air and the darkness, after the intense heat and light I had suffered on my way there. Afterwards, I went up to the terrace, took some photographs and gazed around in search of a better spot to take a panoramic picture of the monument, bearing in mind the position of the sun. Another tomb at the southeast corner of the premises looked perfect.

When I arrived, a woman, a few years younger than me, dressed in a long light green camisole and white cotton trousers – a very Indian outfit and adequate for the climate – with a Nikon FM between her hands and a silver chain around her neck with a golden, oval shaped and antique looking medallion, received me with a welcoming look in her light blue eyes. Some incipient wrinkles marked the corners of her mouth. Her hair was brown, short and slightly curly.

"It seems that we had the same idea," she said in an impeccable English, much better than mine. Later I noticed that she rolled her Rs slightly.

"Indeed, I hope there is space for both of us."

"Of course, be my guest," she answered as she gestured with her right arm, offering me the view in front of us.

"I'm Francisco."

"Hildegard."

"I'll wait for the sun to set slightly."

"Yes, the light will be softer."

"Like you," I thought, "What a serene woman. And she has a certain air of mystery around her."

"With that name, I assume that you are German or Austrian."

"Yes, German."

"Oh God, don't let it even cross your mind," I thought, but rejected the thought of it immediately. We continued exchanging information about our respective trips. It turned out that we were staying at the same hotel, the Ambassador. It was the one recommended in the *Routard* guide book, which we were both using, as the best one in relation to quality and price between the average priced hotels of the city. So, after taking our photographs and enjoying the sunset, we took a taxi back together.

An hour later, we met in the dining room. She had changed and was now wearing a dark blue dress, close-fitting to her slender figure, and on her cleavage the medallion which had already intrigued me a few hours earlier. I could now see that it represented the bust of a woman framed in an aureole. We talked about our lives while we shared a vegetarian dinner and a few beers. She lived in Karlsruhe and was a psychiatrist; she taught at the University and also had a practice.

"You don't look very crazy," I joked.

"The craziness in psychiatrists is inevitable, not like the one our patients suffer," She offered me a smile which seemed to distance her from me and continued, "but you are slightly right. The truth is that those of us who study psychiatry do so because we have personal problems and so want to understand them."

"Well, you seem like a very balanced person."

"Thank you, but I haven't always been this way."

I waited for her to elaborate a bit more but she dropped the subject. She told me she had come to India on holiday for three weeks. She planned to go all the way to Kashmir and Ladakh.

"What a coincidence! We have the same itinerary."

"Oh, really?" Maybe..." she seemed to hesitate for a second, "we could travel together up to Leh if you don't mind. It is better when a woman travels accompanied in this country. I will be very adaptable," she continued, while her hand stroked her medallion. "Moreover, taking into account that you have more experience than I do of walking around these lands..."

"Why not? We can travel together. Although I should warn you, I am a little independent. Maybe too independent. I like travelling alone."

"Me too. That's why we can travel together, we will understand each other. And if we don't, easy, we part ways."

She was leaving by plane the next day to visit the Golden Temple in Amritsar, a sacred place for Sikhs, and from there she was going to Srinagar for a couple of days. Meanwhile, I wanted to stay one or two more days in Delhi and another in Agra to see the Taj Mahal. So we decided that the first one to reach the capital of Kashmir would leave a note for the other one at the tourist office indicating the houseboat where he/she was staying.

The floating houses anchored to the shores of Lake Dal were the typical accommodation here. They had been built by the British in Imperial times to escape the summer heat of the Indian plains. The Maharaja of the time did not allow foreigners to purchase land or houses in his kingdom and so the British had evaded this prohibition by building their residences on the water near the shore.

We parted with that promise. Later on, that same night, I realised how it was actually not a bad idea to have the company of a mature, intelligent and sensible woman like Hildegard after my crazy times in Kathmandu. I remembered how the English poet William Blake had defined women of being made either from soft silver or fiery gold; I felt that in her there was both, gold and silver.

I should have been sad about leaving the Nepali capital two days ago, but I wanted to continue with my project and had to take advantage of August and September to visit the western parts of the Himalayas, with the monsoon retreating and before the arrival of the first snow. I felt like I was abandoning Monique, my fascination, if not my love for her, defeated and crushed. I did not know for certain. In all truth, it was she who had allowed me to leave by myself. I felt my love was betrayed or was it my pride? Should I be hurt by the fact that I had been completely devoted to her and now she had decided not to come with me? But she would have been a burden to my project.

She had almost recovered since I had found her that day, her body had returned to its usual shape, and her face was no longer drawn. In her honey coloured eyes, there was a hint of her old vivacity. She seemed calm and happy, she felt well and sure of having left drugs behind her. But she was in no physical condition to follow me. They were going to be a couple of tough weeks. And the truth was that to really enjoy a trip and the adventures that result from it, one must go alone, free of ties and open to new encounters. So I looked forward, took a deep breath and convinced myself that I felt liberated after all those days of worries and distrust, amen to those very happy moments. "In occasions, life only gives you what you want when you turn your back to it," I thought.

"Are you well enough to stay here alone? Your flight is in four days," I had asked her the afternoon before I was due to leave, while we were sitting in the modest garden in front of Kate and John's orphanage.

"Don't worry," she had answered, while she took my hand between hers. "I feel well here. I have discovered how sweet children can be. I didn't like them in France, but here…" and she gestured towards the dozen children that at that moment ran round over the tired grass. "They are so cheerful and affectionate! They are happy with anything. I think that when I go back to France, I am going to try and become a teacher."

"I exaggerate. Of course, you are not alone," I answered. "For sure they won't leave you alone for a second. And you have Kate and John, and you will be well taken care of by Elisabeth in her house. She understands you and is fond of you," I added as I looked into her eyes.

She must have noticed the emotion in my voice because she put her arms around my neck.

"As do you!" she whispered in my ear. "Be careful, I will wait for you in Paris. And thank you for the flight ticket."

We stayed there for a while, in a tight embrace. I could feel my eyes welling up and also her tears on my face. And so, I said farewell to Monique. She had given me something which had stirred my forty-year-old hardened heart.

I found myself now in Kashmir, in the middle of the night, on my way to an unknown place. My suspicions about the men that were taking me, supposedly to where Hildegard was waiting for me, became certainties when I questioned them.

"But Dal lake is not so far away. Where are we going?" I shouted over the roar of the engine.

The driver slowed down and turned his head slightly towards me.

"What?"

I repeated my question even louder so that they would hear me.

"The houseboats of Lake Dal are full, many tourists, there is no space. We are taking you to another and prettier lake and to a new house. You will like it," he answered.

"Stop!" I ordered.

They spoke amongst each other without slowing down.

"Stop!" I shouted again.

This time the rickshaw did halt. I wasn't very sure of my situation at that point. They might steal everything I had and leave me stranded there.

"Look. Take me back to the bus station. And we'll leave it at that," I proposed in a conciliatory tone.

They quickly talked it over and finally accepted. Back at the bus station, the Tourism Office was still open. There was an advertisements pin board at the entrance. On it, half a dozen messages, some quite tattered. The one that looked the most recent had my name on it:

"I will wait for you at the Victory III house-boat. Take a taxi, not a rickshaw. Hildegard."

Obviously, those men had read the message, some smooth operators! And there they continued, with the intention of taking me, now for real they promised, to the Victory III. I didn't pay them any attention and with my bag over my shoulder, went towards the taxi stand thirty meters further away. They followed me. I opened the door of the first taxi and got inside.

"To the Victory III," I said to the taxi driver. "How much?"

"Forty rupees."

I was not in the mood to argue, so I offered him thirty, and he happily accepted. But both men were still there. They started to talk with the taxi driver. He, a thin man with a sharp nose and white hair turned around towards me.

"They say that you haven't paid them. Fifty rupees."

I quickly explained the situation.

He waved both men away and started off.

"These men have no house-boat nor anything of the sort. You

should be careful here, there are many more men like these trying to trick tourists."

Ten minutes later we were on the small pier, and from there, a shikara took me to the house-boat. I climbed aboard. Hildegard was on deck, resting on a hammock. I noticed in her eyes that she was happy to see me, as she must have noted it in mine. She brought her medallion to her lips, stood up and came towards me, but we only greeted each other with a civilised hand shake.

While we had dinner, we told each other about our adventures since we had parted in Delhi. We retired early, as we both had plans for the next morning. She wanted to buy a *Pashmina* shawl. I wanted to climb a hill which dominated over the lake to take some pictures. When we said goodnight, I couldn't help but ask her about her medallion.

"It seems to mean a lot to you," I said.

"It does. I'll tell you why another day when we have more time."

And now yes, we hugged each other and kissed lightly on the lips.

I liked the accommodation. These house boats maintain the traditional shape of the *bahats*, boats with a flat bottom used to transport goods in the past, and are built with planks of cedar wood from the Himalayas. On the deck, there is a single house of one only floor, also made of wood and unpainted. In its interior, a living room, dining room and two to four-bedrooms with or without a private bathroom. At the front, a porch held up by four columns made of carved wood and a ladder going straight down to the water. Garlands made of carved wood in the flowery style of the region surround the perimeter of the house. The furniture, carpets, brass objects, paintings and porcelain give the interior an

258

ambience of an English country house from the previous century. And offer that intimacy so difficult to find in India.

If India is associated immediately with the splendour and misery in equal parts, the name of Kashmir wakens halos of legends, romantic landscapes and distant pavilions on a background of snowy peaks. The trip from Srinagar, its capital, as we were able to see for ourselves the next morning, raises a suspicion on whether the promises of the Kashmir charm have not been swept away by the Indian perception of progress and buried by abandonment. Decayed buildings, bogs, roofs made of corrugated iron corroded by rust, and shreds of material hanging from the electric cables strewn between posts and facades with no order or sense. Discoloured masses of people (Kashmir is not Hindu but Islamic), noise and rubbish piled up in the corners. We crossed a canal of stagnant waters. At its shore, many house-boats were anchored. Decrepit, congested. There was so little water that rather than floating they were lying in the mud.

Further up, at the top of the hill, the horizon opened. To say "bewitch" is not enough when describing Dal Lake. The ring of mountains enlarged to the north, crowned in white and surrounding the extension of the still waters of the lake; the *shikaras* gliding through it, the poplars, the willows and the vegetation on its shore, the floating gardens where the locals grew their vegetables, fruit and flowers, and the row of houseboats, clean and tidy, offering themselves invitingly.

We enjoyed ours immensely. A lack of worries and pure relaxation. We were maharajas even though it was only for a couple of days. Bathing in sunlight on the terrace roof, reading by the shade of the porch with the daily scenes of the lake developing before us at their timeless rhythm. As soon as dawn broke, the canoes would start floating by, filled to the brim with vegetables and fruits on their way to the market; at each end a woman paddling crouched at water level, her head covered from her forehead to her back with her scarf.

The round of usual suppliers began a while later. "*Salaam sahib*", we were greeted by the baker on his way to the kitchen. The milk woman came from the mountains. She wore an embroidered hat, her hair divided into innumerable braids and large silver earrings. As she passed, she would offer us yoghurt in a jam jar before she left the daily milk ration. A pallet of ordered colours, the florist's canoe was coming: dahlias, hyacinths, carnations and roses. Two young girls apparently shy and with a smile drawn on their lips, turned our living room into a greenhouse full of delicate perfumes and joy, for only a few coins in exchange. Soon after this, one by one, the traders appeared.

"You don't have to buy, you can only look as a pleasure to your eyes," said the first and was then repeated by all the others without variation.

Smart, tireless bargainers, the Kashmir tradesmen were the sharpest and best at sweet-talking that I met on my trip. They always had something to offer and always a reason to praise it. The porch and living room slowly and successively filled up with furs, carpets, silverware, shawls and embroidery. Beautiful things, at bargain prices. The temptation was at our door. But we didn't buy anything. Hildegard was thinking of buying something else apart from her shawl, but on the way back and I, certainly, was not buying anything now nor on my way back. To travel light was sacred to me.

The last afternoon, before tea time, we went for a ride around the lake on a *shikara*. Settled between low cushions under the small pavilion, while the rower, standing on the bow, made it glide softly over the surface of the water, carpeted with lotus flowers and other water plants, I sensed that we were starting to feel attracted to one another. I took her hand; she leaned on my shoulder. The sun began its trip towards sunset. It turned red and descended slowly until it disappeared between a hollow in the mountains. "I'm getting caught up in something," I thought, "but she is a sensible woman." She lifted her head and smiled at me seductively. We kissed softly. But that was all there was that night.

The next morning, we took the bus to Pahalgam, a quiet village hidden among pine trees, in the confluence of two thundering rivers. From there, a shared four-wheel drive till Aru. Food and shelter. We then ascended the valley of the Lidder river to the base of the Kolohoi glacier accompanied by Abdullah and his pony. The man as a guide and interpreter; the animal, to transport our bags, sleeping bags and some food.

The first day we continued on a broad path between forests of pines and fir trees, inhabited apparently, by many brown bears, and extensive alpine grasslands dotted by an infinite number of flowers and covered by flocks of thousands of sheep and goats. At the other end, the white mountains were waiting for us. We felt optimistic. The light, the sky and the environment were ever changing. Valley of flowers, valley of colours, valley of clouds, valley of sun, of the soft lights of dawn and dusk, valley of soft mist, valley of magic, valley of mystery, valley of enchantments, valley of liberation...endless visions. It is the excitement of the traveller: to enter deeper and to continue, to feel how you penetrate a haven of peace and oblivion.

On the second day, the path became narrower at the end of the valley, cut into the glacier. The trees disappeared, as we were at more than three thousand metres in altitude. Only grass, rocks and torrents made of foam. The reddish woodchucks screeched at our appearance, warning each other, and hiding quickly into their

261

burrows.

Just like the previous day, we crossed paths with the *Gujar*. The autumn was arriving, and these nomad shepherd families were descending with their flocks to the winter pastures. There were caravans of children, goats, cows and horses. The women drew our attention. Robust and beautiful, covered with embroidered hats and heavy silver necklaces, they seemed very sure of themselves. Even though they are Muslims, the *Gujar* are a matriarchal society. We had the chance to check this out for ourselves on our way back from the glacier.

Didn't that gorgeous brunette of green eyes invite me into her great tent to offer me tea while she sent her husband to collect the flock for the night? Did she not put a sour face at Hildegard when she followed us inside thinking that she had been invited as well? Didn't she gesture towards a place next to the fire and next to her and left my companion out of the way with the children? Complete hospitality. Didn't she insist that I should spend the night and pointed clearly towards what would be my place next to her bed? We considered it to be fascinating field work for anthropologists, to study in depth the social conducts of the *Gujar* nomads. And, once again, Hildegard showed her balanced sense of humour by not feeling at all offended by the manoeuvres of the nomad woman. I must admit that during the night it rained heavily, the tent was soaked and I for one regretted not having accepted the hospitality of this determined woman.

On the day of our return, dawn broke shining. We still had about five hours walk until Aru and the desired comfort of the small old colonial hotel next to the river. But the way had become at some points quite slippery, and we had to walk slowly. We stopped for a while to take a rest and finish off the nuts we had left. We then had to cross a few torrents, treading carefully on the rocks that stuck out of the water whirls and it was here that, while crossing the third torrent, Hildegard missed her footing and sprained her ankle. It was not serious, but we had to continue the trip with her leaning onto my arm. "How am I going to ride on that poor horse with my more than fifty kilos?" she worried.

But I liked having her hanging onto me, close to me, feeling her breast brushing my forearm. I wanted to lie her on the grass and hug her completely, but I contained myself. We walked like this for a good half hour until four kilometres before Aru, the path widened again and we found an old jeep between a group of houses. "Yes, it was going to Aru, but it was already full." After a conversation between Abdullah and the travellers, a boy offered his seat to Hildegard.

Abdullah, his pony and I continued our way. We got to Aru, crossed the simple bridge over the river, and I saw the hotel. In one of its windows of the third and last floor, a gleaming Hildegard, with her locks even more golden due to the sun rays, was smiling at me.

"I spotted you once you left the pine trees. I thought you weren't coming anymore, that you might have stayed with one of those *Gujaris*."

"No, I couldn't find any more. How is your foot, is it better?"

"With your arrival, I have been cured," she said and laughed out loud.

"I'll be right up, I'll pay Abdullah, and I'm finished," and in private I thought to myself, "and I'd devour you completely."

"I have a surprise for you."

I went upstairs. A splendid bath tub full of hot water, lit by candle light and some incense scenting the air was waiting for me in the bathroom.

"Oh, great! For you or for me?"

"If you make space for me, for both of us," she answered from the bedroom.

"Is that an insinuation, a promise, a commitment...?" I said as I began to undress.

"God, you Latin men!" she paused. "Simply put, there is only one bath tub and only this hot water, you on one side and I on the other. Come on, get in."

I finished undressing and obeyed her. "How splendid! What a woman. I need one like her, who spoils me and doesn't cause me any problems," I thought. I saw her cross the threshold and come into the shadows, totally natural, without hiding any parts of her body, I am not sure if out of pride or simply being completely natural. We stayed in the water for a long while, relaxed and in silence. After, we played a bit tickling each other's feet, but when I insinuated more direct caresses, she decided to end the games and laughing, get out of the tub.

We were the only guests in the small dining room. At first glance, due to its furniture and decoration, it seemed the British had never left. Everything was immaculate and orderly, but the untainted white table cloths full of careful repairs, the heavy brass cutlery with their silver plating nearly worn off and the crystal glasses, barely two the same, showed the passing of time. The menu went according to the ambience: potatoes and carrot soup, roast beef with vegetables and pudding. The old waiter treated us as if we were his own children.

During dinner, we talked about the happenings of our trip and laughed at the woodchucks' games and the peculiar nature of the *Gujar* woman who had invited us to her hut, but during the dessert, we started a more intimate conversation. Hildegard was wearing her golden medallion again. She hadn't during our trip nor during our stay at the house boat.

"I consider you a very wise woman, and I think it is time that you tell me the story behind the medallion," I suddenly came out.

"It is an inheritance which I received from my patron saint," she answered as she took the medallion with her right hand and offered it to me.

"Really? It looks like an antique."

From her bag, she took out a book which I had seen on her before, searched for a page and began to read slowly, as she was translating from German to English: "*In the mysterious vision and in the light of love I saw and heard those words about the eternal wisdom: five tunes of justice sent by God resonate for the human race.*"

"This was written by my patron saint, Saint Hildegard of Bingen, a mystic from the 12th century," she added.

And continued, looking into my eyes as she knew it by heart: "*And those five tunes are superior to all man's deeds because all the acts coming from man are nurtured by them.*" She continued reading: "*Some men don't live according to these sounds, but carry out their deeds with the help of only the five bodily senses. They won't save themselves.*" She looked at me again: "*Wisdom also taught me in the light of love and told me in which way I was educated in this vision.*"

"You overwhelm me, how deep!" I managed to say.

She laughed happily and offered her hand across the table.

"Don't worry, I told you I am a psychiatrist and very rational. The real nature of education is the awakening of the human being, not indoctrination. But one must learn about what our ancestors thought and extract from it what is for us convincing."

"And have you never been married?" I asked her, still marvelled at her speech while surprised at the same time that we had not yet touched that subject.

"And you?" she asked with a cheeky smile.

"I asked first."

"No, I haven't. But I could as well have been, except that I didn't have kids."

She hesitated a silence, an air of sadness. I waited for her to continue and she did.

"I had a boyfriend for more than four years, a good man, handsome, but he exasperated me. He wasn't searching for anything more in life." She leaned back in her chair and sighed. "For him, going and visiting his clients and having a few beers in the afternoons was enough. In the time we were together, he gained twelve kilos."

"And what was his profession?"

"Insurance broker. He inherited a good client portfolio from his father, and he was not short of money. I couldn't stand it." She extended her arms and let them fall in a sign of helplessness. "It exasperated me, and I tried to make him change, for him to have more impulses, more ambition, but to no avail. I tired of it."

"Yes, I understand," I said, trying to make her feel better.

"We see each other from time to time because I still feel affection towards him, but he is quite happy.

"But you aren't, I assume."

"Yes, yes, I am over him. We already broke up a year and a half ago." She was thoughtful for a while and then asked, "What about you?"

"Something similar, six years, except that mine was very complicated, and we lived, first at two thousand and then at one thousand kilometres from each other. And that was sometimes physically as well as spiritually like from here to the moon."

"Wasn't she Spanish?

"Well no, she was German, like you."

"Yes, the women from my generation we are not easy. Our parents had a terrible past because of Hitler and the war, and many of us rebelled against it. We feel like we have an indelible mark in the eyes of the non-Germans. This affects our relationship significantly." she explained while I listened to her intently. "I have seen it in my practice. Deep down it makes us insecure and makes it hard for us to really open up. Do you not love her anymore?"

"Feelings?" I asked myself out loud and lifted my eyes towards the ceiling as if I was searching for an answer. "I don't anymore feel the fascination which I felt for her before, her personality which was so complex that I was never fully able to comprehend. The truth is that after so many years, goings and comings without ever committing fully and living together, I think I have now taken another path. These last months have changed me considerably. I feel like a different man. I don't need her anymore. And anyway, I am excited about another girl."

"That is a surprise; you hadn't mentioned anything until now."

"It's complicated. I'm twice her age. I left her in Kathmandu a few days ago, and I guess she must be in Paris by now," I hesitated for a second. "You might be able to help me understand a few things about her."

I told her how I had met Monique, how I had searched for her

267

for various days around the monasteries of the surroundings of Kathmandu and the city itself. How I had found her hooked to drugs and how I had managed to get her out of it. Or at least that is what I hoped.

"I had never had until then any experience with drugs and I would like to know why they do it," I continued.

"The drug is the symptom, not the cause," Hildegard answered. "I am no expert either. I have started having a few patients, and I looked into it. Look, underneath every story, there is an emotional and subterranean trace, a desperate need to escape from the own identity on one hand, and to assert it on the other; two opposite needs which coexist in a paradoxical harmony."

I listened to her with a keen interest and encouraged her to continue.

"Women's motivation to take them is different to that of men. Women are much more impulsive due to their hormones. There are theories which state that mental or psychological problems lead to drugs, others say that it is drugs which provoke them."

"In Monique's case, I understand that it was her disappointment in the Buddhist monks behaviour during her meditations, added to a love disenchantment and her relationship with her mother and her stepfather, what ended up leading her to take drugs. I now think it was her choice, but I am worried about the sequels that might remain."

"Heroin and hashish alone don't actually damage the organism, or that is what they say. Although I am not so sure. They create a terrible addiction, especially the first one because we have opiate receptors; therefore, the tolerance is maximal, and it tends to be attached to other illnesses due to a lack of hygiene. When you start with heroin, you become addicted immediately."

"The forbidden is attractive, and it is a way to escape reality I suppose," I said.

"Exactly. The typical thing my patients tell me when they relapse is "It is because I have so many problems…". And I say: "Yes, and the way to solve them is like this, very good, your problems are still there, and now you have one more."

I followed with avid interest Hildegard's explanations, some of which I had already thought about and commented on with Elisabeth in Kathmandu.

"And how is a person with a tendency to become addicted?"

"Not very tolerant to frustration, he or she tends to want to be the centre of attention, there is a significant fragility in their affection, they are not strong people, not very sure of what they want."

We went outside and contemplated the sky and all the stars of the northern hemisphere and we each submerged ourselves for a while into our own thoughts while we enjoyed the fresh air of the night. Hildegard felt a shiver and hugged me. We returned to the room. After our corresponding preparations to get ready for bed, I slid under the sheets and entered its orbit of warmth. We continued talking about some of the episodes of our lives until we fell asleep in each other's arms. And I, maybe because I was thinking of the mystic Saint Hildegard of Bingen, contained the material senses of my body. We had sealed a very platonic friendship.

XIX

"If we listened to our intellect, we'd never have a love affair. We'd never have a friendship. We'd never go into business, because we'd be cynical. Well, that's nonsense. You've got to jump off cliffs all the time and build your wings on the way down".

Ray Bradbury

The next day, the ninth and our last day of waiting, we spent it doing exactly the same as the previous one. The only difference was that the weather had become worse. To the East, one could see the enigmatic pyramid of Nanda Devi, the round summit of Bethartoli Himal and the three Trisul peaks appearing over the clouds. These mountains had been our companions for days. They would stay in our memories and be part of us forever. Terrible ones for Jack; good and very exciting ones for me, I hoped.

To the southeast, however, our escape route was covered in clouds. Far away, at the end of the Rishi Ganga gorge where it continued its way to merge with the Ganges, the comfortable world and our usual environment awaited us: our friends, a fridge full of delicious food, and beds with thick spring mattresses. Although this last one I hadn't thought about that much, except the night when the wind had insisted on trying to tear the tent from the ground. When I finally managed to fall asleep, I did so quite comfortably, laid down on the thin mat and well insulated in my down sleeping bag. After the third day, Jack had not accepted using it any longer. He slept with his anorak on, which was much warmer than mine, and covered in the survival blanket which I had carried at the bottom of my bag and which I had needed in previous treks. But the food was a different story, it was scarce, and it increased our sufferings every day.

We waited for night's arrival trying to cheer each other up. We had to thank the solidity of the bond which had been established between us, it would help us greatly on our return to the other world down below. After the tragedy which he had experienced a few days before with his friend's death and his mountaineering experience on snow and ice, Jack was not very worried about the difficulties which awaited us; but I was. As long as there was a more or less walkable path, I could reach the end of the world. But I had no technique nor experience on a more complicated terrain and so I started to feel scared. What if something went wrong? It would not be hard for us to end up lost and incapable of getting out of there. And, consequently, dead. Jack smiled when I told him of my fears. "It's logical, I have them too," he said. "It's even good, that way we will be more cautious. But I am sure we will manage."

I had to sleep to be strong the next day, but I was unable to. I needed peace and quiet next to me. Oh! How calm I would be if I had Hildegard next to me. Maybe I should have stayed with her. I remembered the rest of our trip together.

From Kashmir, we continued to Ladakh. I could see us both in the front row right next to the bus driver in a bus of more or less acceptable conditions except that its back wheels were completely smooth with no tread depth. We were on our way to Leh, the far away capital of that old and undiscovered kingdom in the heart of the Trans Himalaya. A few years ago, in an effective way of invasion, China, Pakistan and India had divided the region between them. India had just opened up its area, the most populated and interesting, to all those who wanted to risk the journey. It was a two-day trip on a dirt track which followed an ancient caravan route, part of the legendary "Silk Route", and which crossed the Himalaya through three different passes at nearly four thousand meters, each one more dangerous than the previous one.

The trip was only possible between the end of May and November when the snow doesn't block the passes. Although recent history tells of the winter march of the Zoji-La pass, where a division of soldiers attempted to cross the pass to reinforce the garrison in Leh during the war of Kashmir with Pakistan in 1947. "With the purpose of provoking avalanches to clear the road, the troupes beat their drums during three consecutive nights... As a result, the crossing occurred without any incidents," was written in the colonel's report.

We stopped for lunch in Sonamarg, "the field of gold" at the end of an alpine valley, a tapestry of green pastures between forests and bordered by precipitous mountain walls. A Rajasthani dressed in a folkloric sorcerer's dress approached us and offered for a dozen rupees something which he claimed, and maybe really was, musk deer glands, that Asian deer which had been hunted for centuries, nearly to its extinction, due to the little bag of intense perfume hiding in its belly. Hildegard tried to convince him of how useless his attempts were as she for one was not going to contribute to the hunting of more animals. He looked at her without understanding and continued harassing us until I had to act angry to send him away.

We then waited patiently for the military convoy from Leh to pass. Every day, some hundred lorries returned from carrying rations for the large Indian garrison established in Ladakh. Until the last truck had not descended from the Zoji-la pass, at the base we found ourselves, the road would not be opened for the civilian vehicles. There was a Sikh official installed inside a tent at the edge of the road, sitting behind a table on which there was a telephone, and who counted the trucks as they passed. With his beard carefully gathered in a hairnet, well-groomed moustache, a pink turban and an irreproachable uniform, he emanated such authority that none of the slovenly drivers dared to question him, regardless of how long the wait.

There were around two or three dozen jeeps, lorries and buses parked in the surroundings of the dirt track, in no order whatsoever and taking advantage of the slightest bit of terrain available. When the last military truck had passed, and the official abandoned his post, the stampede occurred. They all wanted to be the first to attack the slopes of the pass with no consideration of the state, power or load of their vehicle. The majority of the lorries, old and overloaded, but painted in shrill images of Shiva and its divinised partners, together with mantras: "Oh my Lord, protect me", had to climb the first eight kilometres in the first gear. The jeeps would overtake them in the most unbelievable places while the buses tried to push them aside by honking.

The road was not much more than a narrow track of rammed earth that had been carved in successive ribbons between the rocky walls and the hundreds of metres high precipices. Blind curves and vertiginous up hills or down hills. The edges of the road had been eaten up by landslides and only allowed the vehicles to go in one single direction. If one slipped over the precipice, there was no possibility of recovering it, and rarely was one able to rescue its occupants. At the bottom, the narrow valley, more like a canyon really, was a patch of green and rocks, dotted with the flocks and huts of the shepherds; the slopes, black with fir trees, were

273

sprinkled with the white foam formations of the torrents. The clouds closed, high above, the deep carving of the pass between snow capped peaks. The landscape was glorious, as the sensation of danger granted it a fearful beauty.

I noted that Hildegard was tense. Her eyes were fixed on her lap, or she covered her eyes with her hands. I tried to distract her asking her about her life in Karlsruhe.

"I am not up to thinking about that right now," she answered. "What an adventure we got ourselves into. How can there be roads like this?"

"This is not the Alps," I answered. "But don't worry, the drivers are used to it. For them it is normal. They drive through here every day."

"Until they topple down the precipice. I had read that the road was bad, but I didn't expect it to be so dangerous."

I didn't have all my wits about me either. Taking her by the shoulders, she hid her face on my chest. Like this, together, we seemed to be more protected.

As we came out of one of the curves in a hairpin, we saw a lorry loaded with sacks stalled fifty meters in front of us; we would later learn that it was loaded with sacks of flour. All the men, at least twenty of us, had to jump off the bus and push the lorry to help it start again. It took a big effort, but we finally succeeded. The tired engine growled. It seemed to catch speed. The driver tried to switch from first to second gear but failed. The carriage hesitated, stopped, and then started sliding backwards downhill. We threw ourselves against the rocks to avoid being run over. The driver's helper jumped from the cabin, but the driver remained glued to the steering wheel. We saw the lorry gain speed. "It is going to smash against our bus and throw it into the abyss."

"Hildegaaaaaaard, jump!" I shouted from afar, desperate.

But before reaching it, the back end of the lorry hit the mountain wall. The lorry jumped. We saw it turn on itself and tip over. A crash. A dense cloud of white dust enveloped the scene and hid it from sight. Absolute silence. What had just happened? Unending minutes. All of us had our eyes fixed on where the lorry had just disappeared; our ears straining to hear the slightest sound, screams, something that would reveal the lorry's fate. Slowly, the dust settled, the curtain was lifted. The silhouette of the monster lying on its right side emerged. Behind it, we could still see our bus. I ran towards it with my heart bursting out of my chest. I opened the door and jumped inside. Hildegard was still in her seat, immobile, in a foetal position with her hands covering her face. I placed mine over hers.

"Nothing happened, it was only a fright."

She drew her hands away from her face but kept a hold of mine. She looked at me mortified.

"You can't imagine how terrifying it was to see that massive monster coming towards us."

"I was also terrified."

We brought our faces close together, and I kissed her eyelids. We remained embraced in silence. I then noticed that there were four or five women in the vehicle who wouldn't stop sobbing and crying. Some men returned to the bus, and there were a few words of comforts and many orders for them to be quiet.

After the fright, the release and the relief, a few of us met around the damaged vehicle to evaluate our situation. The vehicle was blocking the road completely, and we were told by the locals that it would stay like that until the next morning when a military tow truck would come to take it away. After some discussion, it

275

was clear that many of us were not ready to spend the night there. Altogether, Kashmiris, Ladakhis and westerners, we tried to move the obstacle. Impossible! A useless effort, the lorry seemed to be anchored to the ground. They tried to move it by tying it to another lorry and pulling, but the rope snapped at the first attempt.

It was then that an Italian couple took the lead. As they told us afterwards, they had crossed half of Asia from their native hometown Napoli in a Volkswagen bus and had gained a certain experience in similar situations. He organised, and she gave encouragements nonstop: *"Avanti, Avanti. Forza! Tenere, non smettere."*

First, we unloaded the sacks which had not already broken loose during the accident. Then, we used a metal bar and a thick tree branch as a lever to lift the chassis slightly. A Hundred arms pushed. *"Avanti, Avanti! Forza!"*, Floretta continued shouting encouragements. After an hour of efforts: pushing and resting, we succeeded in pivoting the obstacle a few dozen centimetres, enough to be able to cross. And so our bus hobbled up to the top of the pass and continued between ups and downs, valleys and precipices, the journey through the mountain range. At edge and helpless, my sensitive companion sought comfort in my apparent serenity hanging onto my arm. Night came mercifully and hid the dangers that we still had to face until we reached Kargil, where we stopped to spend the night in a spartan lodge.

In the morning we were woken up by the muezzin: the western part of Ladakh is Islamic. A few kilometres further, in Mulbek, a gigantic statue of Maitreya, the Buddha of the future, carved into a rock wall, announced the entrance to the universe of Tibetan Buddhism. An entirely different world in the physical aspect as well. The previous day we had travelled across the fertile landscapes of Kashmir, fields, flowers, fir trees. Now, we found ourselves in another world, in Martian land, tortured terrain, broken by cataclysms, made of rocks placed one on top of the other, naked slopes, deep canyons and violet, ochre and coppered coloured mountains. An environment of minerals transformed by nature's alchemy.

As we turned the bend in the middle of our descent of the Fotu-La pass, a pass which exceeds four thousand meters, the unexpected and extraordinary image of the Lamayaru temple appeared, the first important monastery of our route. Its white and red cubic mass crowned a steep rocky hill in the centre of a deep depression of yellowish lands. At the far end of the narrow valley at its feet, a path bordered by rundown and ancient *chortens*[25] ended at the foot of a huge wall perforated by hermit cells.

The bus stopped for the midday break next to a few tea-houses made of stones and metal sheets. From them, a path which must have been no longer than a kilometre led to the monastery.

"Thirty minutes" answered the driver. With the help of a few dollars, he accepted prolonging the stop for another fifteen minutes more. Hildegard and I threw ourselves down the path, a saying really, as she had to walk clinging on to my arm due to her sprained ankle, to take a look at the *gompa*, "solitary place" as called by the locals.

Tibetan or Lamaist Buddhism was introduced into Ladakh in the eighth century by the globe-trotting Apostol Padma Sambhava, "the one born in the lotus", who according to tradition, travelled on the back of a flying tiger around the whole Himalayas and Tibet, from Kashmir to Bhutan, founding monasteries and imparting the doctrine. There we found him portrayed in one of the paintings that decorated the walls of the main temple, with his penetrating gaze,

[25] Buddhist shrine, typically a saint's tomb or a monument to Buddha.

his thin moustache and goatee, the large golden hoops adorning his earlobes and a trident in his left hand exuding tongues of fire. "Flames of faith or of terror?" wondered Hildegard aloud.

But the sufferings and excitements of the road had not yet ended. A short while after abandoning Lamayuru, the impressive descend over the Indus river, born here in the Transhimalaya, appeared before our eyes. A thousand meters of a vertical drop which the road descended in thirty-five successive sections. In each one of them, the bus seemed to be suspended for a few meters in the air. Hildegard covered her eyes with one hand while she pushed herself against me. I was not feeling very secure either. The driver was not a Sikh, known to be responsible and trustworthy drivers, but a Muslim Indian and he looked somewhat tired. In one of the curves, luckily with its exit towards the mountain and not the precipice, he did not measure his driving well, and he had to slam on the breaks to avoid hitting the wall. The following manoeuvre, reversing the bus and with its rear hanging above the abyss, provided us with new moments of anguish.

"I am definitely not returning this way," sobbed my companion.

"Well, there is no other way", I thought but did not say it out loud. We continued. Below us, at the bottom of the canyon, we could hear the Indo thundering like a ferocious beast trapped in a pit. The Tibetans call it, *Sin Khaba*; "The one born in the jaws of the lion". They say that its milky waters carry gold nuggets mixed with the lime. Finally, we arrived at the bottom. At the entrance of the hanging bridge was a philosophical sign saying: "You can come and go; but the Indo however, will flow without rest during all of eternity."

At its banks, the village of Khalse, the first oasis born from the miracle of water and the tenacious work of its inhabitants. Hundred-year-old walnut trees provided shade to its only street while the green fields covered in apricot trees descended in terraces down to the river. From here, the road continued down to the end of the valley against the current of the turbulent waters. Every fifteen or twenty kilometres, a small village, an oasis, dominated by an old fortress whose ruins ripped the sky, or by temples precariously standing on pitons of rock, broke the monotony of this unknown land. Partly hidden at the top of the tributary valleys, between the poplar trees and miraculous willow trees, we could see small monasteries. Their silhouettes were born from the cliffs, contrasting with the setting of the snow capped peaks.

The landscape widened as we caught sight of Leh, the "only" city in this dessert of mountains which extends around it for hundreds of kilometres. Not a thicket or bush on its slopes. No pastures, no grass. The naked rock and the sands spread their ochre coloured and reddish tones up to the crests and the snow capped peaks which the violent sun had not succeeded in melting. On the other hand, the capital of Ladakh, on the vertex of a vast triangular plain inclined towards the river, was surrounded by surprisingly green gardens and fields. No middle ground between the desert and the oasis, no middle tone between the arid and the green lands.

The sea of sand and rocks finished directly with the walls of the first houses and the edges of the fields. On the cubic buildings of two floors, crowned by terraced roofs with waving prayer flags, the local people dried barley. The children and the elderly waved at us as we passed, smiling. They had marked Tibetan features, dark tanned skin and red cheeks, and seemed strong and healthy. The women were dressed in long dark tunics and on their heads they wore a scarf or a tall and narrow hat which looked like a top hat. The men had their heads uncovered or wore hats which had a certain British air to them.

"I was expecting something extraordinary and different from what we are used to seeing in our countries or documentaries, but not so different. I am amazed," said Hildegard.

"I am not less amazed than you are, and delighted as well" I answered.

"You must have read "Seven Years in Tibet", by Heinrich Harrer, the Austrian mountaineer who escaped a prisoner's camp in India during the Second World War and crossed the Himalayas until he reached Lhasa," assumed Hildegard.

"Of course, and I have also read Alexandra David-Néel and a few others," I answered.

"I am not sure I know her, who is she?"

"A fascinating Parisian woman: orientalist, opera singer, explorer, Buddhist and the first female in the western world to visit Lhasa. An extraordinary woman," I continued while the bus stopped to allow a caravan of yaks pass, loaded with what looked like freshly cut barley. "She spent eight months travelling across Tibet on foot, in 1924, dressed up as a pilgrim and accompanied by a young lama who she had sort of adopted. She wrote a few books about her adventures.

"Oh! I have to read them then," Hildegard exclaimed.

"Well, I have only read the most famous one of them: "My Journey to Lhasa." I am sure it is translated into German as well. In it, she tells of how she saw levitating lamas and one other moving at great speed without his feet touching the ground. The other books talk more about mysticism and religious matters. By the way," I added, "she died ten or twelve years ago in her retreat in the Alps. She had already reached the age of one hundred. "

"And to think that Tibet is still closed to foreigners! That this place is the closest we can get!"

"That is one of its greatest attractions," I answered, while I looked at the spectacle of Leh's main street, completely absorbed by the scene. "It seems that they will allow the entrance to Lhasa to organised groups, but will only allow them to reach it by plane and not venture out of the city. I am definitely not interested in visiting if it is under those conditions," I replied.

"I completely agree," she concluded, at which our bus stopped, indicating the end of our journey.

In our first sunset in Leh, we had dinner on the rooftop of a Spartan guesthouse, some *momos* washed down by a *lassi* and a liquid yoghurt drink with cumin, while we recovered from the travel's scares. Before us, the panorama of the mountains and the old medieval palace of nine floors on the slope of the mountain that dominated the city. On its peak, white and golden with the light of the setting sun, shone the typical Buddhist stupa.

"We have a lot to do tomorrow," I said.

"By foot, I hope, I am not getting into another vehicle in this land," answered Hildegard.

"Ok, tomorrow we can spend our whole day here, but we can't go by foot to visit the monasteries of the area. We will have to go by bus or collective jeep, short trips and mainly up and down the valley," I answered.

"We'll see. For the time being, the only thing that worries me is the way back. I don't know if I will have the courage."

"We can look for an alternative, maybe we can rent a jeep if it's not too expensive. And we still have a week until we have to make our way back," I said, trying to encourage her.

Leh dazzled us, disappointed us and seduced us successively. After the first impression produced by that gush of life in that remote part of the world that made all the fatigues suffered during the two exciting and dangerous days to reach it worthwhile, we saw another side of the city. An old caravanserai of the Silk Route, mythical door to Central Asia, a perfumed name by the memory of those adventurous explorers of the beginning of the last century, Leh was at our arrival a miserable large village modernised by trowelfuls of cement and meters of corrugated iron.

A tourist market of around twenty stalls with Tibetan objects hundredfold repeated, much too large for the number of travellers who actually reached the place, preceded the local market formed by the only two streets which could really deserve such a name. Until the Chinese invasion of Tibet and the consequent closing of the borders between China and India, Leh had been the centre of active commerce. The meeting point of all the races and ethnic groups of Central Asia, a border city, turbulent and prosperous, in it converged the caravans coming from India, Tibet and Turkestan to exchange their goods. From China came wool, leather, tea, silk, carpets, turquoise stones, medicinal herbs and ponies, among other things. From India and Kashmir, printed cotton, shawls and brocades, opium, indigo, pearls, sugar cane, cereal and grains.

The partition of Ladakh between Pakistan, India and China, and the latent conflict between them had substituted the merchants and caravanners for soldiers and Indian civil servants. The growing tourism – this region had only been open to foreigners for the past four years - had attracted the traders from Srinagar which were slowly taking over the stalls at the bazaar. Western and Japanese travellers now arrived instead of Afghans, Khotanese and Uyghur. The Ladakhi, with their long black tunics and their comic headdresses, together with the already mentioned groups, gave the Bazaar and its adjacent narrow streets a lively and picturesque ambience. The setting was completed with the enormous mass of the ancient palace-fortress suspended over the city. Abandoned, crumbling into dust, its evoking power was enormous. Even

282

further up, at the crest, the old temple of the guardian divinities seemed now unreachable to humans. But we climbed all the way up, ascending with difficulty due to the altitude, to more than three thousand five hundred meters, where the temple was. From there, Leh really did look like a medieval village.

And that is what we did during that week – my companion dared to get into a few vehicles – visiting monasteries and temples, marvelled by the timeless environment of their rooms, the paintings of the kind, beatified or terrifying defenders of religion and sanctified lamas in the lotus position with the ritual instruments in their hands, two arms for the humans and dozens for the gods and demons.

Our most beautiful day began in the monastery of Hemis. We had slept on some thin mattresses on the floor, stuffed inside our sleeping bags, in a room which the monks had prepared for the scarce visitors which reached it. We were woken up by a sound which reminded us of the sea. Completely unexpected in these lands. As the first rays of the rising sun ran across the valley accompanying the Indus in its eternal flow, a couple of lamas stood on the roof of the main temple playing gigantic sea conches adorned in silver. They were saluting the new day, were calling to prayer and warning the evil spirits to stay away.

We went down to the great prayer hall and sat next to the monks – some of them were children no older than eight –, while the lamas played the gongs and drums. When these stopped, it was the clarinets, made out of human tibia bone, that played their penetrating sounds. It was the signal for the prayers and monotonous chants to begin, which were prolonged for a long while. A ceremony so chaotic but so peaceful at the same time. Afterwards, surrounded by the pure air of that unearthly morning, we descended down the path bordered by willows, prayer flags and prayer walls until, after five kilometres, we reached the road.

"Does another world exist apart from this one?" Hildegard kept asking herself.

"I for one, barely remember the one I left behind five months ago," I answered.

Back in Leh, we stopped at Thikse. Already on our way to Hemis, we had admired from the road its fantastic appearance, a group of temples and houses of white and red facades which covered a large rocky hill from top to bottom. At its feet, a group of stupas. Next to them, women wearing their tall hats threshed their barley crops. We visited some of the temples and a school: a simple room with around twenty children sitting on the floor, their backs against the wall and small slate boards in their hands. The teacher was the only one with a stool.

But the ghost of the return journey was still Hildegard's main worry and, due to my fondness for her, so was mine. So much so that the following day on our return from Hemis she began to feel ill, a mixture of the altitude, a cold and the fear of the return trip by bus. We found out that the military base below the city and next to the Indo, received the visit of a military plane from Delhi two or three times a week, bringing supplies for the army. Military men arrived and eventually departed in it, also high-level civil servants and sometimes, the evacuation of a wounded or sick civilians was authorised.

The next day after receiving this information I took a taxi and presented myself at the entrance to the military base.

"I would like to see the commanding officer" I announced to the guard on duty.

"What do you want?"

I explained my reasons. My friend, a German doctor, was ill

and had to be evacuated to Delhi as soon as possible. The guard spoke on the phone, and after waiting for half an hour, a soldier led me to the boss's office in the interior of the base.

The commander Harold B. Singh was a slight Bengali, around forty, with thin features adorned by a carefully cultivated moustache, an impeccable uniform and well mannered; an Indian version of the actor Errol Flynn. We shook hands, and he politely offered me a seat and a cup of tea.

"Milk, sugar?"

"No milk and a little sugar please."

He delivered my indications to his assistant.

"And how is it that you have come to such a remote place?"

I tried to sound important.

"You see, I am a writer and photographer, and have been asked by a major European Publisher to write a book on the Himalayas. I am travelling across a large part of the range, and of course, I had to come here. By the way," I added, "I can see that you are doing a great job in modernising this area which is still so backwards."

"Yes, and don't think it's easy. With this climate the infrastructures don't last, they demand constant maintenance, which is tiring and costly."

"Not to mention that you have to keep the Chinese in check," I said with the intention of flattering him.

"And not only them, the Pakistanis as well. We are respectful of these people's culture, but you can't say the same of the Chinese and Pakistanis. Look what the first ones have done in Tibet and what the others have done with the non-Muslims in their new country."

"Yes, compared to others, Hindu religion is very tolerant," I dared to say as I saw he had a small statue of Shiva on his desk.

"Of course, to tolerate and comprehend each other is the basis for a proper coexistence," he said with satisfaction. He leaned forward towards me. "So, what can I help you with?"

"I am here with a German doctor. We met in Delhi and have been travelling together since then. She is ill, that is why she isn't here with me. She is terrified of returning to Srinagar by road," I continued as I looked at my interlocutor pleadingly. "We saw a couple of accidents, and we could have had one ourselves when a lorry nearly rammed into our bus. We were saved by a miracle.

"I understand, but that doesn't mean you will have an accident on the way back. The road is not in perfect condition, but you must understand, you are crossing some challenging terrain, the Himalayas.

"It is not about me, I will go back by bus, I am used to travelling in places like these or worse. It is for her. She is a great person, very sensitive, and I would like to help her". My interlocutor looked at me expectantly, and so I decided to state what I wanted from him. "I heard there is a military plane coming from Delhi, maybe she could be evacuated on it."

"It's true, and I would love to be able to help the doctor, but it is not easy as it is a cargo plane and there are not many available places for passengers." He thought about it for a few seconds and added, "why don't you ask your friend to come and see me when she feels better? And we will do all in our power to help her."

"Of course. I am sure that with this good news she will feel better tomorrow and we will be able to come and see you."

We said our farewells as politely as we had introduced ourselves and I left feeling quite optimistic.

"At least he didn't say no," I said to Hildegard, who was resting on the bed after I passed on the commander's message. "It is normal that he wants to meet you before committing himself."

"I feel better already. Let's go tomorrow," she answered, while she showed her relief and opened her arms to give me a hug.

"Maybe it would be better if you went alone. He will feel more gallant" I said.

"It would be strange, very ambiguous as if I was offering myself to him."

"Well, what you want is for him to get you out of here, on the wings of his plane or in his arms. And I have to say, he is quite handsome," I joked as I strutted around the room twisting my imaginary moustache.

"Are you ok? I think the altitude is affecting you."

We laughed, and I lay down on the bed next to her.

The next morning, we went to see the commander. After the introductions, common courtesies and tea with little sugar, Hildegard expressed her anguish at returning by road. The man proved to be very understanding but wouldn't give a definite answer. Only the promise that he would send a message to our guest house as soon as he knew of a free place on the aircraft.

"You know, we don't have flights every day, we depend on the meteorological conditions and," he hesitated, "I need to get authorization from Delhi, although in your case I will insist so that they give it."

Two days passed and we didn't hear anything, so Hildegard returned, this time alone, to visit the commander. As she later told me, the courtesies and politeness were repeated, but she didn't receive a concrete answer. She was short of time; she needed to return to Germany. Her plane from Delhi left in seven days. If at the end she had to get a bus from Srinagar, she could only wait for three or four more days for the commander's help. The next day we shared our table with a British couple living in Bombay and who had come to Ladakh as tourists. We told them about our situation.

"The problem with Indians is that, like other Asians, they are unable to say no. It also happens when you ask them for directions. They won't say that they don't know, they will just point in any direction, so you don't think they don't want to help you. I am afraid that he is just leading you on and will continue to do so until you get tired and leave," she explained to us.

The next morning, we went to visit the commander again. He excused himself in many ways. Unfortunately, he could not give us a fixed date, but he had it on his mind and would let us know as soon as it was possible. We left, I convinced of the uselessness of the wait; my friend still hoping. I was getting impatient; I was running out of time for my planned treks across the north of India, around the area where the Ganges is born and the Nanda Devi. The snows of winter would come, and I wouldn't be able to walk in the mountains. Moreover, it was the end of September and of the tourist season in Ladakh. The traders and workers, as well as the travellers, of course, were returning to Srinagar so it would not be easy to find a place from one day to another on the return bus. I pressured Hildegard to start our return trip.

"No, I am not suffering on those roads again," she answered.

"But do you really think that guy is going to get you out of here?"

"I trust him. He looks like a gentleman."

I left her with sadness, and I took the bus to hell again. Or at least that is what the kind-hearted Hildegard thought. "Another woman who I abandon," came to mind. But I quickly pushed the thought away. I was not in the mood for irrational regrets.

XX

Who needs heroes? I think we all need them. They are in a certain way, the ingredient of dreams. For me, they occupy a special summit somewhat less accessible than that mountain, which in my mind has great walls of rock and shining ice, and whose solitary and elusive summit is covered by a blanket of clouds. It is a mountain that I cannot climb, which I will never be able to, but, however, that I dream about."

Thomas Hornbein

When dawn broke, we saw that it had snowed again. The clouds hugged the peaks, and our perspectives were not very promising. But we had to leave. We couldn't wait any longer. With no food, we would only get weaker and weaker. We left the tent and other equipment behind and carried only what we were wearing, a full water bottle, the scarce food supplies we had left, my sleeping bag and the survival blanket for the bivouacs we would have to do that night and the following ones. The Dunagiri's silhouette to our right and the depression of the river's gorge to our left marked the route to follow, right by the bisecting angle formed by both geographic features. The snow remained hard, and our primitive handmade walking sticks aided our way. By eleven o'clock, having walked for four hours already, we had advanced a fair distance, but the snow began to soften, and we were forced to proceed much slower.

At around midday, it stopped snowing. We rested for a long while and were moved by optimism. After continuing for a while we agreed, "Soon, the snow will get hard again, and we will be able to walk faster, we can camp right on the other side of the first pass." However, a while later, the clouds that had remained far away at the bottom of the valley began to rise. In less than half an hour we found ourselves submerged in a dense fog. I wanted to use my compass which until then we had not needed. I couldn't find it, not in my anorak pockets nor in my trousers, nor in my rucksack. I asked Jack. He had never had it on him. "How could it be that I had left it in the tent? I had mentally gone over everything that we had to take with us the night before."

A crow flew above our heads, nearly grazing me, and I had a feeling of weariness. It was as if it had landed on my shoulder and was warning me of the calamities to come. As if it had neared its beak to my ear and had whispered: "You made a mistake, you should not be here. In the mountain it doesn't matter how bad a situation is, it is always susceptible to getting worse." We decided to stop. If we continued, we would end up lost between the precipices on both sides of our route.

Just to our right, a few dozen meters uphill, in the now moderate slope, there was a rock wall. We coincided that it would be a good place to bivouac as it would offer certain protection against the elements, so we sought refuge next to it. However, maybe because at first glance it seemed perfect, I couldn't help but feel a certain uneasiness as soon as we had settled in. With hardly anything to eat, huddled together in the dark fog and leaning against the rocky wall, we got ready to spend the night, with the hope of a more favourable meteorology the next day.

It was a very long night. We moved constantly to find some comfort against the rock and were very cold due to the humidity that enveloped us rather than the actual cold. We would doze off for a while, wake up and doze off again, always the same cycle. "Don't think about anything, sleep; tomorrow you need to feel strong," I told myself without much result. The sleeping bag was wet, and slowly I was beginning to feel the humidity seep through it until it barely protected me from the cold at all. Jack, wrapped up in the thin aluminium layer which was the survival blanket was probably not feeling any better. And then, the unexpected happened, something which continues to make me tremble every time I think about it.

I had dozed off when, suddenly, I was shaken by a succession of rushed thunderbolts coming from the East. The fog had disappeared, and in its place, black clouds were whirling around up in the heavens. The lightning lit the mountains with its brilliant silver light while the blizzard charged at the peaks and ridges. It raised whirlwinds of snow dust, pierced by the blinding spears of the lightning. We stood up as we felt how the storm came nearer. We felt the electric tension increase in the air around us. New lightning and thunder exploded above our heads. A furious wind roared, channelled through the cracks in the rocks. It slammed against us and tried to drag us with it. The snow hurling into our face was blinding. We were alive but at its mercy.

A lightning bolt slithered like an arrow from the top of the crag where we had sought refuge. The thunder broke right above my head, stunned me completely and rendered my mind useless, away from this world. I felt it leave my body while the effects of the electric charge from the lightning which had struck right next to me, travelled all along my arms and legs like needle pins. I ground my teeth, my eyes were about to leave their sockets. The lightning, with its deafening thunder like a divine punishment, wanted to take me with him. Further, further away...

Death wanted to incinerate me, make me a victim of its unrelenting fury, attract me to its fatal lap of eternity. I defended myself by screaming my pain towards the skies seeking an answer to such a black question, and I collapsed in the snow. My body shook, trembled, vomiting electricity under the beatings of the lightning's hammer, I broke into a cold sweat, and the pain my chest took my breath away. I felt like I was in the centre of a strange planet, trapped in the mortal labyrinth of some invisible forces whose laws I didn't understand. Shock after shock, my heart beat accelerated, and I felt what I thought were heart attack symptoms. Seconds or minutes passed. I struggled to calm down. I fought further than all the means of escape I could imagine. I returned to myself. I guessed, rather than saw, Jack's figure coming towards me. He offered me his hand and helped me to stand up. I swayed and would have collapsed again had my friend not held me up.

"We need to leave. If we remain close to the rock we risk getting hit by lightning," I heard him say. He hesitated for a second. "But if we continue we will be swept away by the wind, we will lose our way and end up in some precipice."

I didn't know what to answer. I was still terrified. Jack put his arm around my waist and led me towards a soft depression in the ground, thirty meters from the rocks. We lay in it to mitigate the wind's lashes. I started to recover. The flashes of the lightning bolts, together with the roar of thunder slowly retreated, driven by the strong winds towards the far end of the valley. They illuminated at intervals the silhouette of the Nanda Devi. It's glorious beauty which I so much admired, had turned sinister. It now portrayed its vindictive side. The one that had been the protagonist of so many stories and legends. I didn't know anymore whether I desired her or had started to hate her. The killer mountain, the sacred mountain: neither good nor bad; blind, deaf,

293

and dumb. It was only an enormous pile of rocks, ice and snow with no other value than that which we wanted to bestow on it.

When we felt safer, we returned to the shelter of the rock wall. By now we were not able to sleep again. Silence reigned once again, and I finally felt more serene. We contemplated the clouds, how they slowly opened up, breaking up into various layers. The moon appeared and vanquished the impenetrable darkness. We didn't wait for dawn. We were too uncomfortable, and we knew we had to take advantage of the time. So, at around four in the morning, we re-started our journey. A night out in the open always reduces one's strength. Especially a night like the one we had just survived. Moreover, we continued to dehydrate. There was no doubt that from the psychological point of view and the cold it was more convenient for us to keep going than stay still.

We continued in silence, wrapped in the icy solitude of daybreak. I kept telling myself: "The sun will come out, it will be warm, I won't see it all so dark anymore, and we will be able to walk faster." I thought that Jack, with ample experience of the cold of the high mountains, would be suffering less than I was. After we stopped for the first time that day, after three hours of walking, he confessed that he had also felt that sombre coldness of the morning. The snow was icy, and the incline was relatively steep. I had the feeling that I knew the route even though I had only walked it once and many days before, in the opposite direction. During the bivouac we had heard the sound of running water, so we assumed there was a spring somewhere. I even got up for a second to look for it in our surroundings. I hadn't found anything and now, during the hike, not either. They were like hallucinations, illusions triggered off by my thirst and the moments of weakness.

Finally, dawn broke, but because the sun rose from behind the Nanda Devi massif, it took a while for us to feel its effects. We stopped to rest a couple of times. We filled our mouths with powdered milk and snow and continued our ascension towards the Daranashi pass. It wasn't snowing, but as we continued upwards and the sun started heating the environment, the snow became denser and deeper. There were moments where we sunk into it up to our knees. It was getting harder to push forwards. Our primitive walking sticks were more of a burden than a help, but we had to keep them for when we came across the ice, and then they would only work if it wasn't too hard. At midday, exhausted by our efforts and hunger, we were forced to stop again. I thought we were very near the first pass, but I was ready to drop. I was shattered. Jack was in an even worse shape than me. We rested for a long while. "Come on Jack, one last effort." "Ok, come on, let's go." We reached a very steep slope swept by the wind. The snow had turned into ice. I looked back. Jack wasn't following me. I saw him lying on the snow.

"Go, go!", he shouted, but he made no effort to stand up.

I also felt I had reached my limit, just couldn't go on any longer. I unclipped the water bottle from my belt, raised it to my lips. There was barely any water left, and as I leaned back to drink, abstracted as I was, I lost my footing slipped, fell backwards and began to slide down the slope head first. Everything was white. All I could see was the sky. "I am not getting out of this one," I thought, while I tried to break, driving my heels into the snow. I wasn't succeeding and continued sliding downhill, faster and faster. The bushes, its thorns, scratched my face and tore at my anorak. Then I hit my shoulder against a bush. It turned me over and stopped me slightly. I threw out my arm and managed to hold on to one of the branches of the next one. The water bottle fell out of my grip and tumbled down the mountain. I had a feeling of utter hate towards it as well as the rage of having let go. I saw it crash against a rock and sky rocket upwards, arching through the air and, as it fell, it hit against another rock. Its metallic sound exploded, eloquent to the stillness of the atmosphere. It prolonged during a magical moment, eternal. It raised, unexpectedly, a flock of snow pigeons. I could hear their hasty fluttering as I tried to stand up. "How lucky you are that you can fly; if not, you wouldn't be here like us, a pair of idiots," I thought, incapable of moving. "I need to go back and look for Jack; we need to push forward."

A few minutes passed. I wanted to shout to Jack, but I didn't. I knew that he was in the same situation that I was. "Either I get up, or I die right here and he will also," I thought. The thought of dying did not affect me. I felt like I had no emotions left. I was too tired for it to matter. If I had been scared, I would have of course fought. "Jack helped me last night, now I need to help him." It was that thought that made me react. I managed to stand up and started climbing with difficulty towards him, as I had let go of my walking stick when trying to hold onto the branches during my fall, and so was constantly slipping. I finally made it to him and knelt down by his side:

"Come on Jack, the pass is just there. We shortly can reach it, and we can continue," I said. "One more effort and we'll be there," I continued as I slowly shook him.

"Go on, you go on," he answered; by I could see in his eyes he was pleading for help.

"I'm not leaving you alone. Come on, let's reach those rocks and seek cover there."

"Okay."

But he wasn't moving. I sat next to him to wait for him to recover while a decision hammered my head: "We have to continue; we have to continue."

Suddenly, we heard some shouts. A hundred meters below us,

296

in the last visible end of the slope, four figures appeared. Pemba and his men climbed towards us with great precaution, in the same place where the pigeons had disappeared. They had heard them and seen them fly over their heads, so they told us afterwards. "It was the *sahibs* that scared them," they had thought. And so they had climbed upwards to look for us. At that moment for me, the sky opened up and illuminated me with all the light of its heavens. Jack's face also changed. He grabbed my arms and shook me with all the energy he seemed to have lost a few moments before. We hugged each other, although we hardly had any strength left to shout for joy. While we stayed there, hugging each other, I thought: "We are saved, if they have been able to cross, so will we." And our spirits were flooded by feelings of joy, liberation and gratefulness.

XXI

*Certainly, travel is more than the seeing of
sights; it is a change that goes on, deep and
permanent, in the ideas of living".*

Miriam Beard

The first thing Pemba did when he and his companions found us,
about to abandon our efforts to get out of the funeral chamber of
the Goddess Nanda, was to set up the tent he had brought with
him. He then prepared hot tea, a packet of noodle soup which for
us tasted better than a meal at the Ritz, and rice with lentils which
we shared with our saviours. The snow had covered the passes and
gorges, and so they had needed three days to open a path in the
snow, with the help of some spades they had brought from the
village. We could certainly not complain about their generosity.

As soon as we were slightly recovered and even though we
wanted to stay in the shelter until the next day, our selfless saviour
insisted that we had to start our way back. They had made such an
effort to uncover the path that we couldn't risk another heavy
snowfall covering it, and so we began trekking back very slowly.
Jack and I had to walk leaning on one of the men, and in the more
complicated parts, we had to be helped forward by two of them. At
the last hour of the day, they prepared a platform on the snow
where we would spend the night, right before crossing the gorges.
And from there, only two days and a half until we reached the

village.

The first one was across the hillsides which had been covered in reddish shrubs on the outwards journey and which were now, on our return, covered in white. The view of our beloved, and sometimes hated, mountains framed the four cardinal points, the last hours to enjoy their beauty! But also to reflect on our previous days and the fears and anguish we had suffered.

"Jack, how are you feeling? What are you thinking?" I asked my friend when we stopped to rest, while we devoured some *chapattis* with cheese and some bananas.

"I'm thinking that I can't wait to get out of here, reach Joshimath and call my wife and parents. They probably think I am dead."

"It hasn't been that long for them to think that," I said, trying to cheer him up.

"When Udai, our guide, returned to Joshimath, he probably went to the police to notify our disappearance. From there, they would have communicated it to the embassy, and they would have called our home."

"Of course, you are right. They will be heartbroken. But think of how happy they will be when you call them!"

"I can't wait. But on the other hand, Peter. I shouldn't have let him go in front. He was too proud of having conquered the peak, and I think he lost the perspective of the danger around us. And I also have to talk to his parents. What am I going to say to them?" he was silent for a moment. "And I don't know what they will want to do if they will want to leave him there or rescue his body and take it home."

"I don't know, but from what I have read, if they are buried by an avalanche or inside a crevice, the bodies are left where they fell,

299

right?"

"It is their choice. I have no desire to return to that cursed place."

"You will have to accompany them. You are the only one who can recognise the place."

The next day after we went over the last pass, we set up our tents for the night, just after the starting point of the descent. From there we could see the village, two thousand metres below us, from where we had started – Jack two months before, I less than a month ago -, peaceful, with its roofs of dark slate and surrounded by the terraced fields which descended to the bottom of the valley and its tumultuous river.

On the last day, we abandoned the naked slopes, entered the forest and descended through its beautiful abundance of oak, rhododendrons, conifers and tapestries of fern. The path was quite steep, and during the first hour of our descent, we had to pay close attention to our footing as it was also very slippery. Later on, because I felt very much recovered and optimistic, I allowed myself to enjoy the beauty of the scenery, to also savour the solitude and in that sense the mystery that the great wild forests evoked with the intensity of light and shadow created by the rays of sunlight, its profound silence and its unexpected and inscrutable sounds.

The eyes took pleasure at the variety of colours, from all the shades of green to white and dark red until they reached the coppery brown announcing the start of autumn. The lichen dangled from the branches and formed intricate webs which seemed to move to the rhythm of the birds' songs. I was surprised by how light and receptive I felt after the stressful days we had just experienced. I felt that Jack, even though he was walking at our same rhythm, sometimes before me and sometimes behind me, was not experiencing the same peace of mind that I was. I tried to cheer him up many times with my comments on what we were seeing, but as I wasn't able to liberate him from his worries, I finally opted to keep quiet and not to disturb him.

I am not saying that we had a party awaiting us, but what we did have was a fabulous lunch prepared for us in Lata, as one of the men who had come to our rescue had gone ahead to announce our immediate arrival. They had sacrificed a few chickens in the temple of the village in honour of the goddess to which it was built, of course, none other than Nanda Devi, and had prepared them in a *tandoori* oven, marinated with yoghurt and spices. We even had a beer. I would have stayed there all day, maybe spend the night, well relaxed and relishing the simple hospitality of the Bhotias but, understandably, Jack was in a hurry to call home, and so, with the twang of the spices still in our mouths, we descended in a little more than half an hour to the main road to catch the bus that passed every day before sunset. Pemba came with us so that I could pay his and his colleagues services' as soon as the bank opened the next morning.

We stayed at the Nanda Devi, a simple hotel with a dozen rooms and a few bathrooms, situated at the entrance of the village and on its main road. The same hotel we had stayed in at the beginning of our journey and where both Jack and I had left the possessions we didn't need for our incursion into the mountains. I had no idea how, but the news of our misfortunes had already reached the village, and the owner of the hotel was waiting for us with two large cauldrons of hot water so we could have a bath, and two clean rooms ready for us to occupy. From the hotel's reception desk, Jack asked for a conference call, one with his home and another with his parent's house. Subsequently, I asked for another one to my parent's house. The telephone operator told us that we had to wait for two hours, which actually suited us very well due to the time difference. So we decided to wash while we waited; Jack occupying one bathroom while I used the one next door.

It was a typical Indian bathroom: a wash-hand basin, a squatting toilet, a faucet at medium height and a basin full of water with a small plastic bucket, jug or saucepan. To wash, you lather your body in soap, crouch down and throw water over yourself with the jug. The difference that day was that we also had hot water to mix with the cold water. After the major physiological needs, one could not clean oneself with toilet paper as there wasn't any unless you had brought it yourself, so one did so by using water and the left hand, a method which, in truth, is more hygienic. It is for this reason that in India, as well as in other Asian countries, the left hand is considered impure and one must never touch food nor anyone, nor offer objects or presents with it. To eat, one only uses the right hand.

The conference call wasn't arriving, and my friend felt more and more impatient. I also couldn't wait to talk to my parents, as they would be worried after not hearing from me for so many days. There we were, sitting in front our tea cups, in silence, each one in their own world. Deep down, I felt happy and proud. I had lived days of intense excitement, of dangers overcome. I would have never thought that I would ever find myself in such an extreme situation. And I had saved a man. Although I didn't really see it as such a great feat, it had all occurred unexpectedly and had developed quite naturally. The truth was that I didn't remember that knot in my stomach as being so terrible, the restlessness and uneasiness, at times full of anguish, of the last days and especially the nights where we waited in the snow, and I wondered if we would ever get out alive.

Meanwhile, Jack had decided to call his embassy in Delhi to know what news they had received from him and his colleague, and what they had told their families. This was the first call we received, but in the office of the embassy at that hour, there was only the security personnel who didn't know anything: "Call tomorrow," we were told.

While we waited, dinner arrived. Quite boring. This was a region which was strictly vegetarian, and this resulted in there being little variety food wise in this area of the mountains. But after so many days of fasting, this was like a prologue to the future meals we promised ourselves. And so, for the moment, we were satisfied by the usual chapattis, vegetables, a thick sauce made of spicy lentils and cucumber with yoghurt.

I managed to speak with my parents and reassure them. They told me my sister had had her fifth child, I promised to write to them the next day and that in a little over two weeks I would be back in Paris and after that in Spain. Right afterwards, Jack was able to talk to his wife. I could hear his voice, at first nearly shouting, as on the other side of the line, in Arizona, they probably couldn't hear him very well. Then his weeping mixed with laughter. When he finished and came out, he had a slight smile drawn on his lips and tears in his eyes. He told me about the conversation with his wife.

The embassy had called them a week ago telling them that both of them were probably dead. The family had begun to prepare, together with Peter's parents and friends from the Sierra Club – the mountaineering club -, the trip to come to India with the idea of organising an expedition to retrieve both bodies. Two days ago they had been told by the embassy that it would be impossible to organise such an expedition because there was too much accumulated snow and it would still keep falling. And so, they had had to make do with crying and preparing a funeral in remembrance of both of them.

"At first, my wife didn't believe it was really me," continued Jack. "She nearly started insulting me thinking it was an evil joke. She then began to cry, both of us did. I could feel her emotion and happiness through the line. She is going to call Peter's parents, I don't have the courage yet, so when she talks with them, they will know."

It snowed during the whole night, and the next morning we woke up to see everything covered in white, the streets with more than a hand span of snow matching the mountains surrounding us. Even though the owner warned me that the bank would not be open yet, as the manager lived outside the village and due to the snow situation, would still take a while to arrive. But I went anyway. Jack stayed in his room waiting to talk with his embassy as now that he had manifested his reappearance and confirmed the death of his colleague, he would need a new passport. His had been left behind in his abandoned backpack.

Punjab National Bank was on the main street, right in front of the centre. It was indeed closed, so I sat down in the tea house opposite to wait for it to open which it finally did at eleven o'clock.

"I would like to change money, dollars."

"I am sorry, but we don't change dollars," said the employee.

"And pounds?" I tried, even though I only had a twenty-dollar bill.

"No, no; we don't have change for foreign currency," he answered.

"But how come! I just got back from an expedition, and I need to pay my porters."

The man seemed uncomfortable.

"I am sorry, you should discuss this with the general manager," he answered as he gestured towards the man's office.

I knocked and half-opened the door. The manager was a man slightly younger than me, short hair, olive coloured skin and dressed in a suit and tie. Very British.

"May I come in?"

"Go ahead, come in," he answered while he pointed towards the chair in front of his desk.

"I need to change dollars to pay for my porters and guide."

"Where do you come from?" he asked, the first question of every Indian.

"I am from Spain."

"And are returning from an expedition?" he asked curiously.

"Yes, from the Nanda Devi," I answered. "But I would now like to change dollars for rupees."

"And did you reach the summit?" He then inquired.

"No, no, it was a simple trek to the Sanctuary." I regretted giving so many explanations. I got closer to the table, placed my hands on its surface and continued.

"I now need to change money because my guide is waiting to return to his village," I answered slightly nervous as I didn't see how I could pay Pemba and his men. And I also needed money to get Jack and me back to Delhi.

"Yes, but we don't change money here."

"But I have to pay them."

"I was also a mountaineer before. I'm from Mumbai. I used to come here a lot. I liked it, so I stayed. I have climbed the Kamet, and I nearly reached the summit of Nilkanta, but a storm caught up with us when we were a hundred meters from the top, and we had to turn back."

"This man is going start telling me his life story," I thought. So I didn't let him. I leaned forward towards him.

"Please, I really need your help."

"And have you been in the Valley of Flowers? It is gorgeous," he continued as if he hadn't heard me at all.

I noticed that I was losing my patience and leaned backwards.

"As I was saying, I need to change some dollars. I need to pay my porters and the *sirdar,*" I said raising my voice.

"How much?" he said resigned.

"Three hundred"

"I already said that we don't have a licence to change foreign currency, but go to the State Bank of India." When he saw the puzzlement on my face, he added, "It is at the entrance of the village, on a street that goes down to the river."

I left without saying goodbye, annoyed that he had wasted my time, and went to where he had sent me. The exact same scene was repeated, first the counter and then with the general manager. He was a big man, middle aged, with greying hair and dressed simply, in the traditional Indian camisole. At first impression, he seemed more affable than the previous manager. There were some framed pictures depicting an image of Ganesh, the elephant god, and Krishna, the shepherdess' seducer. But despite his good disposition, the only solution he gave me was to go to Rishikesh.

"But that is twelve hours away by taxi. I would need a day to go and one to come back. If you can't change for me, there must be someone in the village who needs dollars. People go abroad, to

306

England. The traders go to Singapore and Hong Kong to buy watches and electronic devices. I have seen them in the shops. They need dollars. Don't you know anybody?"

"If you come back tomorrow, I might have found someone," he answered.

"I am sorry, but I am very much in a hurry. My *sirdar* is waiting, and he needs to return to his village."

"I understand. Give me a moment, let's see."

He picked up the telephone and dialled. He spoke for a while in Hindi with his interlocutor.

"I have found someone," he said. "Come at two o'clock which is when we close, and we will do the exchange."

"You can't imagine how thankful I am. I knew that you would help me."

We shook hands, and I went to the tea house where I had arranged to meet Jack for lunch. I told him about my bank negotiations, and he told me about his with the embassy. They were going to ask the Ministry of Interior to prepare him a travel authorisation so he could fly to Delhi. He had to go and pick it up in forty-eight hours at the local police office.

At two o'clock I returned to the bank and was led directly to the manager's office. The staff left. Ten minutes later the doorbell rang. The manager left his office to open the door, I heard him talking, the door of the office opened. The surprise nearly made me jump off my chair. The newcomer was none other than the manager of the other bank. He smiled at my puzzled face again. "This pain in the neck", I thought but smiled back.

"We meet again. But this time I can help you."

"Good…" I waited for him to continue.

"But please, sit down," the manager of the State Bank told us both.

We did. He settled in behind his desk, and the director of the Punjab bank sat in front of me leaning back in his chair and with his legs crossed. A boy appeared with tea, he left it on the table and disappeared.

"And how many dollars would you like to change?" said the manager of the Punjab Bank.

"Three hundred," I repeated.

"I can give you eighteen rupees per dollar", the man continued smiling.

"But the official change is at twenty-six! I saw so this morning in the newspaper."

"You must understand. You have a problem, and we are doing you a favour. We don't know when we will be able to recover the rupees and at what exchange rate. The black market fluctuates."

I was outraged. The black market! They would then sell the dollars for at least thirty rupees. But, at the same time, I knew I depended on those unscrupulous men, even if they didn't see themselves that way. This was how business was done in India, the Muslim influence. I resorted to the argument that had served me so well in similar situations.

"Look, I am not a wealthy American. I love India, and I go everywhere I can by foot, like Gandhi. I try to follow his teachings. You know them?"

"Of course, *Gandhi-ji*. Who doesn't?" he answered somewhat annoyed. "I am one of his followers. He rid us of the English."

"And don't you think that Gandhi would have helped me instead of thinking of how to make the maximum profit?"

308

They looked at each other and exchanged some words in Hindi.

"Ok, I will give you twenty-two," said the Punjabi.

"I still don't think it's right, at least twenty-four."

He shook his head from side to side, which in India is a sign of agreement, and put a wad of notes on the table.

"Ok, and your dollars?"

Counting six notes of fifty I put them also in front of me on the table. He pushed the rupees towards me. I counted them. Exactly, seven thousand two hundred. What a pig! He had come prepared to change them for twenty-four from the beginning, no more and no less.

Bidding farewell to both of them and satisfied with my money negotiations I returned quickly to the hotel as Pemba was waiting for me, his bus back to Lata left at three in the afternoon. I paid him, gave him the corresponding amount for his colleagues, added a tip and walked with him to the bus. On our way, we passed the market, and I bought some kilos of rice and lentils for him to share between the people of the village and left him settled in the bus. Then I continued down the road in search of the only shop in the village that sold beer. A moment later, the bus overtook me. "Goodbye Pemba, my great friend," I thought. "One day I will come back even if it is only to see you again".

The liquor shop was in a small alleyway to which one gained access through the main road and down some steep stairs. One couldn't go inside, as the door was protected by a thick iron gate. It looked like a prison instead of a shop. This was due to the strict prohibition law which regulated the selling and consumption of alcohol in this very religious state.

I bought four three-quarter bottles of beer for Jack and me and returned towards the hotel. A few yards along the way I bumped

309

into Pemba. He had left the bus and was returning to his village on foot, with his sack of provisions on his shoulder. I understood immediately. Why would a keen trekker like him spend twenty rupees to avoid doing what he liked the most in the world, walking? We faced each other. He looked at me confused but I patted his back, and we smiled. I hugged him, and he hugged me back, satisfied, we parted ways, and he continued. Observing him as he walked away, I thought, this is what a real man looks like! I doubt I'll ever see him again, what a pity."

After a few more days in Joshimath to recover from our hardships and intense emotional sufferings, Jack and I travelled together to New Delhi, a total of thirty hours by bus and train. When the train left the station of Haridwar, I leaned out of the window to look at the mountains. But those giants of rock and ice, the reason why I had been roaming around for months, were not visible anymore but instead some brownish-grey hills dressed in forests. I wanted to say goodbye, but I suddenly felt that it could not be a goodbye forever. One day I would return, and it would be the same. I would again feel the call of the high peaks, the tempest would howl above them, and my thoughts would be vast and free. Although this time, neither Pemba nor Jack, would be with me.

That last evening together in New Delhi we went for dinner to an excellent restaurant situated in the porches of Connaught Place. White table cloths, china dinner plates with golden rivets, silver plated cutlery, crystal glasses and waiters in a black uniform with a white shirt and tie. Very British. We had Rogan josh, a lamb stew Kashmir style, very spicy, accompanied by vegetables and watered down by a bottle of fine Australian wine. But the wine, instead of cheering us up, left us slightly sad and melancholic. Our adventure and comradeship had come to an end.

The next day, we said goodbye with a long and heartfelt hug.

Jack was going back to the United Stated in search of reconciliation with his wife and long afternoons of play with his son Jimmy. He also had the cruel task of explaining to Peter's parents the circumstances of their son's death and decide if in spring they would or would not, try to recover his body or, if on the contrary, they would leave it there, undisturbed, offered to the eternal ice. I was returning to Kathmandu to finish my voyage with a trek in the Annapurna region, to complete my selection of photographs and the information for my book, bid farewell to my friends and pick up some of my possessions which I had left in the Hotel Shakti. We promised to write and visit each other.

I obtained a ticket only for the last plane of the day. A while after taking off and to our left, a large section of the Himalayan mountain range presented itself, well illuminated by a setting sun. I was able to recognise some of the mountains: The Machapuchare, with its peak in the shape of a fish tail, between the triangular Daulaghiri and the summits of the Annapurna massifs and, more to the East, those of the Gurka Himal. I had trekked the slopes of some of them, and the rest were waiting for me. I would never grow tired of walking their paths. I remembered my days in the Nanda Devi; the gorgeous scenery, the fears and thrills I had seen and felt, and the intense happiness and gratifications. Mountains are contradictory. One remembers their magnificence but not the adversities lived and the agonies. Maybe because they are harder to remember than beauty which one can be seen, while fear is a feeling and so, is invisible.

I thought about the past. A terrain mined with holes. What dam opposed itself to the torrent of my memory, was it the passing of time or a self-defence mechanism coming from the subconscious? What was left of me, what could I see and feel from who I was before and what did I feel and see now? Who had I become? Had I been lying to myself all those years in my commitment to earning money and social status? There I was, I was facing my own mirror, something that the majority of us try to avoid as it can lead to unexpected discoveries, it's hard to open the door to one's shadows.

"I am forty already," I thought. I am at the chronological equidistance from the maternal womb and the hole in the earth of the cemetery. I have lived half of my life. In theory, the most fruitful, the most intense, of youth and maturity. But no, I still have the other half left, and it can be of even more value. A total change. A new life of no ties and commitments, of no dogmas and structure, a pure life in all its simplicity. Only sensations and wherever the wind pushes the desires, with no defined itineraries, aims or destinies. And this life makes sense when one aspires to nearly everything without sacrificing anything. I wasn't going to go back to my old antics. What does not progress is destined to disappear.

To travel is to nourish ignored appetites, hidden or rejected. This is what had happened to me these past months, with the experiences I had lived and with the memories brought by the encounters, the solitude, the wait and also the terror I had experienced. And it was those invisible things - forgotten or put aside, but which were there and formed part of my past, and at that moment, of my present – and were going to define my future. Ghosts, doubts, life... Where at the end of the day, you always search for certainties.

If we forgot about the desire of knowing the future and were able to liberate ourselves at the same time from the ties of the past, acting only in and for the present, then we would be able to achieve absolute freedom. In those moments, I was very conscious of it in the mountains and the landscapes, the further away from civilisation the better, is where one is the closest to this ideal. It is

312

there where the daily problems disappear; the relationships and conflicts with the others are seen so far away, that one doesn't worry about them, due to the simple reason that one can't resolve anything. It was decided: never again would I work for a company, nor in an office or in a factory. For the time being, the coming years at least, I would spend them travelling, exploring and learning about the world in detail. I would continue with India, then the rest of Asia, then…

How my existence had been transformed in little more than a year! Before, always in a shirt, tie and Italian shoes; now my attire consisted of corduroy trousers, anorak and mountain boots. I had changed the luxury hotels and luncheons of caviar, foie gras and Arcachon oysters, with Burgundy or Bourgogne, for rice and tea. Before, gastric problems, headaches and heavy legs. Now, I was healthy and strong as a yak. For the moment, I loved the idea of returning to Kathmandu and its temples, streets, life and smells. Monique wouldn't be there, but I would see her in two or three weeks in Paris.

Monique or Ursula? Ursula or Monique? With which of the two was I in love? Why couldn't I be in love with both of them? I recalled the film by Truffaut: "*Jules et Jim*" where a young Jeanne Moreau plays the main character, in love with two friends. Or rather, the two friends were in love with her. Therefore, the threesome was perfect. Since I had watched that film, I believe that it is possible to be in love with two women at the same time and not be crazy, as also claimed by Antonio Machín.

But, Ursula? Was that chapter of my life closed? Had I really pushed myself away from her existence? Did I still love her? Can hope survive the passing of time? Can it exist in relation to the past? I had thought about her on many occasions, but as she was far away, I felt she now was part of my past. But soon I would be close to her again. We had had so many stories in common, much ecstasy and many conflicts. But no future. That had already been made clear. Her complex personality and her image would always be present in me. "Love...fire and flames for a year, and thirty of ashes", wrote Lampedusa in "Il Gattopardo". Our relationship had been very strong, impossible to forget. But in six years we had been unable to find a place to live together, impossible to continue. So many adventures, so many encounters had diluted my love. When love dies, there is nothing left. Where does it go?

And Monique? Was I in love, infatuated, seduced? Vain hopes. I was twenty years older than her... "Time will tell," I concluded.

And my home? Where was it now? It changes and broadens with the path of one's life. The far off distance caresses you and calls you, and the memories, those pieces of life ripped out to the abyss, your darlings, your lovers, bind you to the different places through which you travel. With time the number of places increases. On the one hand, they broaden your horizons and perspectives, they enrich you, and you become more adaptable to places and people; on the other, it is a burden, a danger which has a name: solitude, rootlessness. In the Western world, we believe that we have a right to life. Here in the East, they consider it a privilege. And one lives according to this belief. Only those able to place their soul outside of themselves are able to contemplate the world and learn to live truly.

I had discovered new ethical values. Their synthesis: those of the primitive Buddhism, those from the disciples of the historical Buddha before the moral teachings of the master had been transformed into an organised church of monks and cults to the god that never wanted to be; those of the philosophical Brahmanism, not the popular Hinduism full of superstitions and rituals, as empty as they were cruel, to the benefit of the superior casts.

I had learned to appreciate the aesthetic qualities of the new landscapes in faces, in customs, sediments of history, in the interrelation of the worlds and their values. The thoughts built up with their numerous doubts and scarce certainties. They fought to get out and did so impetuously, untidily. "Have I reached the horizon I was after?" I asked myself. "I have been very close. And by doing so, it has now moved further away and broadened. Better, it will lead me to greater learning, to meet more people, to discover them, and appreciate them in one way or another, even to love them". But there was no doubt that I felt like a different man. "There will be many days in my life and in each one, like this one about to finish, the individual that I am will continue to be moulded by the happenings of each day and by every being that he finds on his way. I am, definitely, one of those born under a wandering star. I sometimes don't know where I am going, but I like being on the road; that is what matters."

The plane began to descend. The reddish sun rays signalling the end of a day caressed the snowed peaks of the Langtang and the Ganesh Himal. I was arriving in Kathmandu again. Someone wrote that to where you have been happy you should not return.

XXII

The world has a life of its own. It rotates and rotates ignoring the past, unmindful of the future, without hesitation of its inexorable progress. If life did not have in its final death and this one did not precede life, neither would make sense. We must die so that our lives have reason to be.

When I arrived at the hotel in Kathmandu, it was already night time. I had a few letters from home: encouragements, worries about my whereabouts and news which I had already received via a phone call two days before, and a postcard from Delhi: *"My plane back home leaves in a few hours. Travelling with you was wonderful. I would like you to come and visit me in Karlsruhe one day. I finally returned from Leh to Srinagar by bus. I was able to endure it. I was running out of time, and the "handsome commander" was still promising but not delivering. Love and kisses. Hildegard."*

I had also received a message from Elisabeth. She told me she had left to accompany Ang Rita on an expedition to Manaslu. She was planning on staying at base camp while her companion would go with the climbers up the mountain. She also explained to me that Monique had not left for Paris. At the last minute, even though she was very well health wise and had not relapsed into heroin, although she did smoke some weed here and then, she had not had

316

the courage and strength to return home and had decided to stay in Kathmandu, at least "until Francisco returns," she had said. Elisabeth added that a few days before leaving to Manaslu she had spoken with Jean Pierre and he had not seen any inconvenience in Monique staying in his house for a few days.

At first, I felt a surge of happiness. I was going to see the little French girl again, hug her, kiss her, maybe hold her in my arms and love her. But after that first spurt of enthusiasm, worry inundated me. I looked at the date of the message; it was from two weeks ago. On the one hand, I was worried that Monique would relapse without Elisabeth by her side, and the very relaxed ambience in Jean Pierre and César's house was not going to help. On the other, I was disappointed about not having any welcoming message from her or that she had not told Elisabeth to leave one in her name.

With these concerns and as I had not eaten for many hours, I decided to go out for dinner and reflect on what I should do. I went to KC's, my favourite restaurant to eat meat, amen that it was one of the few that were still open. Even though it was late it was still bustling; the majority were people who had just returned from the mountains or that were about to leave on their trek.

There were a couple of Frenchmen who worked as tourist guides and which Jean Pierre had introduced me to at some point. I sat with them. They asked me about my adventures. I only gave them a resume, as I wasn't really in the mood of extending myself and I wanted to have a quick dinner and go to bed.

"Let's see if our friend Jean Pierre finds a leopard," said one of them.

"What do you mean?" I asked, alarmed at guessing the possibility that Jean Pierre had left Kathmandu.

"Indeed, you know him as well. Always looking for new adventures. He had the opportunity and grabbed it. He left two days ago with a group of Americans. They have just opened the Valley of Dolpo to foreigners. You know which one I mean, the one where Georges Schaller went looking for snow leopards."

My heart missed a beat. All my exhaustion disappeared. Monique was alone with César. In his clutches. I remembered the scenes I had witnessed a few months before when that American girl, barely an adult, had left his room uncombed, half dressed and with a few rupees in her hand. And the Colombian's comments. Without waiting any longer, I got up and ran to the street, in the direction of his house, running at full speed. Half way I slowed down. Two minutes more were not going to change the world, and I had to keep my strength in case I had to face that piece of garbage. But as I crossed the Royal Square, already at two hundred metres from his house, I couldn't help it. I felt the fear like a noose around my neck and started running again. As I turned the corner, I banged my head against a beam that was protruding from a facade. I brought my hand to where I had banged it and withdrew it stained with blood.

From the street, I could see the house, with all the lights out except a faint glare from César's room. I pushed open the door. Complete silence. I wondered whether my suspicions were justified and if I was doing the right thing by coming to his house at this time of night. I climbed the stairs, dark and still, trying to keep them from creaking. The first floor, where they had their workshop, storage space and kitchen was deserted. I got to the second floor. The blood trickling down my right cheek and I wiped it away with the back of my hand. "Where could Monique be sleeping?" I wondered.

Lanterns shone in the living room between cushions strewn on the floor. Thrown untidily over them, a shirt and trousers. Due to their size, they must have been César's. The door of his room was ajar. It was only illuminated by the scarce light coming from the bathroom, from where I could hear the sound of the shower. It was enough light to see Monique lying on the bed, her naked legs open, an arm hanging by her side with small droplets of blood in the interior face of her elbow, the sheets were strewn on the floor, and her shirt pulled up over her small breast until it covered her face.

For an instant, I didn't know what to do but then ran towards her. "Monique!", I whispered as I uncovered her face and covered her body with the shirt. She opened her eyes and looked at me in fright. She curled up, trying to disappear towards the headboard of the bed and hid her face behind her hands.

"It's me, Francisco."

"No, no, go away...demon!" she screamed.

She took her hands away from her face and extended her arms towards me in rejection and fear. Her eyes seemed like they were popping out of their sockets, and reflected the horror she appeared to be feeling.

"Go away, go away!" she continued, her fear escalating.

I saw that she must have been high and my face covered in blood must have scared her even more. A look towards the bedside table confirmed it. There was the needle and a little jade box open with the white powder in its interior. I tried to calm her down, although I knew from previous experience that she could not really see me and would not be able to reason with logic for a long while until the effects had passed. The sound of the shower had stopped. I didn't wait for the bastard to come out. I left Monique and went towards the bathroom door. It was there where we met. He, big and sure of himself. I, blind with fury. I clenched my fists and did as if

I was about to punch him with my right. He covered himself, and it was then when I kicked him in the groin. The towel that covered him cushioned part of the blow, but it was enough to get him writhing in pain. I then kneed him in the face. I didn't hit him fully but was able to then grab him by the neck with both hands pretending to choke him. My hands were sweaty on his skin, and I wasn't able to squeeze tightly enough while he fought to break free. It didn't take him long and managed to shake me off separating my arms with his large hands.

Monique was screaming even louder. Her shrieks resonated inside me. She must have now seen not one but two demons fighting, shouting and making disjointed sounds, growing and coming closer to her. They would soon reach her; she must have thought. While I tried to defend myself from César, I saw her look towards the open door which led to that sort of terrace which Jean Pierre had built on the roof. A slanting surface with hardly any protection. The light of the moon, shining through the undulating curtains made of light blue gauze, must have seemed like an exit towards liberation.

I received a blow from César; slipped and fell to the floor. I moved backwards, sliding on my back to where Monique was. She had managed to get out of bed, and her back was glued to the wall, her arms extended and shaking. She screamed again as she saw me lying at her feet. "The demon is coming; it is going to possess me again." Leaning with her hands against the wall she pushed herself towards the door, leapt and, hugging the curtain, flew into space.

I had jumped up but was unable to hold her back, and César was still facing me boiling with rage. I stumbled over a small chair of solid wood, grabbed it, raised it above my head and with all the fury in the world, bashed it against his head at the same instant that he was about to tackle me. He was left immobile. Without verifying his state, I threw myself down the stairs.

The streets of the old Kathmandu, witness and refuge of so many miseries and miracles, moments before empty but now with a gathering crowd, received Monique's body with no mercy. I pushed myself through: "Moniiiiiique!" A scream of anguish and desperation, of loss and helplessness. She was lying on the floor, motionless. As white as the curtain that she had dragged with her and which now covered her body. She looked like a butterfly born at the break of dawn without having had the time yet to be painted by daylight. Her eyes open, fixed, lifeless. Blood between her lips. I kneeled down and took one of her arms, feeling for a pulse. I couldn't find it, so I brought my ear to her chest, over her heart. Silence, silence. Dead, dead, dead. But I surely could revive her. My mouth on hers. Still warm. I covered her nose with my fingers and blew air into her lungs, and then I let it out. I repeated the procedure. Over and over again. Nothing. Nothing. "I've lost her," I said to myself as I lifted her torso and hugged her, without comprehending how it could have happened, so fast, so easily.

The tears flowed freely while I imagined what had happened. Monique, with no willpower again, had been seduced by the drugs that César had given her. "How had Jean Pierre been able to leave her alone with him? Yes, he had seen so many people like Monique that he had stopped caring what happened to them," I answered myself. "The fault really was not his, but mine. Why? Why did I leave her? Why didn't I wait a few days until I had seen her safely on the plane? How was I not able to foresee that this would happen? I was too selfish. If I loved her so much, why wasn't I patient enough? Why, why...?"

XXIII

"Pain, I don't want you to leave,
the last form of love.
I feel like I am living,
When you hurt me, but not in you, nor here,
Further away: in the earth,
In the year where you come from,
In the love with her,
and everything that was".

Pedro Salinas

I felt a hand on my right shoulder. Two men in white coats who signalled me to move away. I did so with a ray of hope, but no, they confirmed it immediately: she was dead. They covered her with a sheet; then, the police arrived. I stood back, at the side of the crowd. I saw César leave the house with a bag in his hand, he sneaked away, glued to the facades to try and pass unnoticed. I felt my blood boil and rise to my head, and I flew like a bullet towards him. He saw me coming and started running, got to the corner of the street and hesitated, enough for me to throw myself upon him, clinging on to his back and trying to grab his neck. We fell to the ground, wrestling. Then, the police arrived and pinned us down.

They took us to the police station but were precautious enough to put us in separate cells. In the morning they brought us before the judge. They gave me forty-eight hours to leave the country, but they retained César. Afterwards, I learned through Jean Pierre that he had been sentenced to four years imprisonment for reoffending in drug trafficking, but with his contacts and a couple of thousands of dollars he managed to reduce it to expulsion from the country. Monique's death, one more of the many of unbalanced westerners, was considered an accident.

I asked the police officer where they had taken her body. He told me it was in the Tribhuvan University Hospital and that they had already contacted the French embassy. I took a taxi and left for the hospital, still with an undefined hope. When I arrived, I realised it was absurd. They didn't allow me to see the body, they were doing the autopsy. No other person had asked about her, so they asked me if I was going to repatriate the body or I was going to take it to Pashupatinath for its cremation. Incineration in ovens did not exist in Nepal. They advised me about an agent who could take care of both proceedings. I decided that it was the embassy who had to take responsibility. The attaché was a friend of Jean Pierre, and I had met him a couple of times. I felt my friend's absence again, if he had been in Kathmandu, this would not have happened.

Maurice, at first, looked at me with suspicion and wasn't very happy at having to take care of the issue. They were trying to get in contact with Monique's family in Paris through the ministry, but because of the time difference, they didn't expect to be able to do so until mid-day. From previous experience, they knew that the family would not cover the costs unless they had insurance, something neither him nor I believed they did. According to Nepalese law, the body needs to be disposed of before twenty-four hours since the death has passed, so we had to be ready for its cremation. And so it was to be.

Monique's body consumed itself in the funeral pyre at the banks of the sacred river. It was the sunset of a dry and hot day, with not a wisp of wind in Pashupatinath. The sun set over the roofs of the temple and the smell of burned flesh mixed with wood and dry cow dung used as fuel filled the air. Kneeling down on the earth, following with my eyes the smoke columns which in its ascension to the skies were maybe leading Monique's spirit, I struggled to understand. Collapsed, shipwrecked. Sadness overcame my whole being and soul. How had we, she and I, ended up in this situation?

When I had arrived, an hour previous, accompanied by the civil servant of the French embassy, they were washing the body in the river, a narrow streak of water at that time of the year, while the usual *sadhus*, a few monkeys and some stray dogs, prowled around the stairways of both river banks. They had wrapped the body in a shroud, scattered some flowers over it and placed it on a sort of stretcher made of wooden planks and bamboo cane. One of the helpers placed five *ghee* lamps (clarified butter) around the body and painted a few signs of divine protection on her cheeks and forehead with saffron. Then, they transported it twenty meters down the river to the last cremation platform, the one meant for poor people and foreigners. The pyre was ready, and they placed the body on it.

Monique had her arms crossed over her chest, her eyes closed and her beautiful face, framed by her black locks adorned with flower garlands, was pale and calm. The officiating priest walked around her three times. The first for her birth, the second for her life, and the third for her death, while he sprinkled the body with holy water. Afterwards, he covered her completely with the shroud. In front of us, on the other bank, a woman dressed in a white sari began to sing a ritual song accompanied by a zither.

Until then, the scene had seemed so unreal to me. No, it wasn't Monique who was lying there immobile. But when they brought the torch to the wood in various different points and this one began to burn, the flames also set fire to my heart. I had an impulse, I lifted my arms and stepped forward, slightly indecisive. Someone held me back. I clenched my fists, closed my eyes and dropped my head forward. But I could still see her, her body enveloped in the white material, the flowers. I lifted my eyes and, she was moving! I jumped towards her. The smoke blinded me, and the heat forced me backwards. I was held back again. The priest maintained the body still with the help of a pole. I heard a small explosion. I fell to the floor, weeping, incapable of looking at her any longer, unable to keep her company.

When I recovered, there were hardly any remains of Monique or wood left. I would never again be with her. She had become ethereal. The image of her when we were watching that sunrise in Kolkata, innocent and beautiful, appeared before my eyes. I made an effort to keep a hold of it. It lasted for a few seconds. The image of her body on the pyre returned, between flames about to be extinguished.

"But she was moving," I said to my companion.

"No, it was the muscles that contract with the heat and make the body shake," he answered.

"And the snap?"

"That was the cranium".

I stifled a scream.

"I am sorry, I shouldn't have told you," he apologised.

We waited for a long while until only the ashes remained and then until these got cold. The assistant proceeded to collect them and handed them over to the priest. He approached us and gave us a handful. Then, he threw the rest into the river, we did the same. The civil servant bid me farewell with a "Good luck". I walked towards the pyre to see if there was anything of Monique left which I could keep as a memory. I only found a small flower on the floor which must have fallen off before the pyre was set alight. With it in my hand, I climbed the stairway up to the road and began the seven-kilometre walk that separated me from Kathmandu. I felt as if I were dead. As if the world had ended. Despite the chaos of the taxis, motorbikes and people around me, I only felt the silence, as if I was submerged in the depths of the ocean.

I left Kathmandu the following afternoon with a broken heart. Literally. I told myself that Monique had been fleeting passion, an impossible love that had left as it had come, unexpectedly. A fantasy to which I had succumbed with the excitement of a child and with the commitment of a redeemer. A chapter in my life which had made me, I'm not sure if a better person like my adventure with Jack, but at least wiser and stronger.

I took an Aeroflot plane to Munich, via Moscow, with the intention of visiting Ursula, like I had planned some time ago. We had to certify the end of our relationship. After spending the night in the Soviet capital, I showed up at her student residence without any prior warning. She wasn't there, so I went for a walk around the city. I found myself wandering down Maximilianstrasse with its luxury shops and fashion boutiques. I stood before some of the shop-windows. After seven months in India and Nepal, travelling across their mountains, living with their people in a simple and austere lifestyle, in their cities and villages, I kept asking myself why the need for so many clothes and objects which were displayed before me. Never until then had I been so conscious of the frivolity of our society, the futility of life in the West. "How many useless things. None of this is necessary to live. Material possessions, indulgence, and compensations for the lack of time people have to really live and enjoy the essential in life," I reflected.

I returned to Ursula's residence. When she opened the door of her room, loyal to her character, she didn't throw herself into my arms. She looked confused and surprised, her questioning eyes staring at me. I wasn't sure how to start either.

"Ursula, I need you."

"What's happened? You don't look very well," she said, a hint of compassion in her voice.

Now yes, I stepped forward to hug her, and she accepted.

"A lot of things have happened. To intense to tell you by letter. Anyway, I have arrived sooner than they would have. These last days have been terrible. Exhilarant, dangerous...tragic.

I poured it all out, mixing Jack with Monique, the Nanda Devi with Kolkata and Kathmandu, life and death, unfinished sentences and long silences, nervous laughter and contained sobs. She just looked at me, at times affectionately, at times surprised, astonished; at times unimpressed. But we ended up hugging and sobbing. Afterwards, we went to a restaurant for dinner. It was then her turn to talk.

She had told me in her letters. She had suffered by my departure even though she knew that our relationship had no future.

"You were never able to understand why I was so hurt with you leaving for Nepal. It was the way you told me, or actually, the way you didn't tell me about your ideas and plans," she said once we were seated at the table and after having ordered. "I saw it as a great lack of love from your part," she continued, her voice sounded upset and her eyes looked sad, "that you didn't consider that the person with whom you had the most intimate relationship was eager to know every single detail of your trip, especially if you were saying that you didn't know for how long you were leaving or when you would be back."

"Forgive me, I guess that that last part was a joke, you know what I am like."

"It is forgiven and nearly forgotten. I have recovered. I also accept that it was partly my fault because I didn't want to go and live in Paris with you. And I don't regret it. I already explained it to you in my letters. Of course, it is a good experience to live there but how? Without any money? With no possibility of finding an exciting job related to my studies? You know it; I can't live depending on a man. Here, on the other hand, things are going very well for me. I have succeeded in obtaining a job as a History of Arts teaching assistant at the University, and my thesis is nearly finished. I will present it in March."

We slept in my hotel, in the same bed, but we didn't make love. In that sense, we felt like strangers, far away from one another. We had become old friends. For a few years, we wrote to each other regularly. But little by little the letters became less regular. Until one day, she or I stopped.

I returned to Paris with a conviction enclosed in my solitude, floating around in my melancholy. Neither Monique's death nor the confirmation of the end of my relationship with Ursula would be allowed to interfere with my intentions, in making me deter from the decisions I had taken on the flight from Delhi to Kathmandu after having said goodbye to Jack. Nothing would be the same now, but it would be better.

EPILOGUE

"Now I know that when a newborn with his little hand, squeezes his father's index finger for the first time, he has trapped him forever".

Ten years had gone by since that tragic night in Kathmandu. I found myself alone, in the semi-darkness of a room in a clinic in Madrid, at four o´clock in the afternoon of a hot day at the end of July. The noise of the traffic in the crossing of Juan Bravo with Príncipe de Vergara seeped through the walls. Slightly more than an hour had passed since Bárbara and I had arrived. After fifteen minutes, they had taken her to the operating room, and I was left waiting. Excited? Perplexed? I had never imagined that I would find myself in this situation.

We had come from San Rafael, just at the top of the "Alto del León" on the northern face of the Guadarrama mountain range. There, under the shade of its pine trees, we had sought refuge from the heat of the summer in Madrid. I remembered our stay fondly. A few beautiful weeks in a small house we had rented next to the public swimming pool. How cold the water had been! Bárbara, unscathed by her pregnancy, was sewing baby clothes at the shade of a tree while I read or swam. At home, she cooked or waited patiently for me to wake up from my "siesta" to go for a walk until the sun set.

Sitting next to the bed I recalled Ramón J. Sender, my favourite author when I was young, with his *Crónica del Alba*, *Imán* and *Réquiem por un Campesino español*. He also spent his summers in San Rafael. It was here that he had spent the last moments with his wife. When the civil war began, Franco's army took control of the area. He left to Madrid to join the Republicans and sent his wife to her parent's house where Franco's supporters, frustrated at not having caught the writer, murdered her a few days later. Now that I had a wife myself, I could imagine Sender's pain. Even though it didn't occur like this in real life, I had always imagined him married to Valentina, his childhood love, pure and rebellious, from his first book, *Crónica del Alba*.

I had met Bárbara three years previously in FITUR. For the past seven or eight years, I had been working as a travel writer and photographer for various magazines and newspapers. This helped me to soften the impact and loneliness of the failure of my intense relationship of six years with Ursula and the tragic end of my romantic and impossible love with Monique. I met other women during my travels and in Madrid, I had company, affection and sometimes even emotion and excitement, but none of them found a place in my heart. During those years there were moments when I believed that my sadness would be eternal; but I continued surprising myself, again and again, laughing uncontrollably and feeling happy. There were moments when I stopped believing in love; until the person appeared who made me love again, more and more every day.

Back to FITUR. This travel fair was the perfect place to establish contacts with tourism offices and airlines and to collect information to plan my trips. I was at that time going over a particular issue which needed to be solved. The publishing house with whom I collaborated mostly and which published the travel magazine "*VIAJAR*", the in-flight magazines of Iberia, and some others having to do with cars, banks or other companies, had received a few months ago the offer of producing Visa Spain's new magazine, "*ORO*", a magazine to be published every three months, dedicated to luxury and with a run of five hundred thousand copies.

Every number featured an article of six or eight pages on one of the best and most luxurious hotels in the world. I had been assigned the job, writing the text and taking the photographs. Strictly speaking, it was I who had to choose and suggest the hotels. And it had been like that in the first number, where I had written an article on the Hotel Dorchester in London. However, for the next number, Visa magazine had asked us to feature the Fairmont Hotel in San Francisco, as it was there where the famous TV show "*Hotel*" was filmed. The editor of the magazine and I thought that it would be logical to take advantage of the trip to the United States to write another piece, this time of a hotel in New York. I chose The Pierre, a grand establishment of European style and which was at that time seen as the most exclusive one in Manhattan.

So that morning at FITUR, I kept asking myself, as I had done the days before, how was I going to get those two famous hotels to invite me for four days, I, an unknown Spanish journalist who wrote for a magazine which had just started. I couldn't even begin to imagine at that point the great interest of those extremely expensive hotels to promote themselves through media devoted to luxury and style. And then I saw them, the logo and her. The logo said "The Leading Hotels of the World", the most prestigious hotel association in the world and to which I knew both hotels belonged. She was pretty, elegant, blonde, big blue-grey eyes, and was dressed in a tailored suit; forty years old? I threw myself in her direction with my expectations, I imagine, portrayed on my face.

"How can I help you?" she said with a welcoming smile.

But I thought: "The reason this lady is here is to promote her hotels, not to give free rooms to a stranger in exchange for the promise of an article." I hesitated and said, "No, I don't think so."

A sparkle of a challenge shone in her eyes.

"What do you mean? What do you need exactly?"

"It is for a magazine. I...," I hesitated again before continuing.

"If it for an advertisement, then you are right, it is not my area. We have an advertising agency in New York."

"No, it's not that. I am a journalist," I ventured. "We would like to do several articles of two of your hotels."

"Oh! Very good! This is something else then. Interesting." Her smile returned. "You see, I am not the one in charge of press, but I can help you. Which hotels do you have in mind?

For a moment I was distracted by her eyes and mouth, but I recovered.

"The Fairmont in San Francisco and The Pierre. For the magazine "Oro" by Visa Gold Card," I added.

"Great. I am the sales manager for Europe, but I have a person in the London office who takes care of the journalists," she went towards the table, opened her leather wallet and returned with two cards in her hand. "This is her card, and this is mine," she offered both to me and pointed at one of them, "her name is Susan, just send her a fax with the details. I will tell her about it when I return to my office."

"Thank you, thank you so much," I answered, incredibly relieved.

"Lovely to meet you, I am Barbara," she added, while she offered me the directory of their hotels. "Here are all of our hotels with their characteristics. We take care of the marketing and communications. You can contact us for anything you need."

She then offered her hand, and I shook it extremely happy about the successful outcome of the meeting.

"You are English?"

"No, I am German, but I have been in living in London for more than fifteen years."

More people were waiting to speak to her so, with another smile she finished the conversation. I left thinking: "What a piece of luck! I am on the right track. What a woman! As pretty as she is professional! And a German... Thank god she lives in London."

I wrote to Susan. She answered immediately, and everything went smoothly. I spent four weeks in the United States. I visited the Fairmont first where I photographed both the hotel and the city, San Francisco, freely and extensively. It was my first time in the city of the Golden Gate and the gay revolution, and I made good use of the time. Afterwards, I visited a good part of California and gathered material for various photographic articles on Yosemite Natural Park, with its spectacular landscapes of its almighty rock walls; of the valleys of Napa and Sonoma to the North of San Francisco, devoted to Wine and the so called "The King's Highway", the series of missions founded by the Franciscan order of monks in Upper California. Afterwards, I went to New York. In The Pierre, I was treated fabulously, just as I had been treated in The Fairmont. I submerged myself in the rhythm of the city like a local, not going up the Empire State Building nor visiting the Statue of Liberty, but I allowed myself to be surprised by the audacities of the MOMA and enraptured by the art pieces at the Metropolitan.

During the following months and years, I got to know and photographed the Ritz of Paris, the Oriental of Bangkok, the Copacabana in Río, the Okura in Tokyo and many others. In all of them, I slept in their celestial beds, ate in their Michelin star restaurants and was treated like a VIP.

Since then, I alternated my vagabond trips across the less discovered paths of Asia, America or Oceania with stays at the the most luxurious suites. Occasionally in my suitcase, suits, shirts, ties and shiny shoes would share space with mountain boots or sandals, a backpack, jeans, and a sleeping bag. When I finished my work at the hotel in Rome, Beijing, Acapulco or Hong Kong, I would leave my suitcase at the hotel and would travel across Umbria, the unknown Laos, the stages of the "Silk Route", the colonial cities and jungle of Brazil, or the mountains and monasteries of Japan or Burma.

I had not forgotten Barbara. From time to time, she would come to Madrid to present a new hotel and would invite me, together with other journalists and travel agents to the usual cocktail party. She showed me she followed my adventures in her hotels and she even found out about my visit to the Mandarin of Hong Kong with my girlfriend of the time. And it was that one day she appeared in Madrid, and this time to stay, as she came to open the company's office in Spain and Portugal. Nevertheless, it took a few months until we saw each other. She was very busy looking for a flat in which to settle and to find suitable premises for the office, to choose her staff, and to obtaining the necessary administrative permits to open the office as well as other pertinent matters.

Noises and squeaks of doors and footsteps down the hallway of the clinic, coming toward the room, took me out of my thoughts. I sat up anxiously, headed for the door, and opened it slightly. No, it wasn't for me. A nurse passed pushing a stretcher on which lay a brunette with long hair, hooked to a dropper and apparently sedated or asleep. I returned to my seat and to the memories of my relationship with Barbara.

It was clear that we had liked and were interested in each other. One day, after a very professional interview we had in her new office in the Tower of Madrid, I invited her for dinner at La Bola, still my first choice for taking foreigners and providing them with the pleasures of the enjoyment of the pure, traditional Madrid. The next day, a Saturday morning in spring, we went for a walk, around the hills of La Pedriza, to check out legs and spirit. The girl deserved top marks. And apparently, I deserved them as well because we continued seeing each other day in and day out.

I remember the nights on the terrace of her beautiful attic of Princesa Street, and our weekend trips around the villages and landscapes of Spain. Apart from her many physical and social qualities, she was an excellent cook, and she appreciated good wine. And I also remember that morning when I returned from México, and she was waiting for me at Barajas airport. She was flying to Barcelona for a meeting, but she delayed her flight to be able to meet me. She looked stunning in her white Chanel suit. We found a seat in a discrete corner, and we whispered sweet nothings to each other and kissed until we heard her flight's last call. I left Barajas happy as I hadn't been for a long while, with my insides full of feelings which I had believed dead until now, with forgotten emotions which I thought I would never feel again. She had woken me up from my loveless existence, defeated the resistances of the memory of my broken loves and had stirred my heart.

Summer arrived, and we went on holiday to the beaches and mountains of Asturias. The Volkswagen Golf, a tent, mattresses, sleeping bags and a minimal amount of clothes, she followed my suggestions quite faithfully. I have to admit that I, very much influenced by my experiences in India and the Himalayas, had become a very frugal man, perhaps even too much. A saucepan, a frying pan, two plates, two forks, a Swiss knife, two glasses, one to share water and the other to share wine, was our kitchen and dining room.

The first night we slept in the foothills of the Picos de Europa, next to a stream and at a couple of kilometres down a dirt track from the Pontón pass, past Riaño. A shepherd who was sleeping in the area with his flock came to have a coffee with us.

"Don't leave anything outside the tent, especially food. There are wolves in the area, but they won't come close, they are more interested in the sheep," he said, scaring Barbara and giving me the chance to show off my bravery by not giving the man's words much importance.

After a trek to the base of the Naranjo de Bulnes, we continued down to the wild and nudist beach of Torimbia, near Ribadesella; across the valleys and villages of the interior of Asturias, the depths of the forest of Muniellos in search of bears, the remote and gorgeous collegiate church of San Pedro de Teverga with its mummies, and we ended in the magical lakes of Saliencia, in the Natural Park of Somiedo, home to the ancestral spirits according to the Theosophist and thinker, Mario Roso de Luna.

We enjoyed our days of a million kisses and holding hands, of picnics under shady trees and picking fresh figs of farmers yards, of dancing at village fiestas, of discovering Roman Arches and towering gothic Cathedrals of the Spanish past. We did not mind sleeping in a, sometimes, uncomfortable and cold tent. She laughed at me being drunk on cider in a village Church yard and then bull fighting a cow. We were sorry about burning forests and the news of a threatening war in the Balkans and sad about the end of a summer and the return to reality... But best of all was the tenderness, love and affection travelling with us all the way.

I heard noises in the hallway again, it was the rolling of a crib. It stopped when it reached the door. A nurse opened it and pushed it into the room:

"Your daughter. We will bring your wife in a few moments."

I brought my chair close to the crib, and I looked at that little animal shaking its arms, looking for the light in her sleepy eyes, and now yes, tears of happiness came to my eyes. I brought my hand close to hers.

"Hello, Cristina."

She took hold of my index finger and looked at me. I swear I heard her say.

"Hello, papi."

A new life had been born. And in my heart as well. And this one, forever.

THE END

I hope you enjoyed reading my book.

Please consider writing a review. Thank you.

Printed in Great Britain
by Amazon